IMAGES
of America

STATESBORO

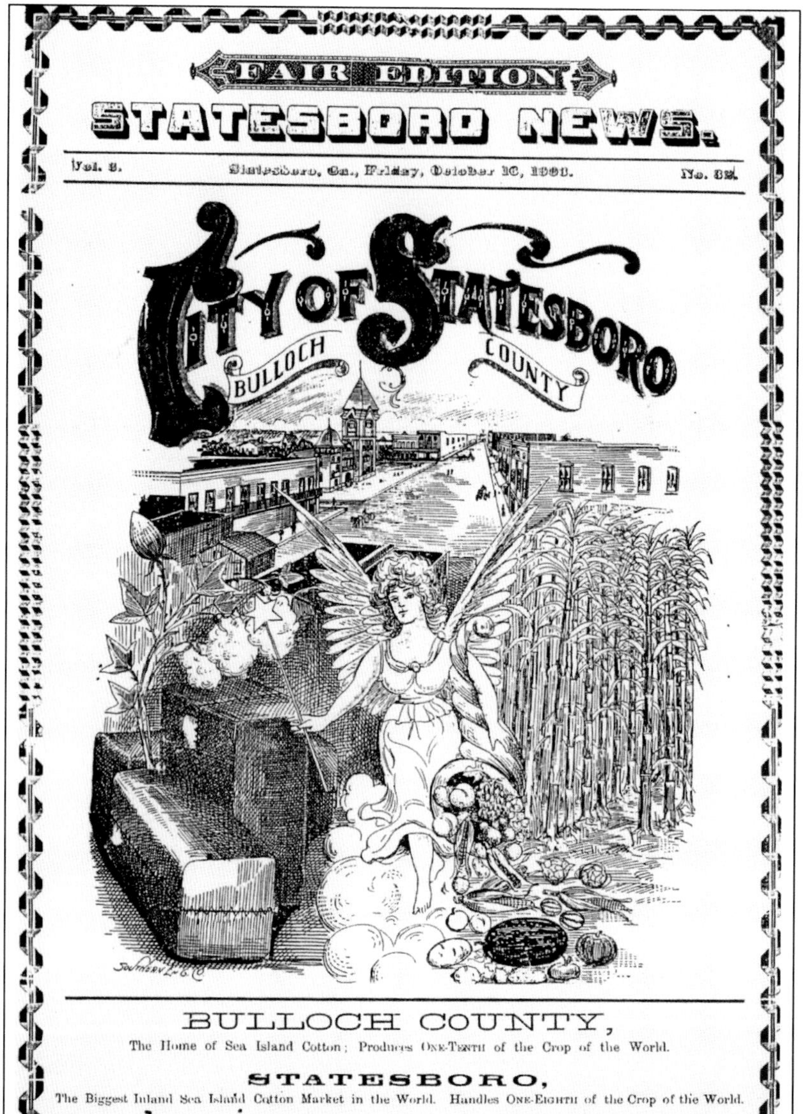

FAIR EDITION

STATESBORO NEWS.

Statesboro, Ga., Friday, October 16, 1903.

CITY OF STATESBORO

BULLOCH COUNTY

BULLOCH COUNTY,

The Home of Sea Island Cotton; Produces ONE-TENTH of the Crop of the World.

STATESBORO,

The Biggest Inland Sea Island Cotton Market in the World. Handles ONE-EIGHTH of the Crop of the World.

The October 16, 1903 cover of the *Statesboro News* depicts the Angel of Plenty as she admires the bountiful harvest of Bulloch County. The Georgia State Fair edition of the newspaper showcased how much Statesboro depended upon the business generated by local farmers. The city achieved its leadership in south Georgia by serving the needs of an agricultural economy.

(*on the cover*) William Jennings Bryan of Nebraska, the famous orator, editor, and statesman, delivered his lecture "The Prince of Peace" in Statesboro on June 13, 1911. Nominated by the Democratic Party for the Presidency on three occasions, Mr. Bryan had a wide following in the South and was popular among citizens of this region. He was a guest at the Jaeckel Hotel, and was welcomed by a large delegation of local leaders. Slightly bald and wearing a vest, he stands near the center of the front row. The man and woman standing on the front porch in the background are Mr. and Mrs. R.L. Paschal, who managed the Jaeckel.

IMAGES
of America

STATESBORO

Delma E. Presley and Smith C. Banks

ARCADIA
PUBLISHING

ISBN 978-0-7385-1495-6

Published by Arcadia Publishing
Charleston, South Carolina

Printed in the United States of America

Library of Congress Catalog Card Number: Applied For

For all general information contact Arcadia Publishing at:
Telephone 843-853-2070
Fax 843-853-0044
E-mail sales@arcadiapublishing.com
For customer service and orders:
Toll-Free 1-888-313-2665

Visit us on the Internet at www.arcadiapublishing.com

With appreciation for her service of almost 50 years to Statesboro and southeast Georgia as director of the Statesboro Regional Library, and for her diligent efforts to preserve our history and heritage, we dedicate this work to Miss Isabel Lane Sorrier. "Miss Isabel" collected many photographs which appear in this volume. We honor her memory.

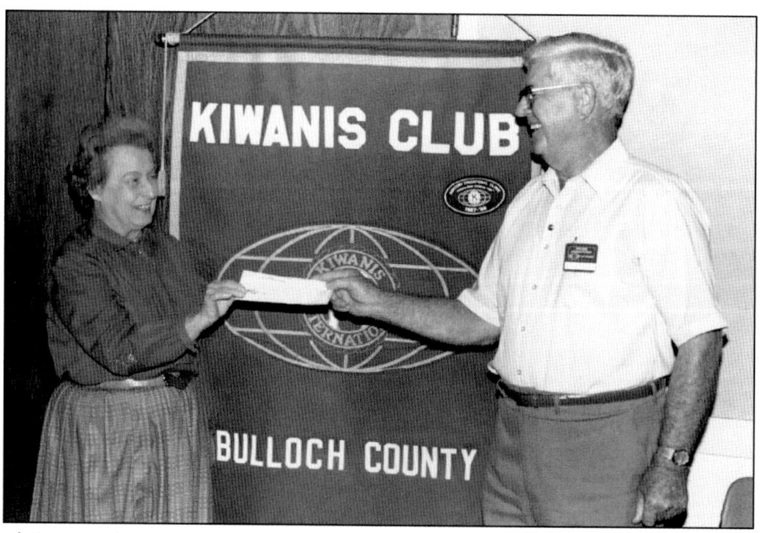

In 1944 Isabel Sorrier became the new director of the Statesboro Regional Library. She held that position for 48 years until her retirement in 1992, ending a career of 50 years in the library profession. Under her leadership the region grew to five counties in which she planned and built eight new library buildings and two major library additions. She is shown here in the 1980s as she accepts a donation in appreciation for the club's use of the meeting room from E.T. "Red" Mullis, president of Statesboro's Golden K Kiwanis club.

Contents

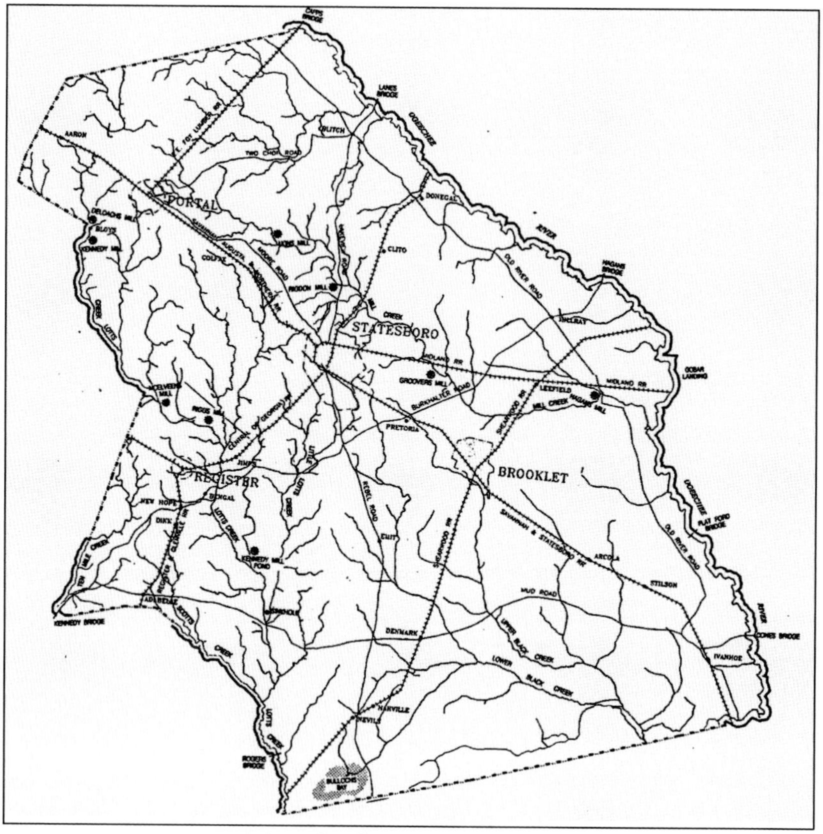

Map of Bulloch County in 1914.

ACKNOWLEDGMENTS

We acknowledge with gratitude two publications by *The Statesboro Herald*, our local newspaper: *A Century of Progress* (1966) by Leodel Coleman and G.C. Coleman, and *Spirit of the People* (1996), edited by Larry Anderson and Kemp Mabry. We could not have completed this project without the valuable and informative work by the late local historian, Dorothy Brannen, *Life in Old Bulloch: The Story of a Wiregrass County in Georgia* (1992). We recommend these publications to anyone who wishes to explore the rich and fascinating history of Statesboro. Many members of the Statesboro Bicentennial Committee have assisted the authors, as well as the staff of the Statesboro Regional Library. We are especially grateful to Heather Brown, who scanned most of the images found in this book, and to the Georgia Southern University Museum for providing technical assistance.

INTRODUCTION

Statesboro is a gift. It arrived in 1801 when George Siebald of Augusta donated 200 acres for a centrally located seat of government for Bulloch County. Over two years later, in December of 1803, the Georgia Legislature created the town of Statesborough, located some 50 miles northwest of Savannah.

Smaller than a "borough" for the next 80 years, Statesborough seemed irrelevant to a county that was bustling with immigrants whose roots traced to the British Isles. In 1866 the state legislature granted a permanent charter and changed the name to "Statesboro," but growth did not follow. The census for 1880 reveals 25 residents in the fledgling town, while 8,052 lived in the growing county.

Leadership for the new 'Boro came from outside of Bulloch County. The original visionary was a young lawyer named J.A. Brannen, who moved here from neighboring Bryan County in 1879. Back then locals still talked about an incident from the autumn of 1864. It seems that during Sherman's infamous "march to the sea," a Union commanding officer approached a saloon in the middle of a forest in Bulloch County. He asked for directions to Statesboro. The proprietor replied, "You are standing in the middle of town." The invaders torched the wooden courthouse but spared the town's three homes and nearby farms.

Within a few years conversation in Statesboro shifted to what Mayor Brannen and other outsiders were accomplishing. First came a newspaper. Then local businessmen funded a vital link to the Central of Georgia Railroad. Municipal services began to multiply. New stores sprang up along the town's four major streets, each named Main. Banks quickly followed.

If Bulloch County residents ignored the county seat during its first 75 years, they could ignore it no longer. Led by enterprising newcomers, Statesboro's leaders developed a progressive local government and nourished an economy geared to serve the interest of regional farmers. During the first decade of the 20th century, cotton became king in south Georgia. Statesboro was poised to become the market of choice. In 1908 it led the world in sales of the longtime staple, Sea Island cotton. For each bale of cotton sold in Savannah, 10 bales were sold in Statesboro.

After the boll weevil decimated the cotton crop in the 1930s, local farmers shifted to another cash crop: tobacco. The transition allowed this community to recover from the Great Depression quicker than most. By 1953 over 20 million pounds of tobacco passed through warehouses in Statesboro, making it the largest market in the "Bright Tobacco Belt" spanning Georgia and Florida.

Why did Statesboro emerge from its long slumber to become a central town in southeastern Georgia? The answer, simply, is that city and county learned to work in tandem. A notable example is the movement in 1906 to obtain a college. Skillfully, local citizens outbid several other communities with similar aspirations. Within a few decades the institution became Georgia Teachers College. In 1990 the state designated the old A&M School as Georgia Southern University. Early in the 21st century, it is a comprehensive regional university serving a diverse, residential student body some 15,000 strong.

A number of major industries moved to Statesboro during the last decade of the 20th century. Boosted by manufacturing and service industries, the current economy, nevertheless, depends heavily on agriculture. Taxpayers acknowledged this fact in 2002 when they overwhelmingly approved public funding of an innovative agricultural center.

Art and music, important in the community, are symbolized by a blind guitarist and singer who led the blues movement in the early 20th century. Statesboro knew him as "Doog," a nickname for Willie McTell ("Blind Willie"). The university contributes greatly to the community's quality of life through a museum, wildlife education center, and botanical garden. Its state-of-the-art Performing Arts Center hosts touring Broadway shows as well as drama, dance, and other public performances.

The census for 2000 recorded 56,000 residents of Statesboro/Bulloch County. It is the largest inland city/county in the southeastern quadrant of Georgia. The population is 68.7% white, 28.8% black, and 1.9% Latino. The authors worked with all segments of the community to obtain images that tell Statesboro's common story. We are grateful and somewhat overwhelmed that we uncovered over 800 images. Sadly we have space for only one-fourth of them.

Dozens of generous citizens aided us throughout the project. While we do not have space to recognize them by name, we hope each will take pride in this pictorial history of Statesboro. Many contributors, both living and dead, have made possible this gift to the future. We are grateful that proceeds of this publication will support the work of the Statesboro Bicentennial Committee.

Delma E. Presley and Smith C. Banks

One

How We Lived

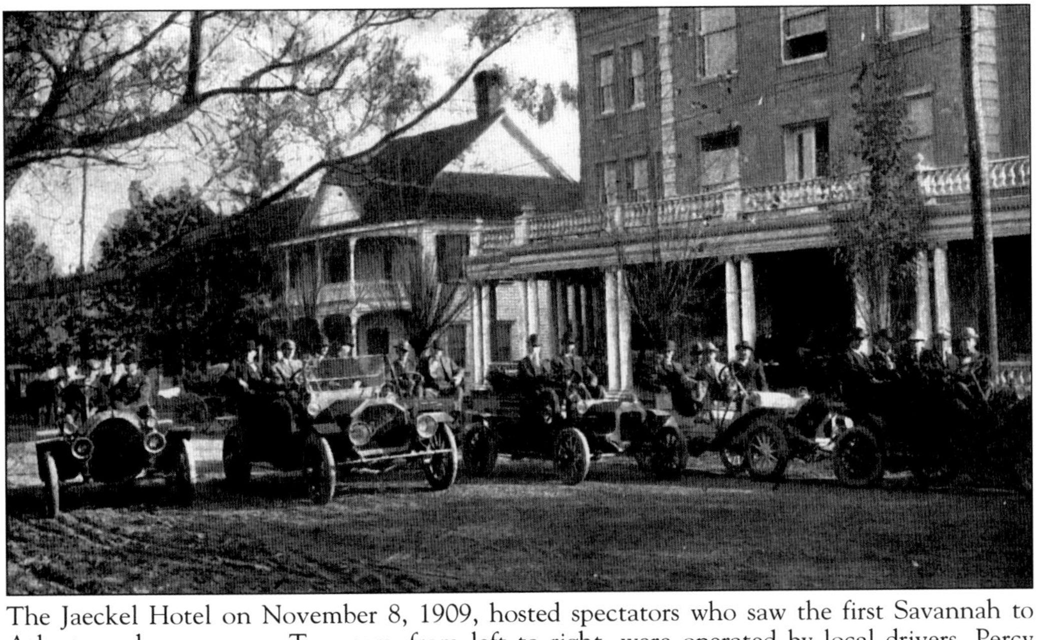

The Jaeckel Hotel on November 8, 1909, hosted spectators who saw the first Savannah to Atlanta endurance race. Two cars, from left to right, were operated by local drivers, Percy Averitt's 1909 20-hp Buick and Jack Blitch's 1909 30 hp-Buick. The next car is probably a 1906 Reo, operated by spectator B.B. Sorrier Sr. The Roundtree Hotel, formerly known as the Drummer's Home Hotel, was located east of the Jaeckel. Mr. Gustave Jaeckel managed this hotel until the three-storied Jaeckel was built in 1905.

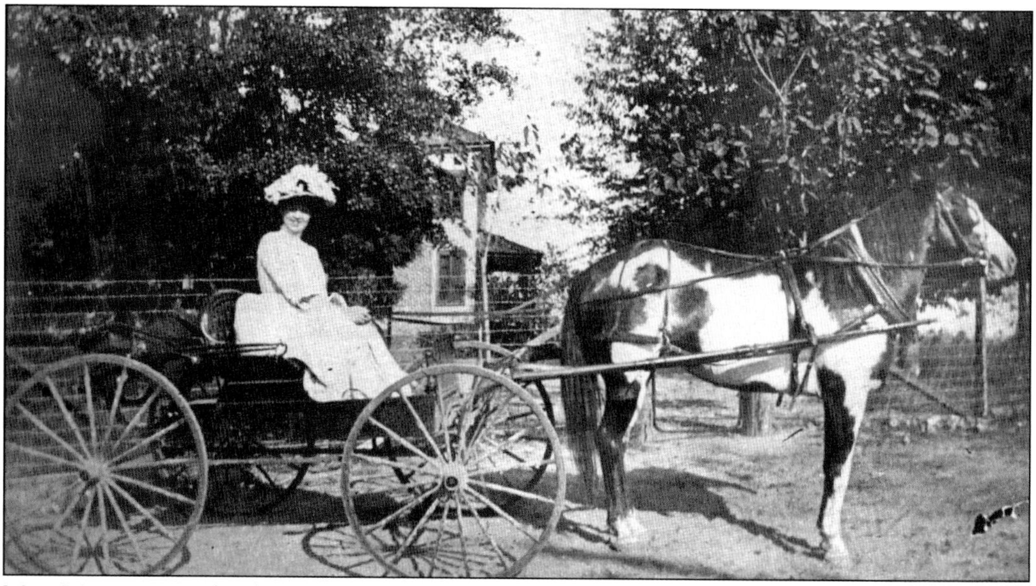

Miss Margaret Outland Johnston, daughter of Mr. and Mrs. Greene S. Johnston, sits in her buggy as she drives her horse named "Maude." In the background is Crackerhurst on Savannah Avenue, in 2003 the office of attorneys Edenfield, Cox, Bruce, and Classens. The photograph was taken around 1900. Mr. Johnston named his home "Crackerhurst," or the home of a Georgia Cracker (of which Mr. Johnston was proud). For many years this was the location of Smith-Tillman Funeral Home. After this photograph was taken, the house was remodeled and a two-storied columned portico was added.

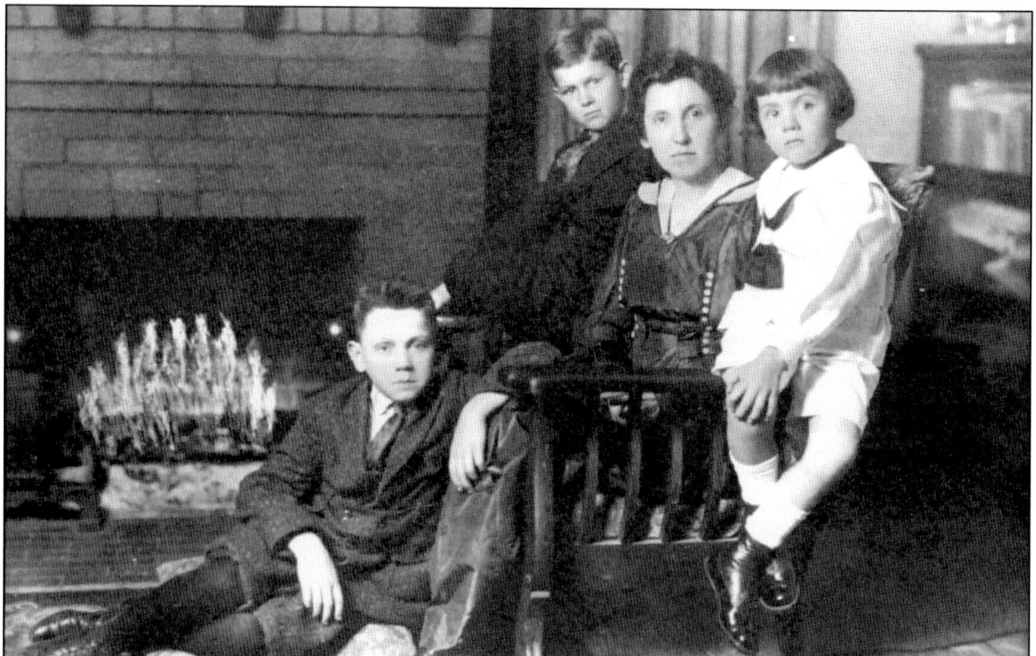

The stylishly dressed family of Greene S. Johnston posed for this photograph around 1910. The young man in the center, on his mother's right, George, became the longtime attorney for the City of Statesboro, following in his father's footsteps.

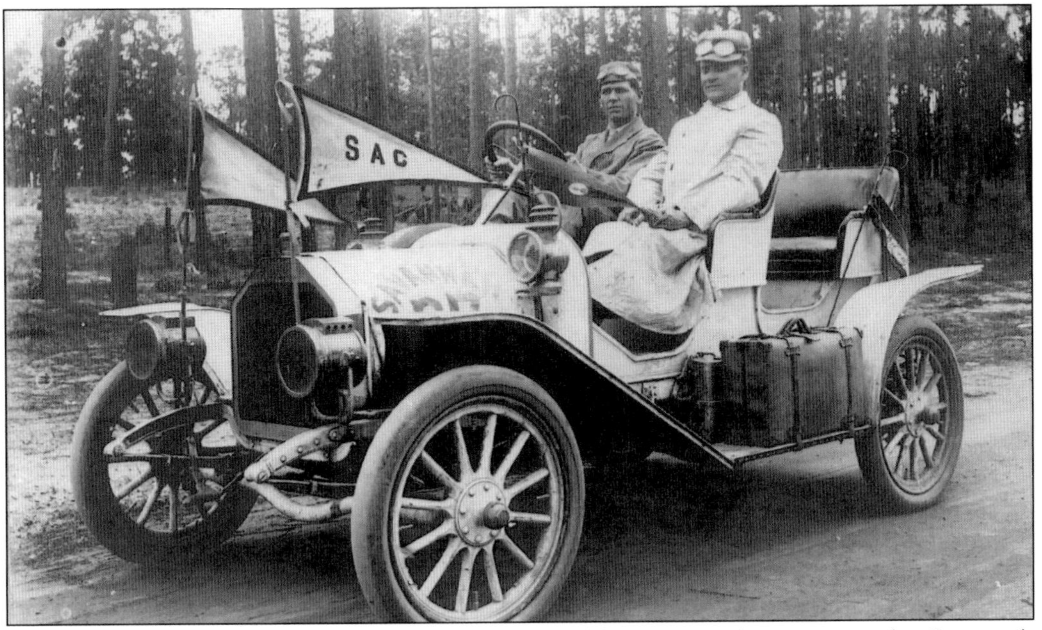

In 1909 on Lakeview Road, Percy Averitt (left) celebrates a perfect score in the Savannah to Atlanta endurance race. The event began on November 8 and was sponsored by the Savannah Auto Club (SAC). Notice the SAC pennants on the hood. Joining Mr. Averitt is E.L. (Ed) Smith. Note Mr. Smith's stylish duster and driving goggles. Mr. Averitt's Buick is a 1909 20-horsepower model. Mr. Averitt is said to have been the first to drive a car into the city of Statesboro.

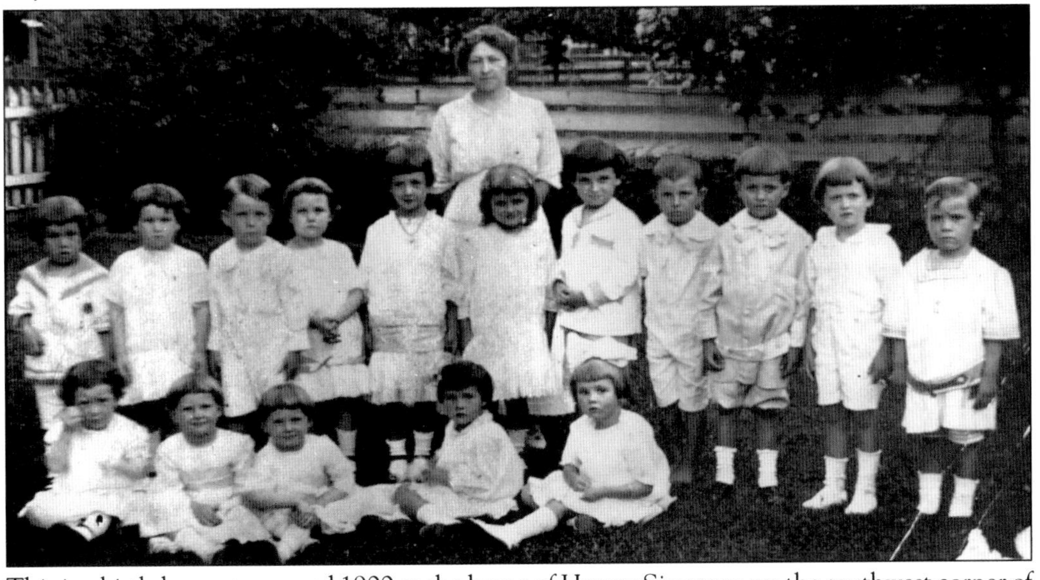

This is a birthday party around 1900 at the home of Homer Simmons on the southwest corner of North Main and Church Streets, which is still standing in 2003. Standing from left to right are Frank Mikell, Marguerite Cail, Carl Renfroe, Margaret Kennedy, unidentified, Lila Preetorius, J.E. McCroan, Ed Kennedy, Homer Simmons, John Mooney, and Howell Cobb Cone. Sitting from left to right is little Miss Cone, Mary Groover, Martha Groover, Evelyn Simmons, and James Brett.

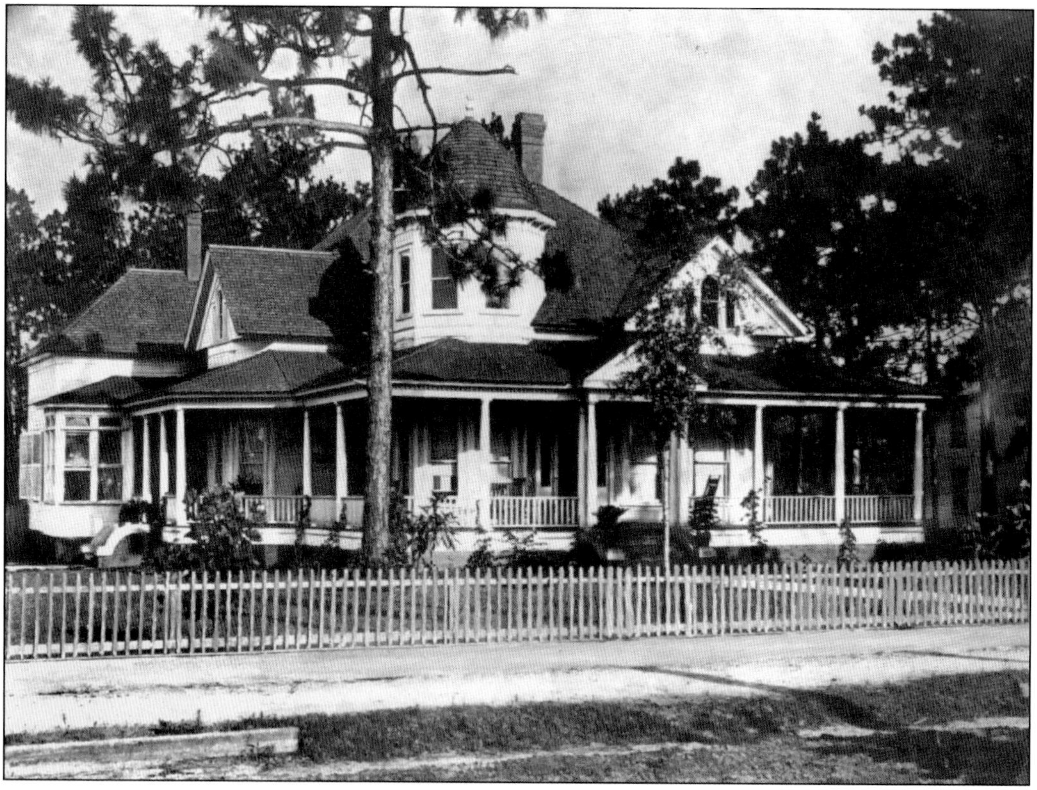

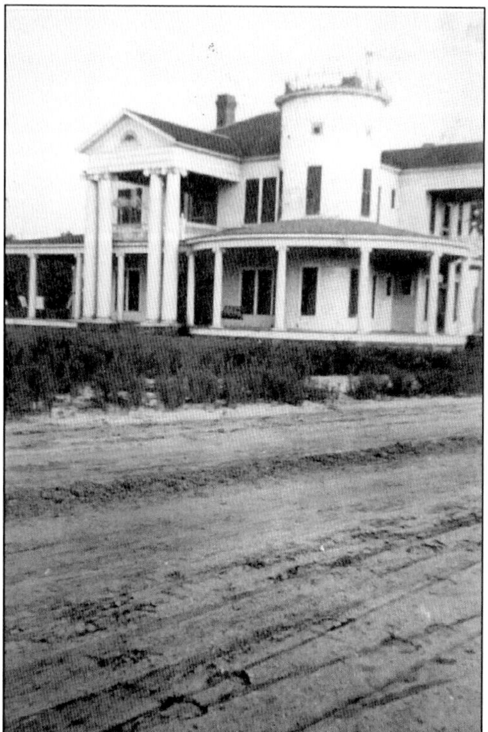

The Robert F. "Sonny" Donaldson Sr. home was located at the northwest corner of North Main and Church Streets. The Queen Anne–style home, built at the turn of the last century, stood on the site of the earliest school in Statesboro, the Statesboro Academy. In the 1950s and 1960s the home was beautifully landscaped with azaleas. Wisteria vines climbed into pine trees, and the beautiful cone-shaped, purple flowers led tourists to believe that pines actually produced the gorgeous blossoms. The home was demolished in the 1970s and is the site of the Northside Office Center.

The home of attorney J.J.E. (Julian) Anderson stood in the forks of South Main Street and Fair Road. The large home featured two twin columned porticos, two stories in height, facing both South Main and Fair Road. Destroyed by fire in 1930, the site became prime commercial property.

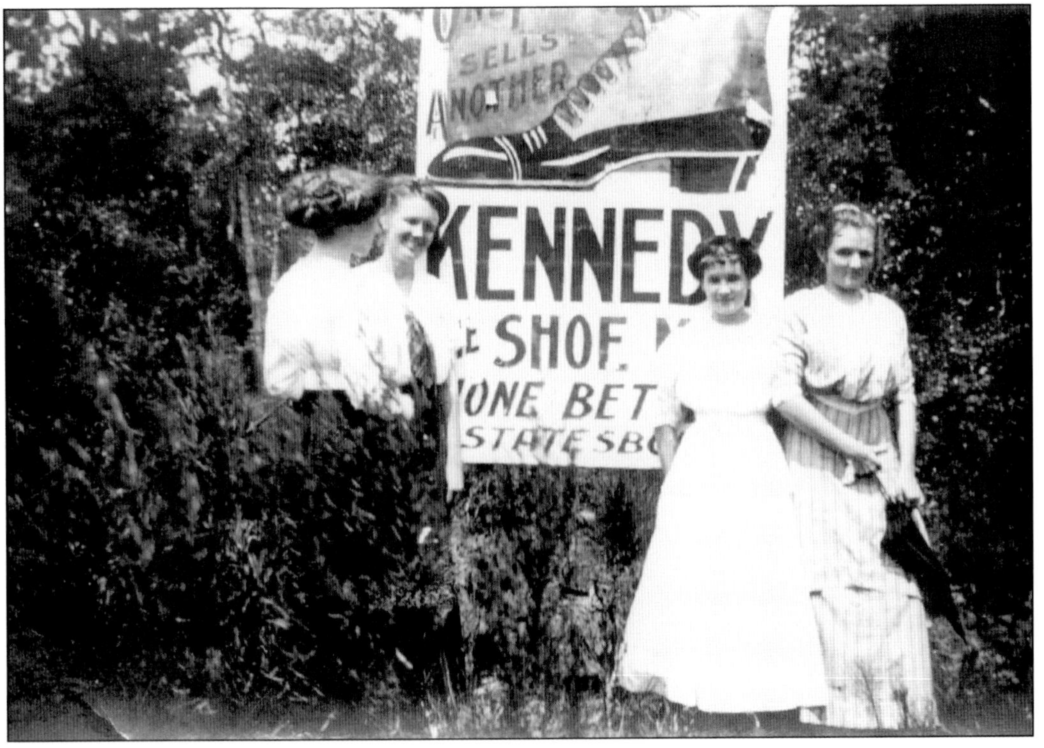

An early roadside sign near Statesboro advertised high topped, lace-up shoes at Kennedy Shoe Store. Unidentified ladies, in shirt-waist dresses with parasols (umbrellas), posed for the picture.

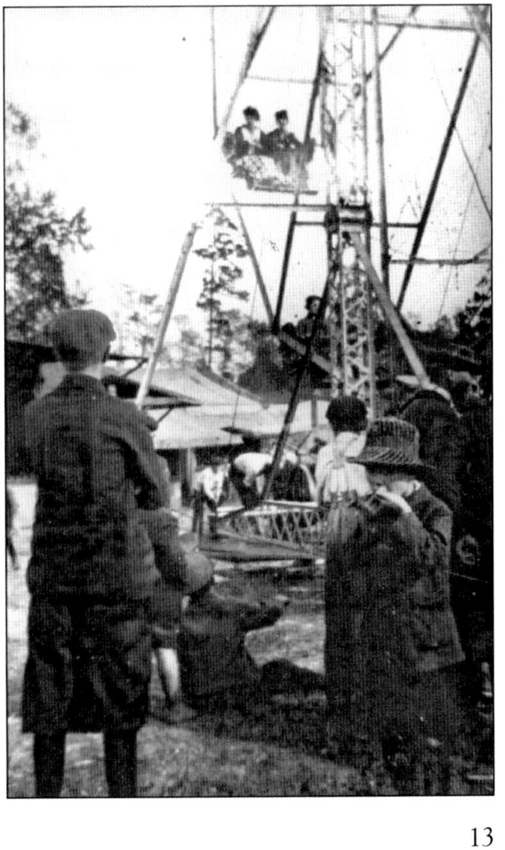

Bulloch County Fair, located at the fairgrounds on Fair Road *c.* 1918, was a special occasion for all citizens. In 2003 it is the site of the Statesboro Recreation Center's Memorial Park. Exhibits of farm products included livestock, canned goods, sewing, crafts, and food items. The exhibits were as attractive as the exciting games of chance and amusements, such as the primitive ferris wheel. The operator, wearing an apron, cared for the equipment and accepted tickets.

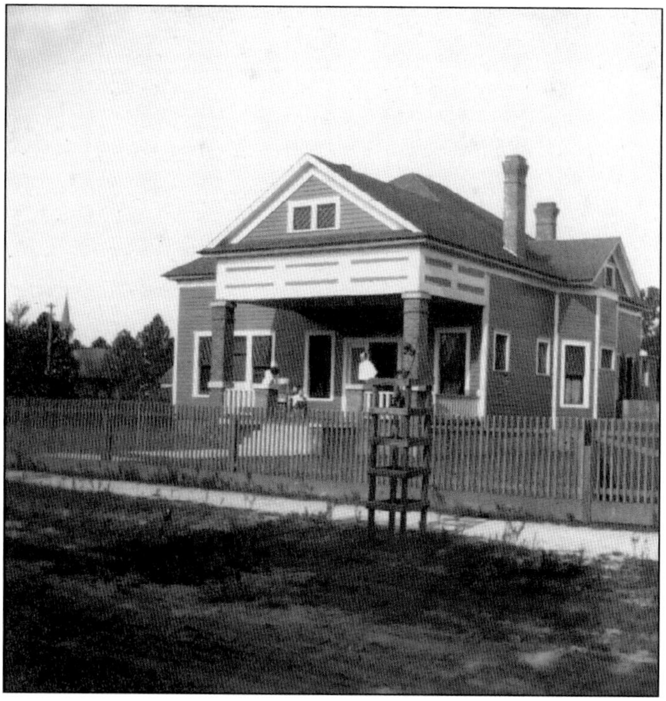

This home, located on South Zetterower, was built as a wedding gift c. 1912 for Mr. and Mrs. Dell Anderson from Mrs. Anderson's parents, Mr. and Mrs. W.H. Sharpe.

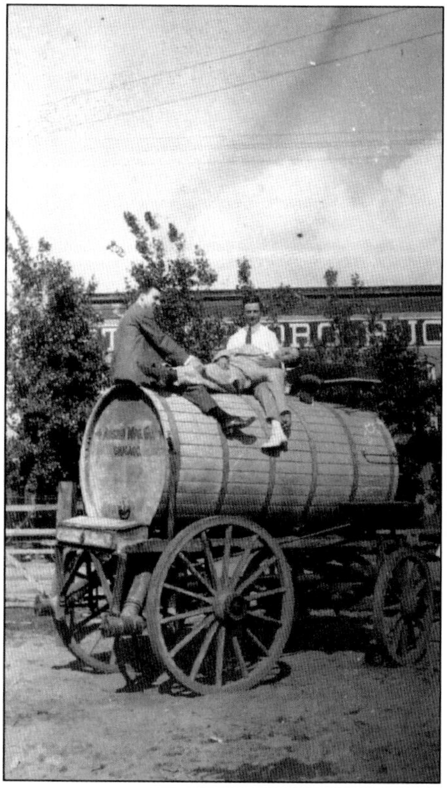

Three unidentified Statesboro young blades engage in shenanigans atop the Statesboro water wagon c. 1910. The vehicle carried water that was used by the local fire department. The city also used it to sprinkle the dirt streets to prevent dust during dry seasons. The wagon is parked on North Main Street across from the Statesboro Buggy and Wagon (the entrance to Simmons Shopping Center in 2003).

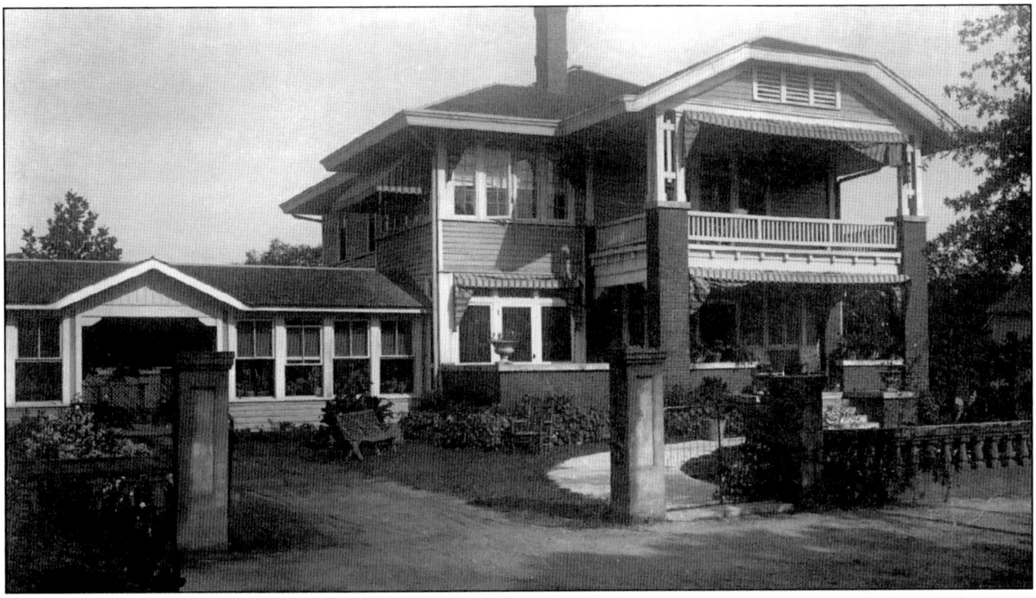

The W.H. Sharpe residence on South Zetterower was constructed *c.* 1913 on the north side of the home of Mr. Sharpe's daughter, Kate Sharpe Anderson. Note that the homes are joined to each other by sun rooms with a covered drive-through. Mr. Sharpe was a prominent businessman in the community, having a large turpentine operation and farming interests. He also owned the Jaeckel Hotel at one time.

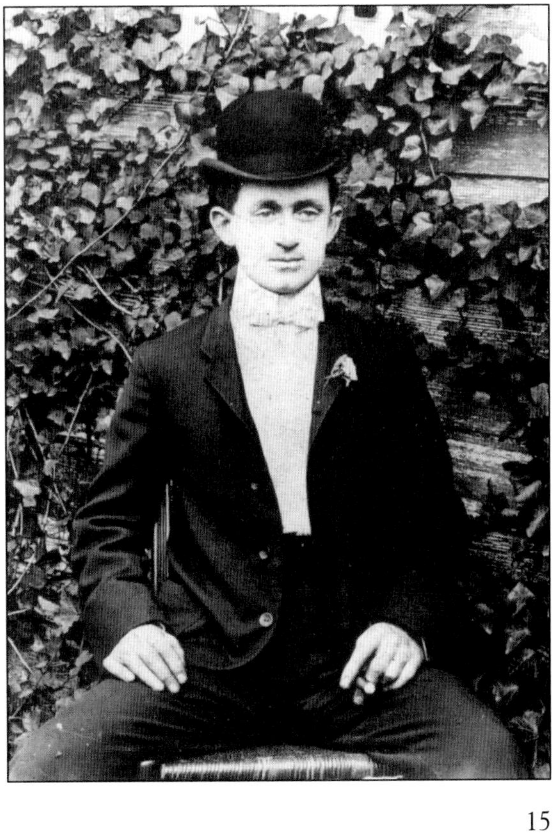

The distinguished looking gentleman is Mr. James Shields Kenan Sr. He worked for the *Statesboro News* as a printer and typesetter during its early days, around 1905. He went into the printing business for himself in 1909. He also was a correspondent for newspapers in Savannah, Augusta, Macon, and Atlanta. His son, J. Shields Kenan Jr., later ran a printing company and bought the *Bulloch Times* from Mr. D.B. Turner and operated it until he sold it to the *Bulloch Herald.* The younger Mr. Kenan remained in the printing business until his retirement in the 1970s.

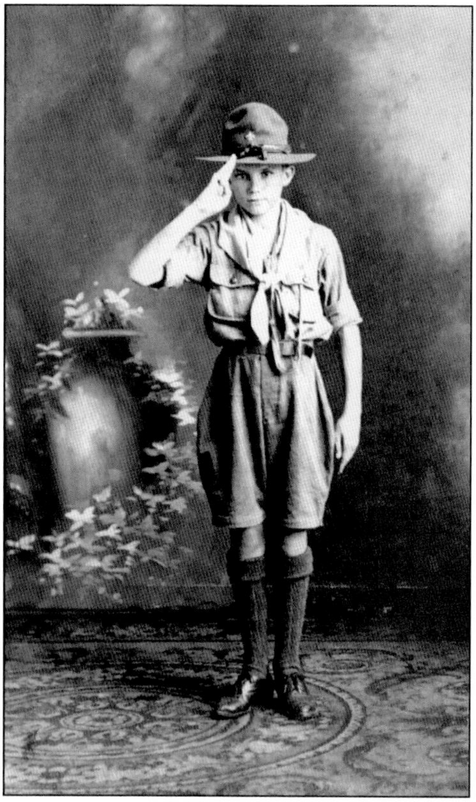

Robert F. "Bob" Donaldson Jr. snaps to attention as he poses proudly in his Boy Scout uniform in 1918. He was a member of one of the earliest Boy Scout troops in Bulloch County. During the 1930s Mr. Donaldson was a professor of journalism and publicity director for South Georgia Teachers College. For many years he was correspondent for the *Savannah Morning News*, *Augusta Chronicle*, and the *Atlanta Journal*. Later he was a successful insurance company agent. He especially enjoyed assisting with the tobacco market each year.

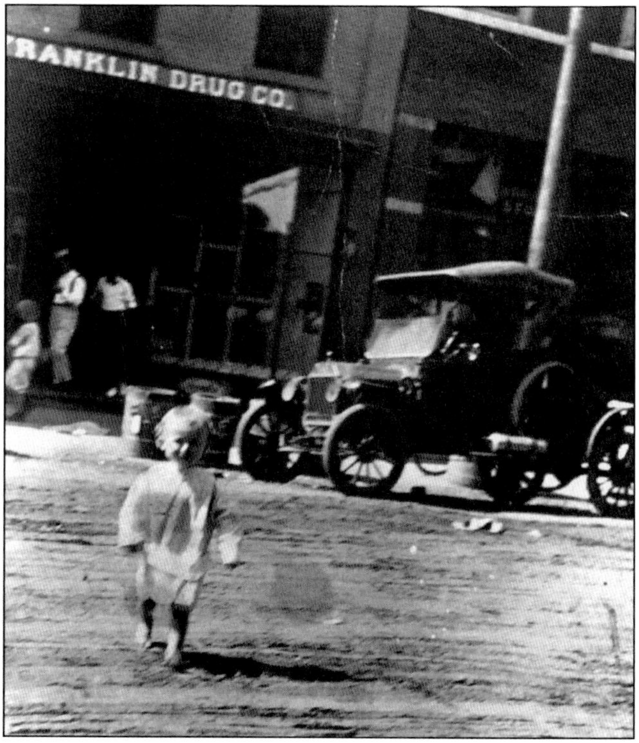

Young Paul G. Franklin Jr. toddles along the unpaved East Main Street across from the Court House Square in 1915. Note he is wearing a shirt tail—a one-piece "dress" young boys often wore until they were old enough for knee pants. He is shown in front of his father's drug store. Note the early model Ford with spoke wheels parked beside a raised wooden sidewalk. Following in his father's footsteps, he became a pharmacist and operated Franklin's Rexall Drug Store on North Main Street until his retirement in the 1970s.

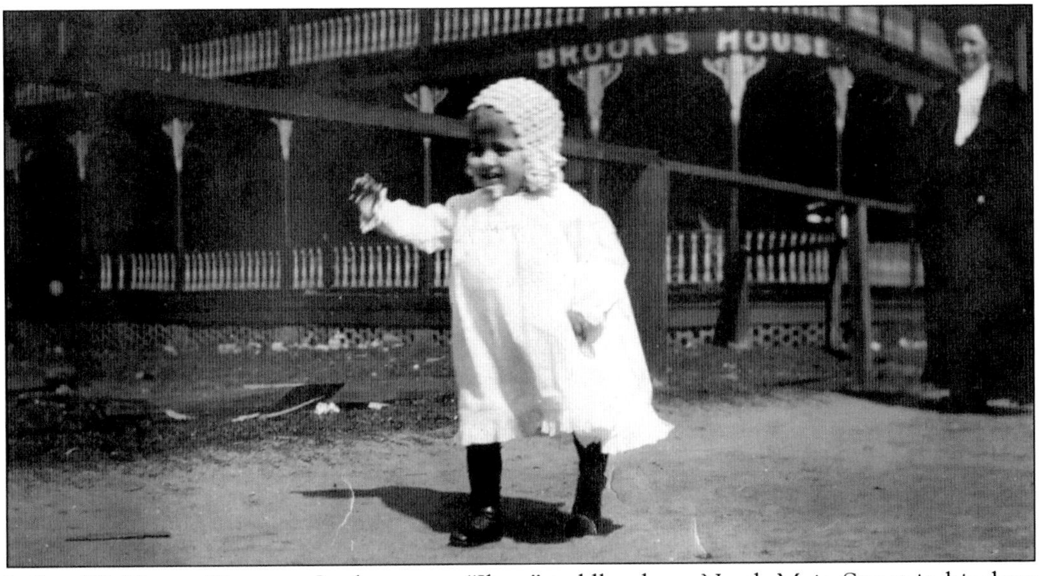

Infant W. Homer Simmons Jr., known as "Ikey," toddles down North Main Street in his dress and bonnet with his nanny, Miss Dody Lichenstein, at the turn of the 20th century. In the background is the famous Brooks House Hotel where the Simmons family lived while their home was under construction. Still standing in 2003, the home was built on the southwest corner of North Main and Church Streets. In 2003 the Brooks House Hotel is the site of a parking lot north of the brick building at the entrance to Simmons Shopping Center. His father was a member of the family of Simmons merchants and was president of the Statesboro Mercantile Company. In later years "Ikey" Simmons was an owner of Statesboro Men and Boys Store on East Main

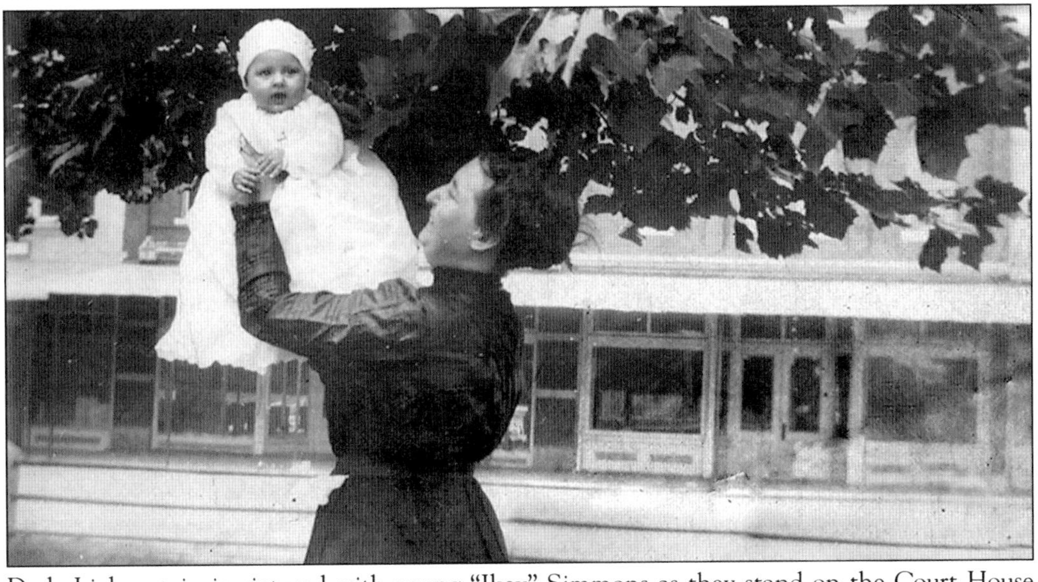

Dody Lichenstein is pictured with young "Ikey" Simmons as they stand on the Court House Square on a sunny afternoon. He received his nickname because as a child he loved to listen to a family friend read the comic strip, "Ike and Mike." Note the fence around the courthouse lawn and a row of stores on the west side of North Main. Also evident is one of many Sycamore trees that once stood on the courthouse lawn and in many neighborhoods throughout town.

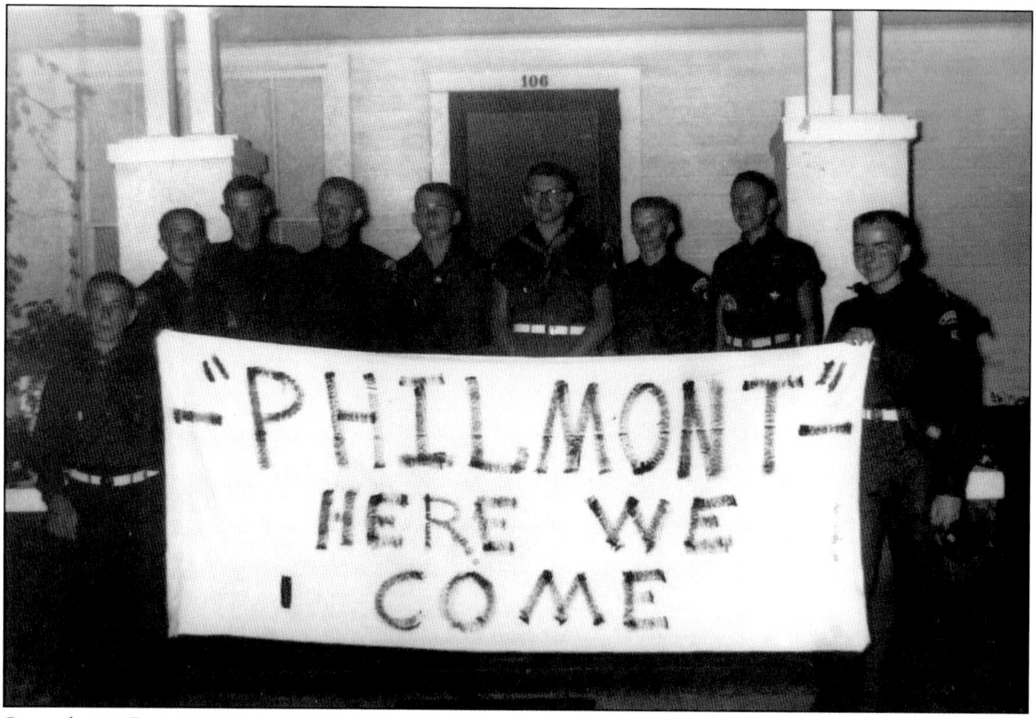

Statesboro Boy Scouts are prepared to leave for Philmont Scout Ranch in New Mexico in August of 1955. They pose for a picture on the steps of the Reppard DeLoach home on Zetterower Avenue. From left to right are Al DeLoach, John Marshall Jackson, Billy Huggins, Phillip Howard, Kenneth Chandler, Dennis DeLoach, Mike Kennedy, Al McDougald, and Winton DeLoach.

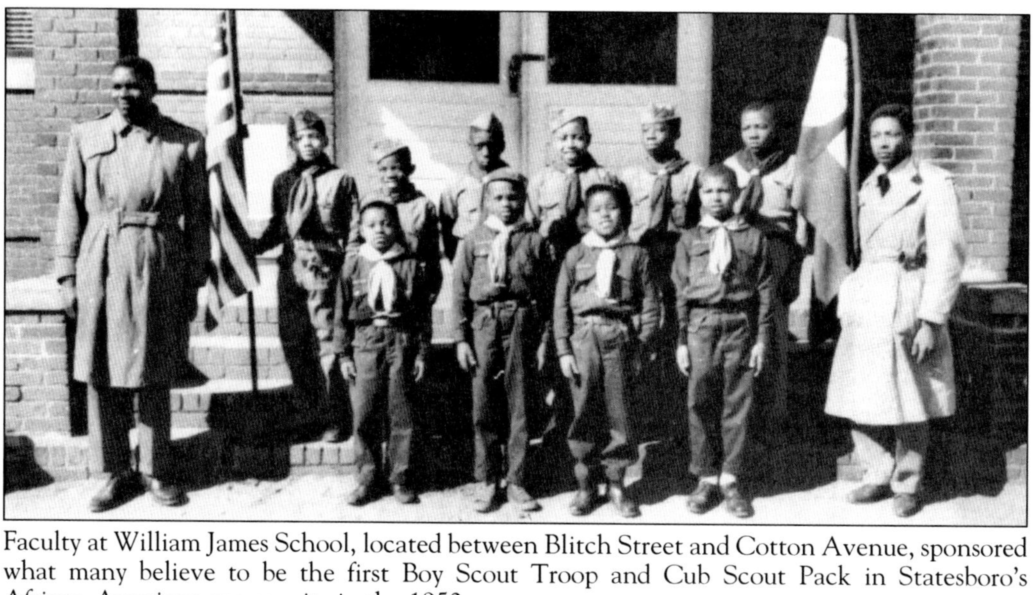

Faculty at William James School, located between Blitch Street and Cotton Avenue, sponsored what many believe to be the first Boy Scout Troop and Cub Scout Pack in Statesboro's African-American community in the 1950s.

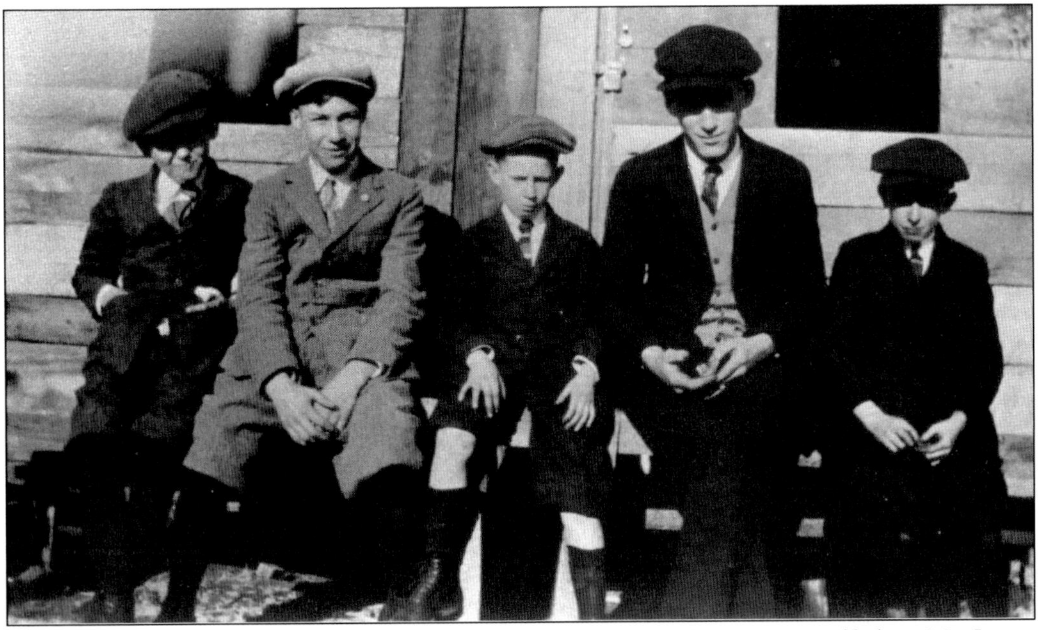

"Five Star Gang" was a group of five young men who shared the same grandfather, Mr. James Moore. They are pictured sitting in front of their club house in the forest behind the Paul G. Franklin Sr. home on Savannah Avenue in 1921. From left to right, they are young Paul Franklin Jr., Robert Benson, Gus Sorrier, "Shot" Hall, and Brooks Sorrier.

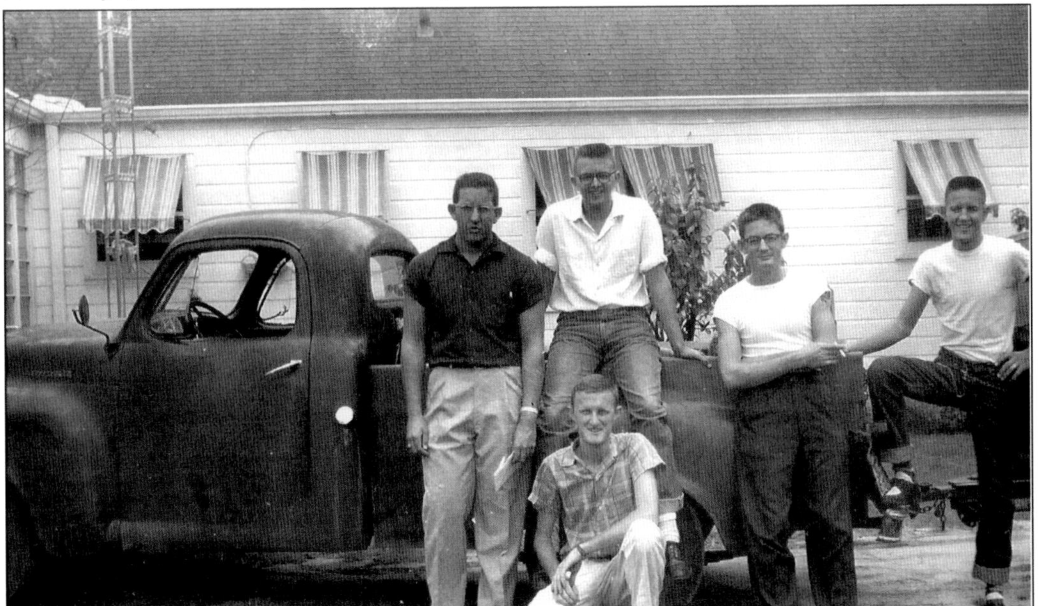

"The Crew" hung out in the backyard of Mrs. W.C. Huggins on Donaldson Street in 1956. They are planning a camping excursion to Canada, including Nova Scotia and Niagara Falls. From left to right, standing, are Fred Dyer, Dennis DeLoach, Allen Sack, and Al Mc Dougald; hunkered down in front is Billy Huggins. The truck is Billy's 1950 Ford. Note in the left background the television antenna that allowed the family to watch broadcasting channels in Savannah and Augusta.

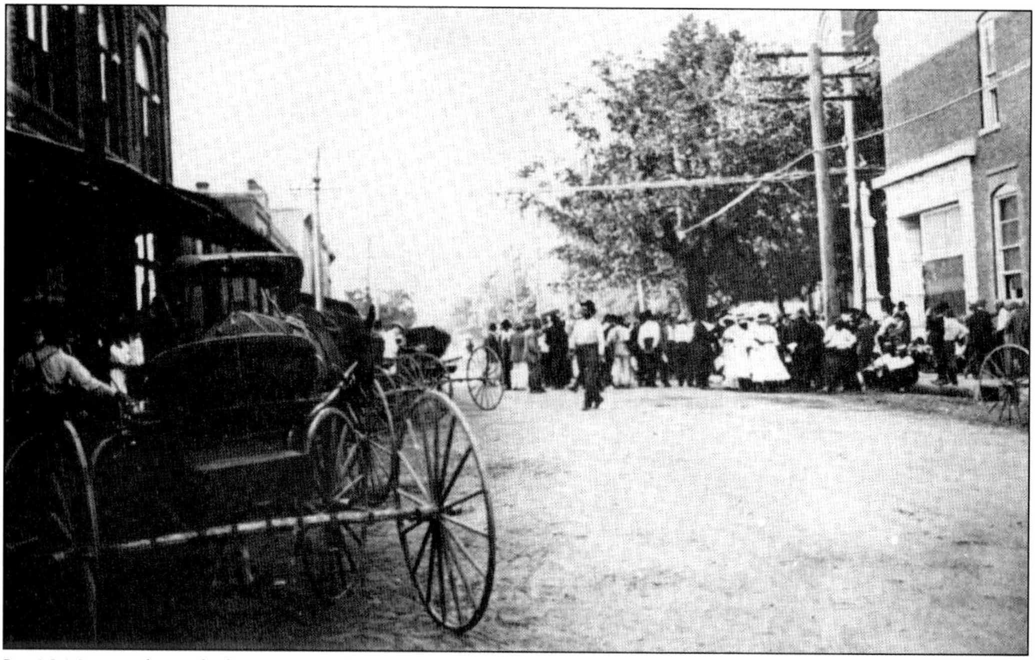

In 1910 people rode buggies in from their county homes and listened to political speakers hold forth on the East Main Street side of the Court House. The view is from South Main, facing north, with the R. Simmons building on the left and the Statesboro Mercantile Company (later Sea Island Bank) on the right. Especially large crowds gathered on Confederate Memorial Day and for political rallies.

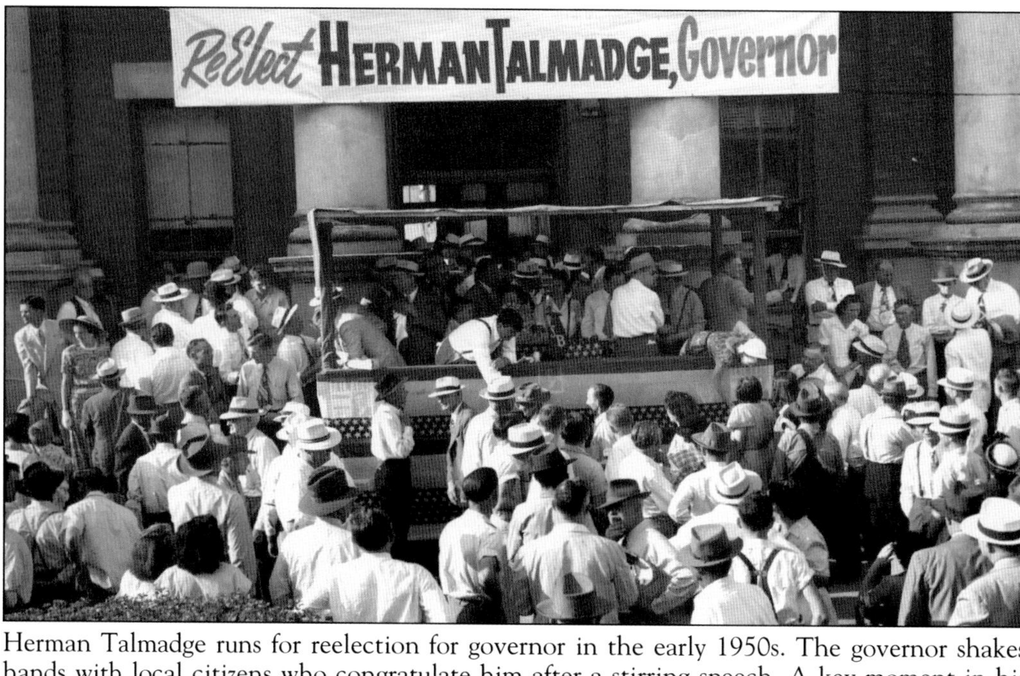

Herman Talmadge runs for reelection for governor in the early 1950s. The governor shakes hands with local citizens who congratulate him after a stirring speech. A key moment in his rally came when he removed his coat and flapped his red suspenders—the trademark of his father, Eugene Talmadge, an earlier governor.

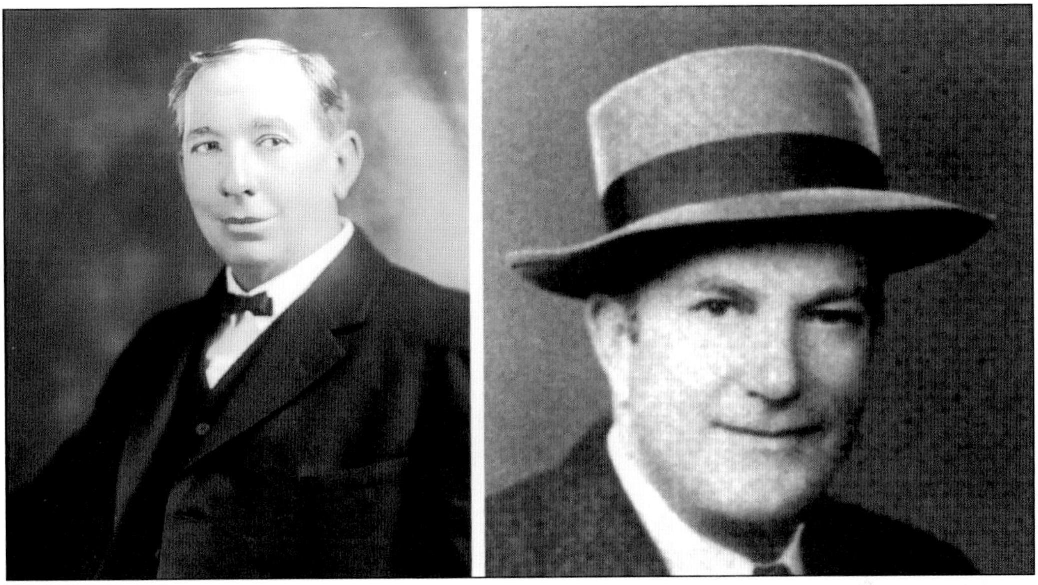

Two of three United States Representatives who called Statesboro home are R. Lee Moore (1923–1925) (left) and Homer Cling Parker (1931–1935) (right). Admitted to the bar in 1890, Mr. Moore served as mayor of Statesboro and held other offices of the court. He died in 1940. Mr. Parker served as mayor of Statesboro and was brigadier general of the Georgia National Guard; later he was elected comptroller general of Georgia, a post he was serving at the time of his death in 1946.

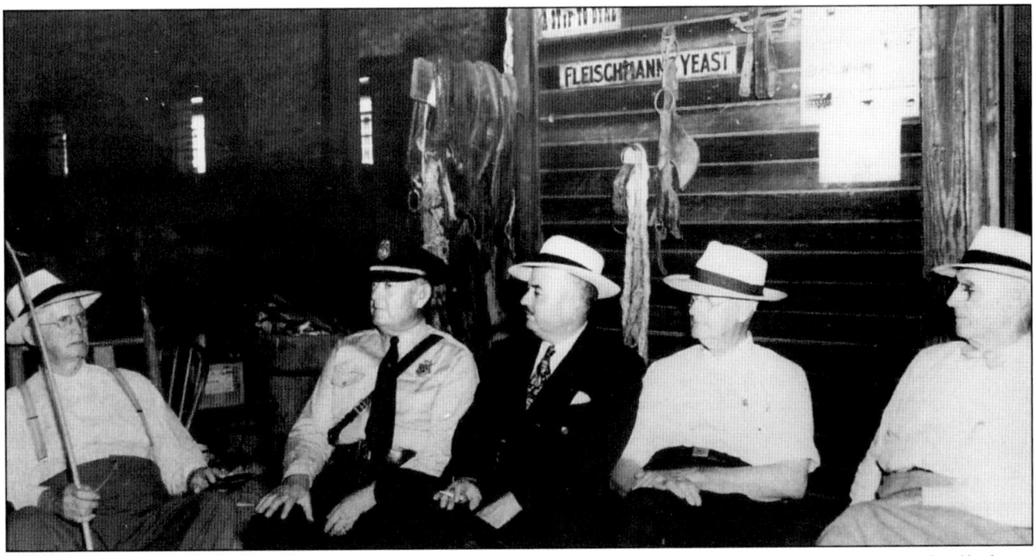

Prince Preston practiced politics the old fashioned way, by "chewing the rag" with (left to right) Josh Zetterower, police chief Henry Anderson, Congressman Preston, Josh Hagan, and veterinarian F.H. Hook. They gathered at the Buggy and Wagon stables on the corner of Courtland and Siebald Streets. Preston was admitted to the bar and began his law practice in Statesboro in 1930. A member of the State House of Representatives from 1935 to 1938, he served in World War II as a captain in the Army. He served six consecutive terms in the United States Congress (1947–1961), and the Prince H. Preston Federal Building on North Main Street is named in his honor.

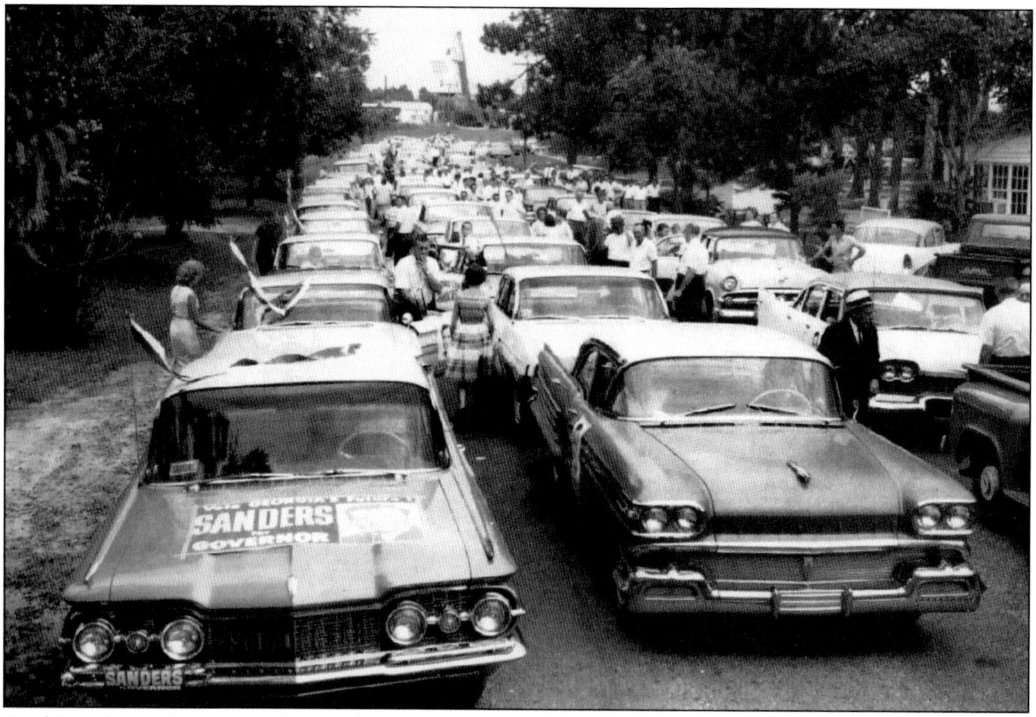

Carl Sanders, who married Statesboro native Betty Bird Foy, began his race for the governorship of Georgia with a huge rally on the Bulloch County Courthouse square in the spring of 1962. A parade composed of enthusiastic local supporters begins with a line-up at the Statesboro Recreation Center at the junction of Fair Road and Sharpe Street (now Max Lockwood Drive). Note the tower of Kennedy's Concrete works in the center background.

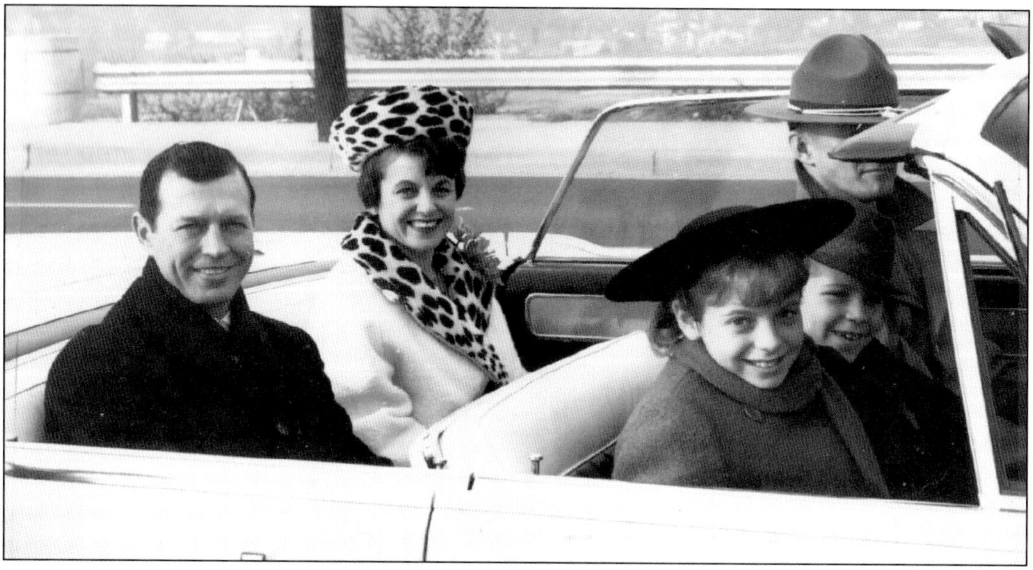

Inauguration ceremonies took place on a cold January day in 1963. Governor-elect Carl E. Sanders and his wife, Betty Bird, are in line for the inaugural parade through downtown Atlanta. In the front seat are the driver, a Georgia State Patrol officer, and Little Betty and Carl Jr. Mrs. Sanders was the first and only first lady of Georgia from Statesboro.

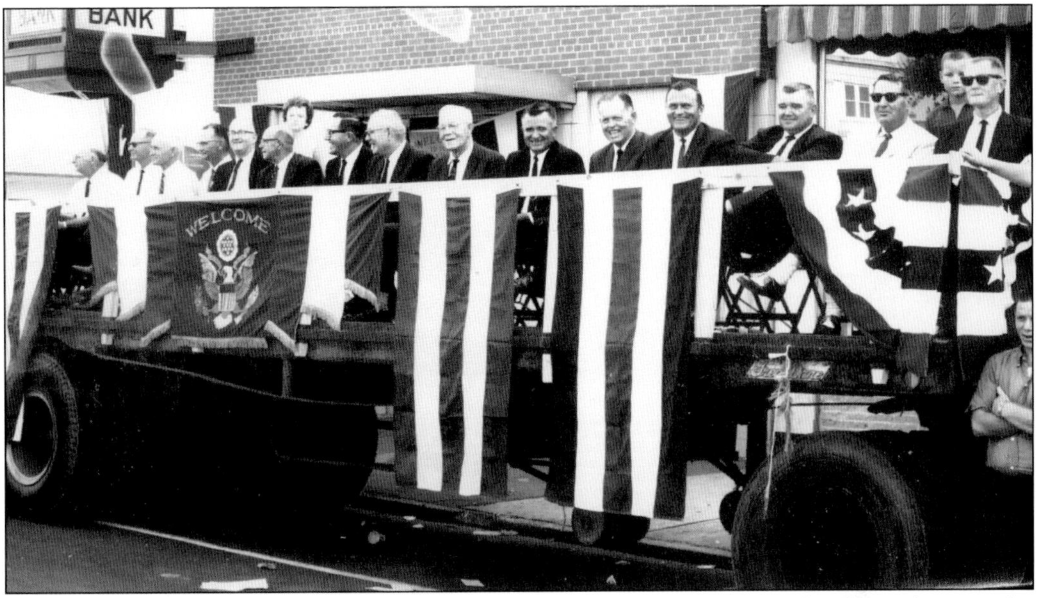

In the early 1960s local political leaders, including county and city officials, gather on the reviewing stand for the annual Fall Harvest Festival. The stand usually stood in front of the Bulloch County Bank at the corner of West Main and North Main Streets. From left to right are four unidentified men in shirtsleeves, city councilmen J. Brantley Johnson, T.E. Rushing Sr., Bernard McDougald, Osborne C. Banks, unidentified, county commissioner John Paul Ellis, state representatives Paul Nessmith and Jones Lane, county commissioner Edgar Wynn, mayor of Statesboro W.A. "Bill" Bowen, and city councilman Albert M. Braswell. Note the street clock on the corner of the bank.

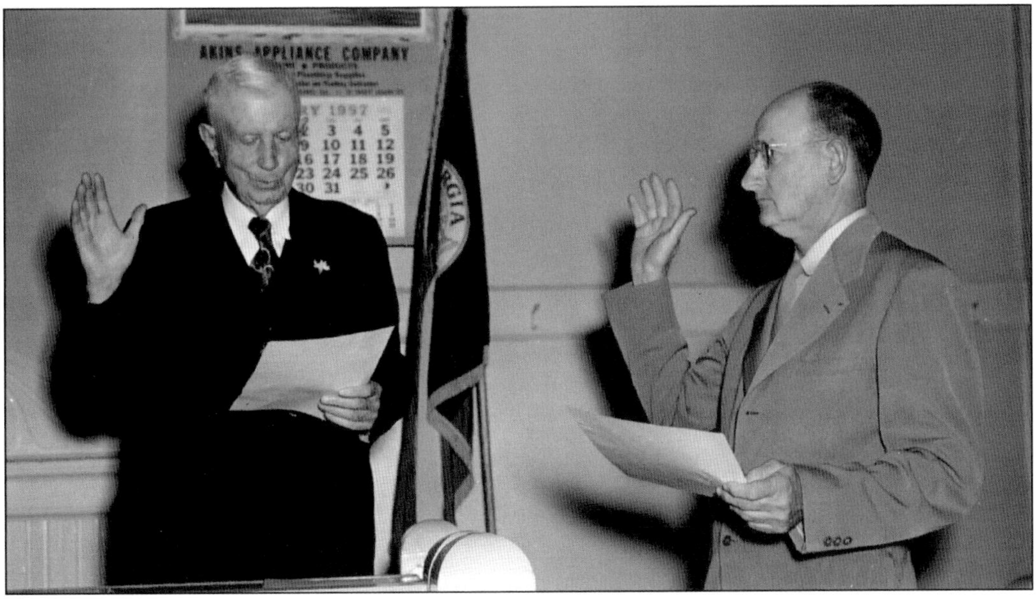

Superior Court Judge J.L. Renfroe swears in R.P. "Bob" Mikell as ordinary of Bulloch County, an office that later became the judge of the Court of Probate. They are shown in the courtroom of the courthouse. The calendar, advertising Akins Appliance Company, indicates the exact year—1957.

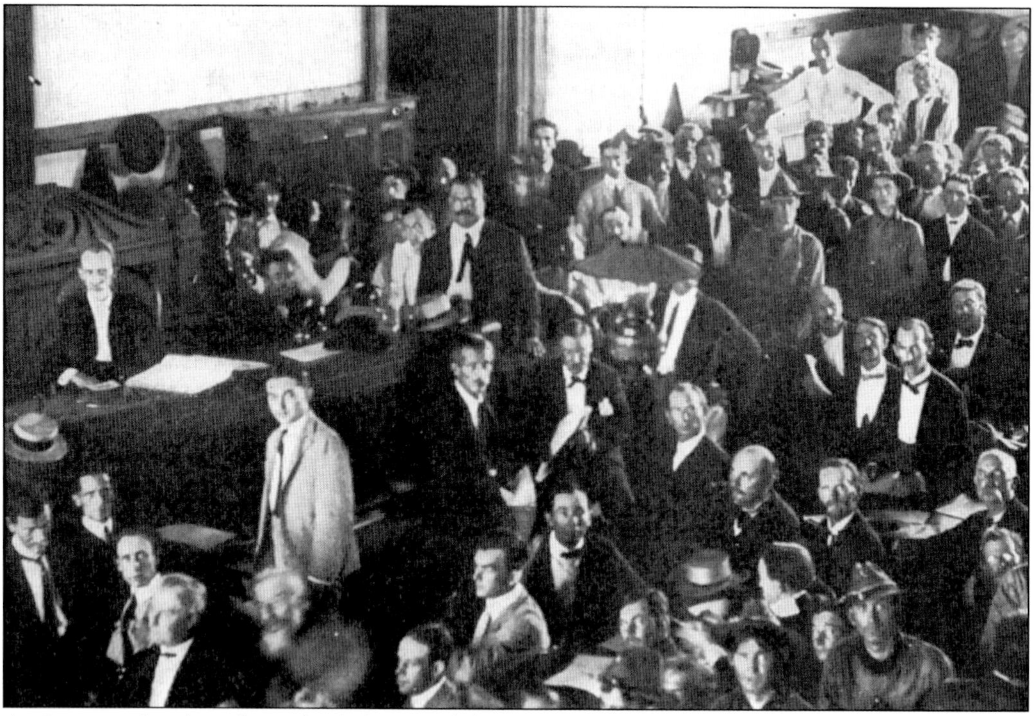

A photograph taken from the balcony of the courtroom reveals the public's great interest in a court trial of 1904. Presiding is Superior Court Judge Alexander F. Daley. He is seated at the judge's bench on the left hand corner. Note the ornately decorated woodwork behind the judge's chair.

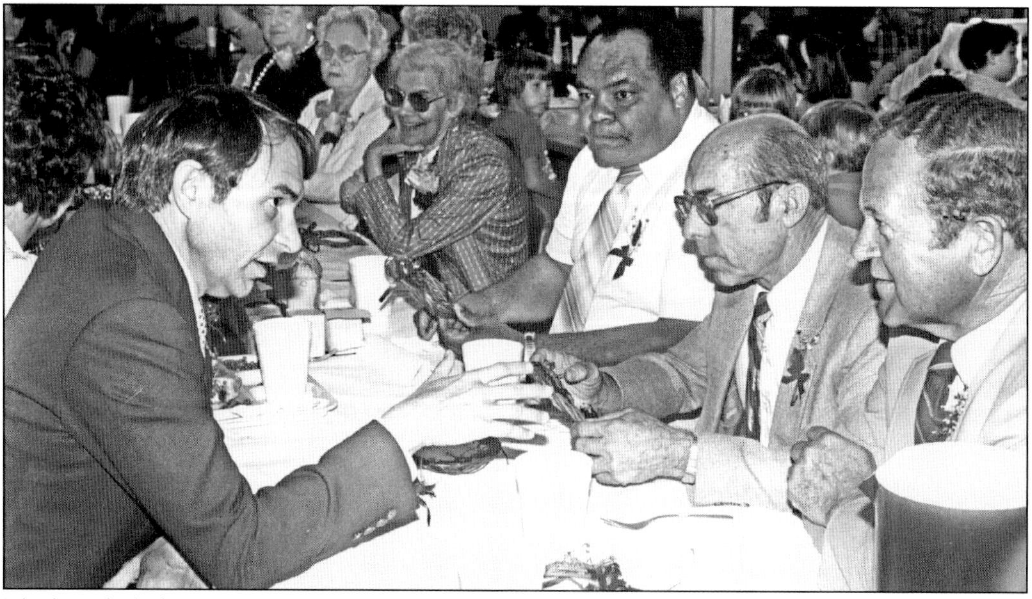

The board of education meets with county commissioners in the 1980s for a yearly public meeting known as "eggs and issues." Gordon Alston, commission chairman Robert Cox, commissioner Thomas Anderson, and unidentified ladies in the background are shown. In the foreground is attorney and education board member Charles Brown.

Statesboro mayor William S. "Bill" Hatcher II addresses an audience gathered at Blitch Street Recreation Center on a cold February 6, 2003, on the occasion of the dedication of Martin Luther King Jr. Drive. The city council voted to change the names of two streets. The newly named MLK Drive was formerly Institute Street from West Grady to West Main, which connects with what earlier had been Blitch Street. The new drive ends at West Parrish Street. A former member of city council, Mayor Hatcher began his tenure in January of 2002.

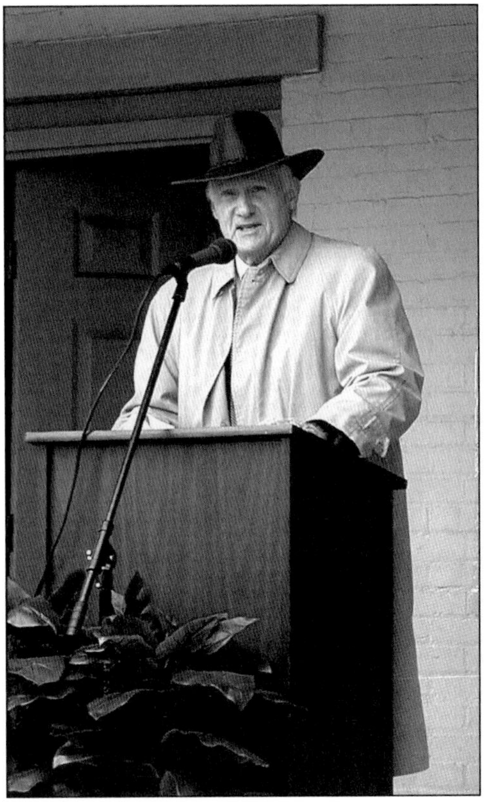

Mayor W.A. "Bill" Bowen with city councilmen Osborne C. Banks, Tommy E. Rushing, J. Brantley Johnson, and A.B. McDougald pose with the new fire truck, which arrived in Statesboro on November 12, 1964. The new truck was capable of pumping 750 gallons of water a minute, and it had a 500-gallon auxiliary tank. They appear at the Statesboro fire department located on the corner of Siebald and Courtland, the site of the Bulloch County Judicial Annex in 2003.

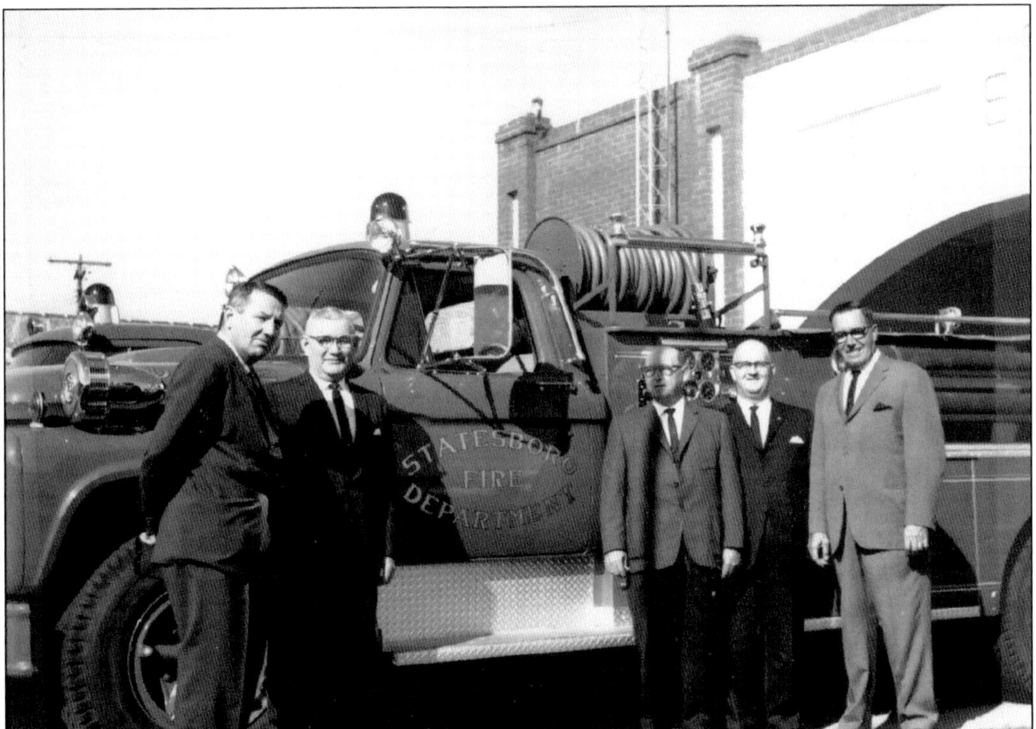

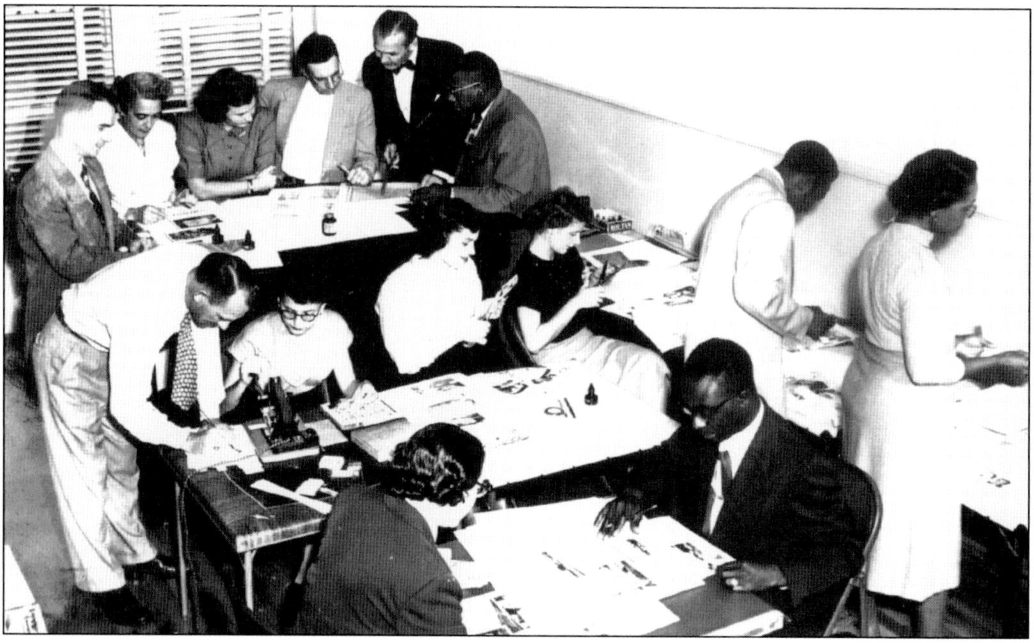

In 1951 all segments of the Statesboro community met to prepare material for the All American Cities Contest scrapbook. It was sponsored by the Georgia Power Company. The interracial cooperation took place three years before the Supreme Court rendered its Brown vs. Board of Education decision.

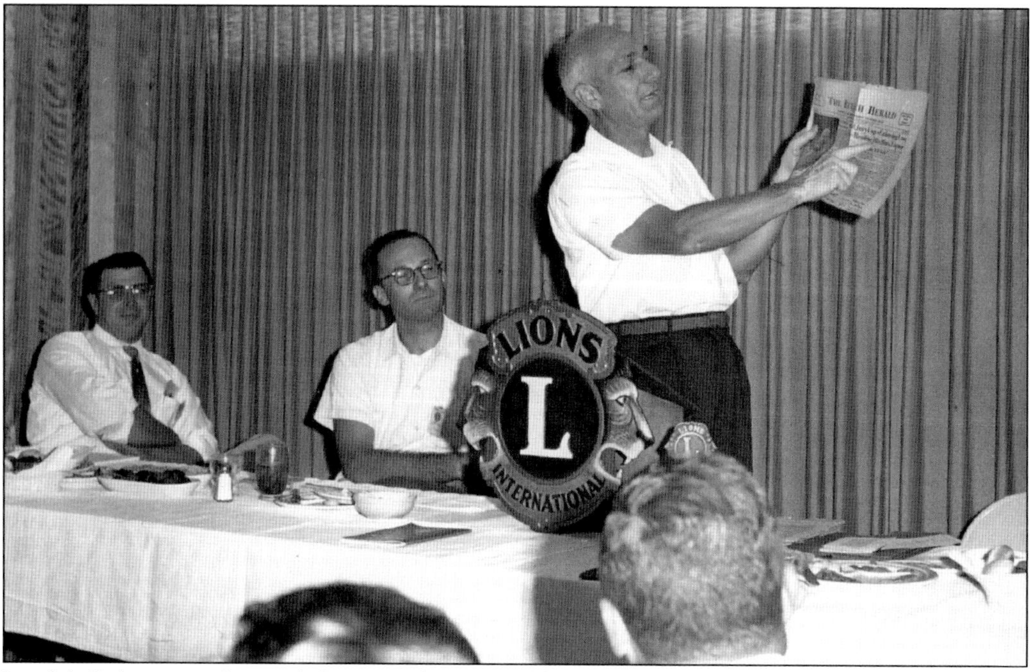

Leodel Coleman, editor of the *Statesboro Herald*, is guest speaker at the Statesboro Lion's Club in the 1960s. Their regular meeting place, as shown here, is the banquet room of Mrs. Bryant's Kitchen on South Main Street. The Lion's Club was established in 1941 as a community service club.

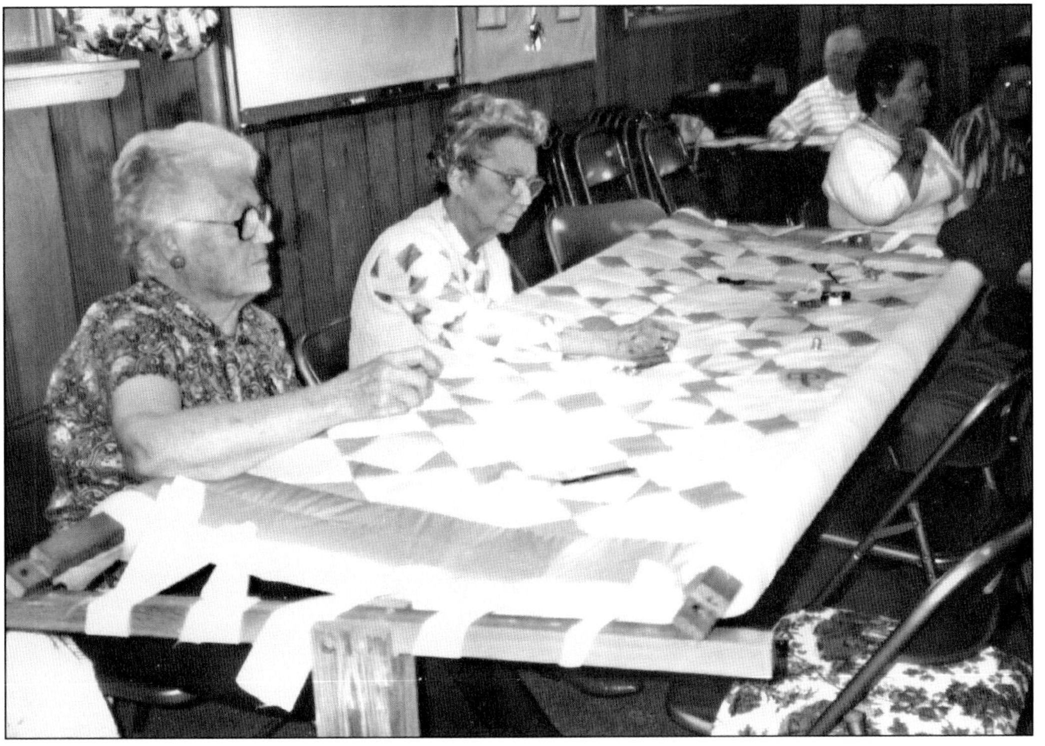

The Statesboro Recreation Department's Senior Center was located in the corner of Northside Drive and Hill Street in the 1970s. Shown are local quilters working at the frame that holds their artistic work. The frame secures the cotton batting or filling, attached to the top of a sheet. Using colorful pieces of cloth, the ladies sewed intricate geometric designs. Later the work was exhibited and sold at a raffle to support the work of the center.

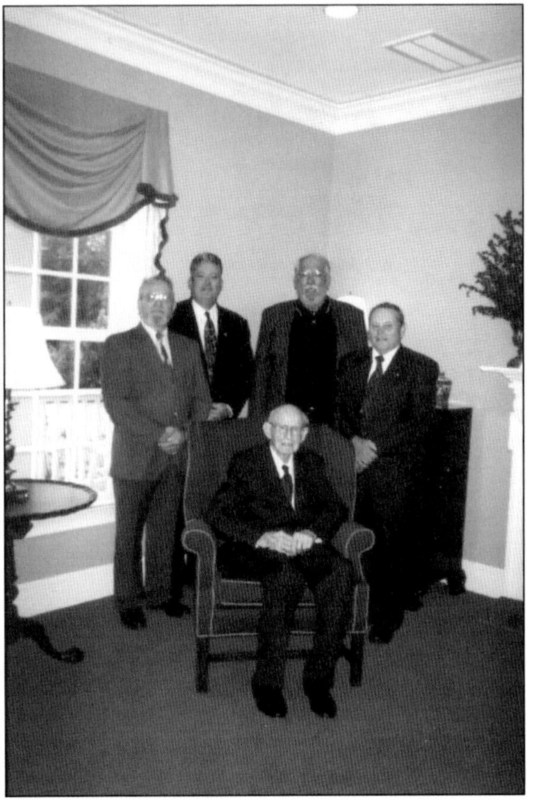

The Ogeechee Masonic Lodge # 213 was organized on April 24, 1857, at the Union Methodist Church on Old River Road. The Lodge moved its meeting place to South Main Street in 1874, near the site of the First United Methodist Church in 2003. The present building stands on the site of the original structure and was dedicated in 1941. Shown are (seated) Hamp Smith, age 100, Past Master, and standing left to right are Gene Parrish, Keith Barber, Tom Thornton, and Ken Bennett. In 2003 Mr. Smith had been a Mason for more than 75 years, a rare accomplishment, since membership can only begin after age 21.

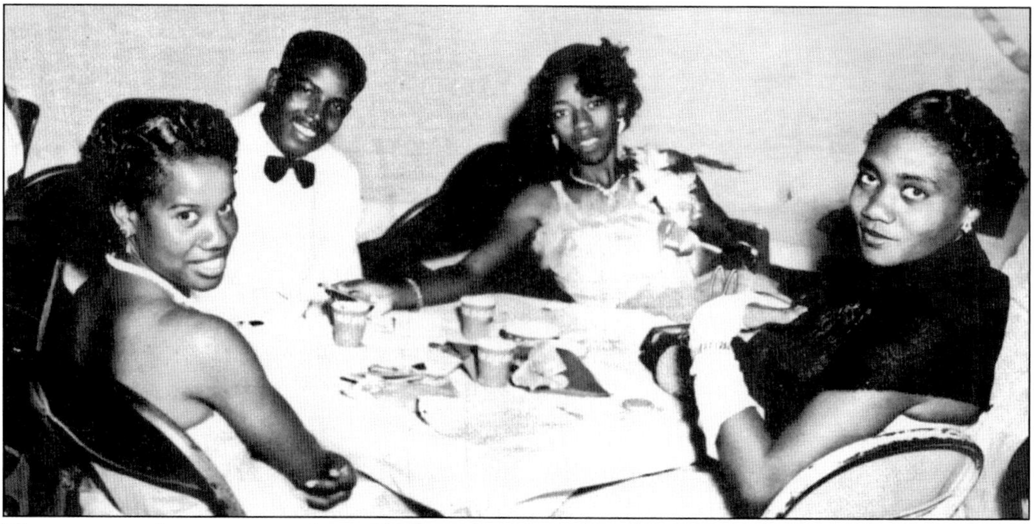

This scene is from prom night at William James High School in the mid-1950s. Fashionably dressed students enjoyed one of the social highlights of the year. Live music, delicious food, and elegant decorations made the evening memorable. From left to right are Hazel Allen, Vernon Pryor, Maggie Sue Fleming, and Eulee Holloway.

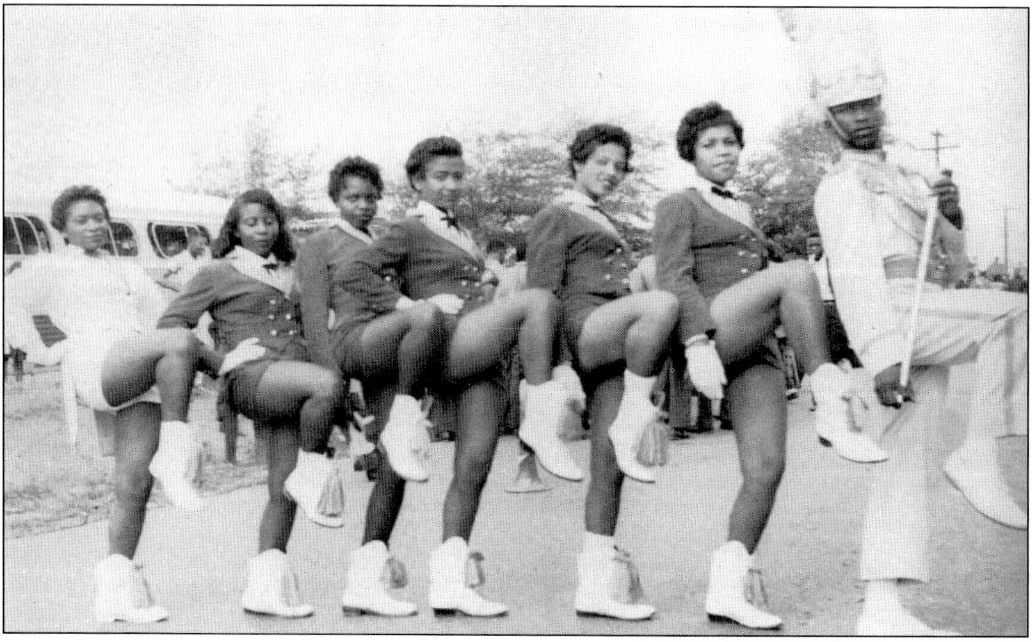

In the 1950s the drum major and his high-stepping majorettes of William James High School were much in demand for parades in Statesboro. The William James Homecoming parade was a highlight of the year. It featured floats, school dignitaries, academic clubs, and out-of-town bands. From left to right are Nora Williams, Helen Brown, Frances Burton, Willie Mae Manning, Elaine Garrison, Gloria Groover, and drum major Billy Cole.

Miss Sherrie Ann Williams, elegantly dressed, joins her escort, Kenneth Moore, as they promenade along the entrance to the Miss Blitch Street Recreation Center contest. From left to right, seated, are Mrs. Julia P. Bryant, for whom Julia P. Bryant Elementary School was named, Mrs. Amy Deigh, Mrs. Ethel Talbert, and Mrs. Gertrude Everett.

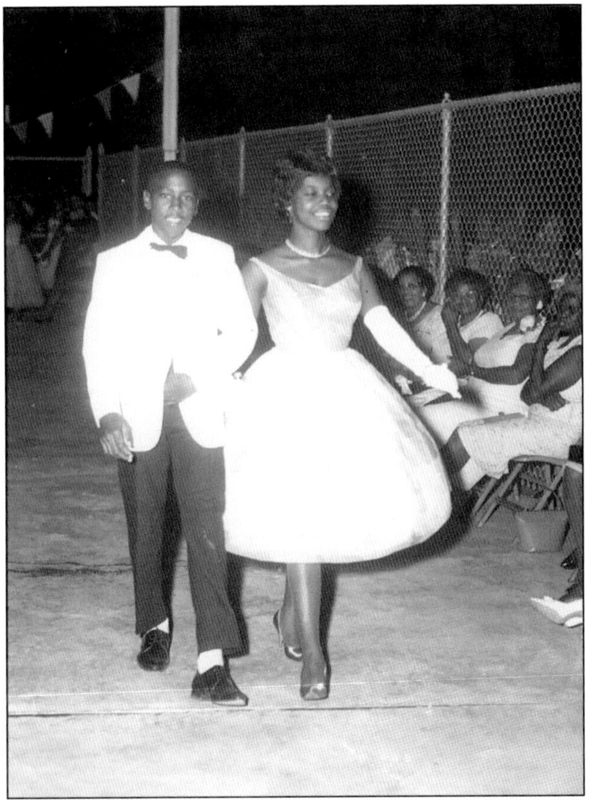

The Blitch Street Center teen council provided information and advice to the Statesboro Recreation Department. From left to right are Leon Grimes, Beverly Jean Brown, Lee Daniel Hill (who later became a legendary basketball coach at Statesboro High School), Pedetha Grant, Pamela Smith, and unidentified.

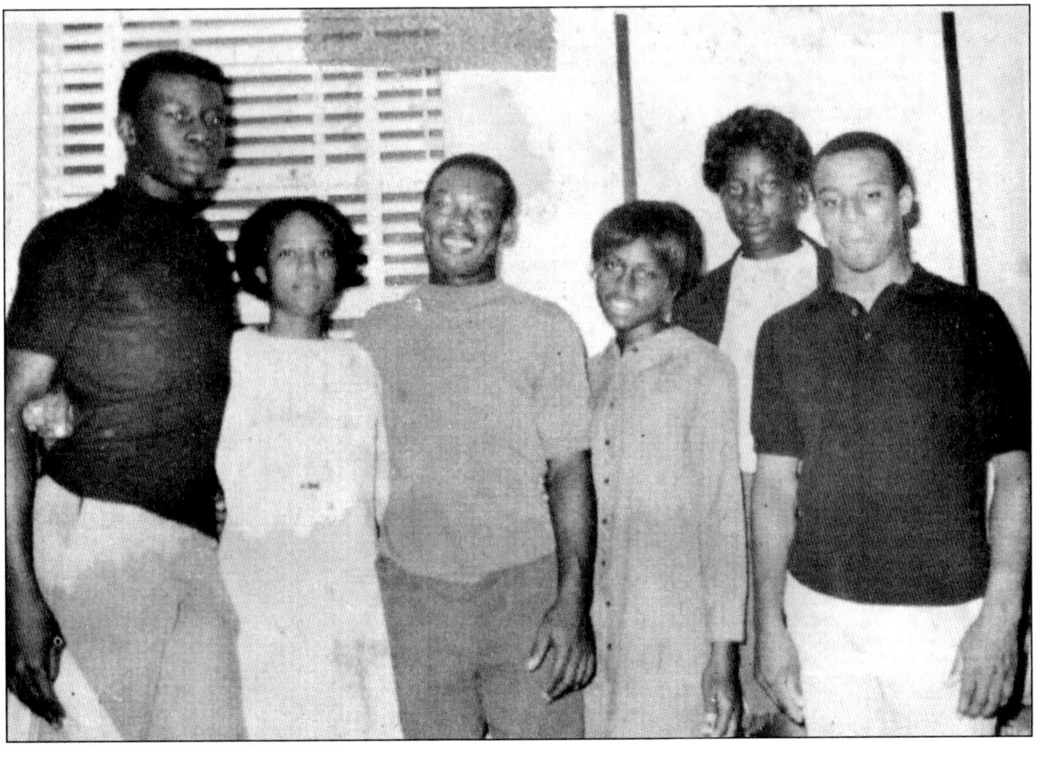

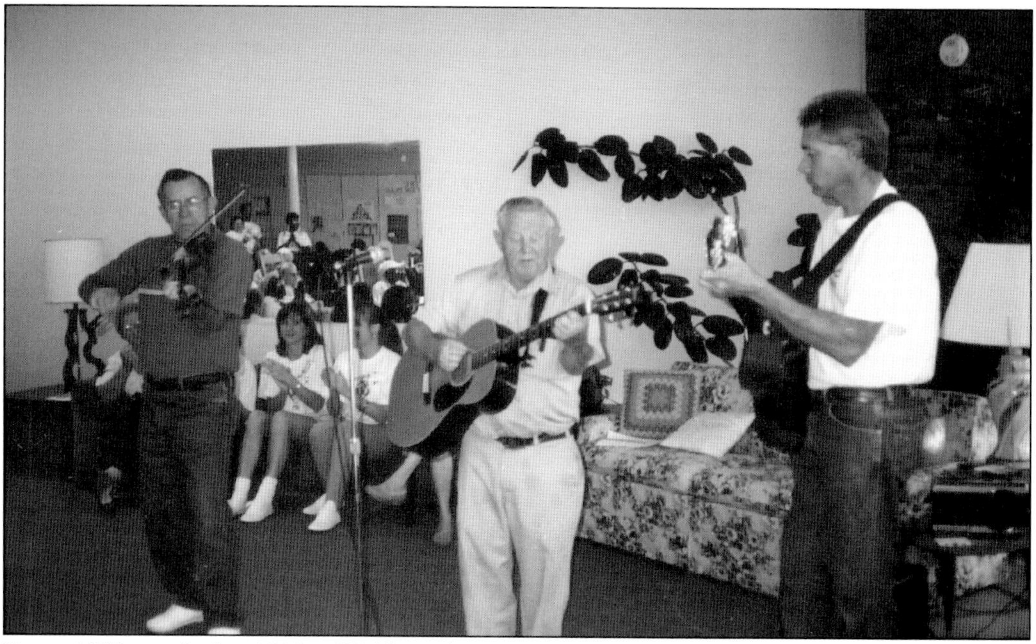

From 1950 until the 1990s, Waldo "Shorty" Smith entertained local audiences with his band, the Georgia Peapickers. They performed a variety of music—from country and western to religious—and often they could be found in churches, nursing homes, and senior citizen centers. In the commons room of the Statesboro Nursing Home in the mid-1990s, from left to right, are James Smith on the fiddle (Shorty's brother); Shorty at the guitar; and William Lee at the guitar. Waldo's son, Gerrald Smith, continued the family tradition in music by composing, singing, and recording country music in Nashville, Tennessee, where he is known as the "Georgia Quackerjack."

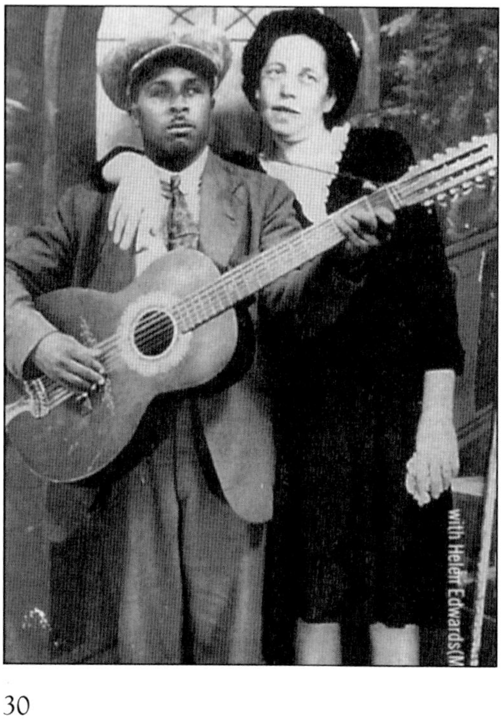

In a Library of Congress interview of 1940, Willie McTell says "Statesboro is my real home." Blind from the day he was born in 1898, he learned to play the guitar as a youngster. He became a leader of the blues movement in the 1920s. A familiar figure on the streets of Statesboro, as well as Atlanta, "Blind Willie" recorded 100 songs. Perhaps his most famous is "The Statesboro Blues," rediscovered by several rock bands in the 1970s. Locally known as "Doog," Blind Willie returned home often, especially during the tobacco season when he sang and played in warehouses and at the Jaeckel Hotel. He is shown here with wife Helen Edwards McTell in 1955. He was inducted into the Georgia Music Hall of Fame some 40 years later.

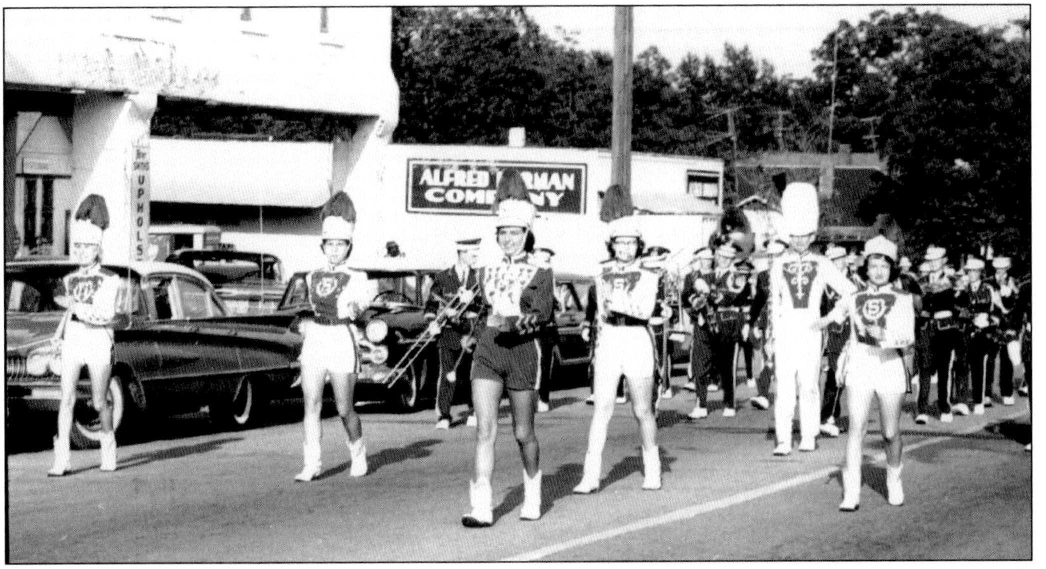

The Statesboro High School band in the 1940s and 1950s participated in a weekly ritual each Friday afternoon of all home football games. A parade began at the First Methodist Church and moved up North Main to Hill Street, to East Main, West Main, and back to the church. When the parade reached Courthouse Square, the cheerleaders who led the parade would conduct a spirited pep rally. Families brought children, and stores emptied of clerks and customers who lined the sidewalks to enjoy this festive moment on autumn afternoons.

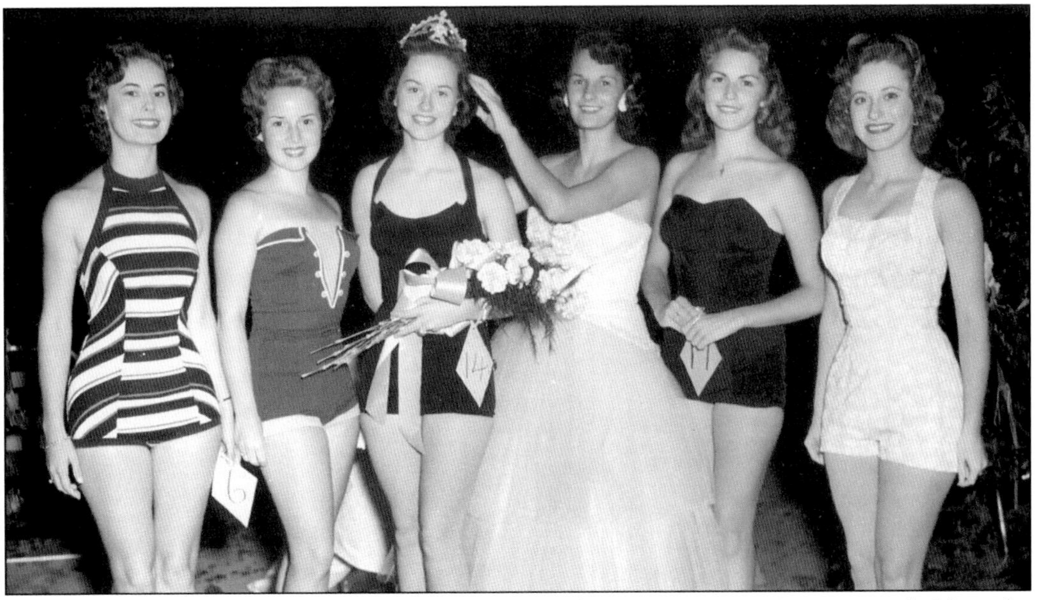

In 1957 the Miss Memorial Park contest at Statesboro Recreation Center was held at the Swimming Center on June 5. Judges were Mrs. Charlie Joe Matthews, Mrs. G.H. Byrd, Lewis Hook, and Don Coleman. Selected to serve on the court were (from left to right) Glenda Banks (fifth place); Annie Laurie Sain (second place); Miss Memorial Park Patricia Redding (who is crowned by Edwina Paul, Miss Memorial Park 1956); Marsha Hayes (third place); and June Iler (fourth place). A dance honoring the queen and her court was held at the new Pavilion with music provided by Emma Kelly and her combo.

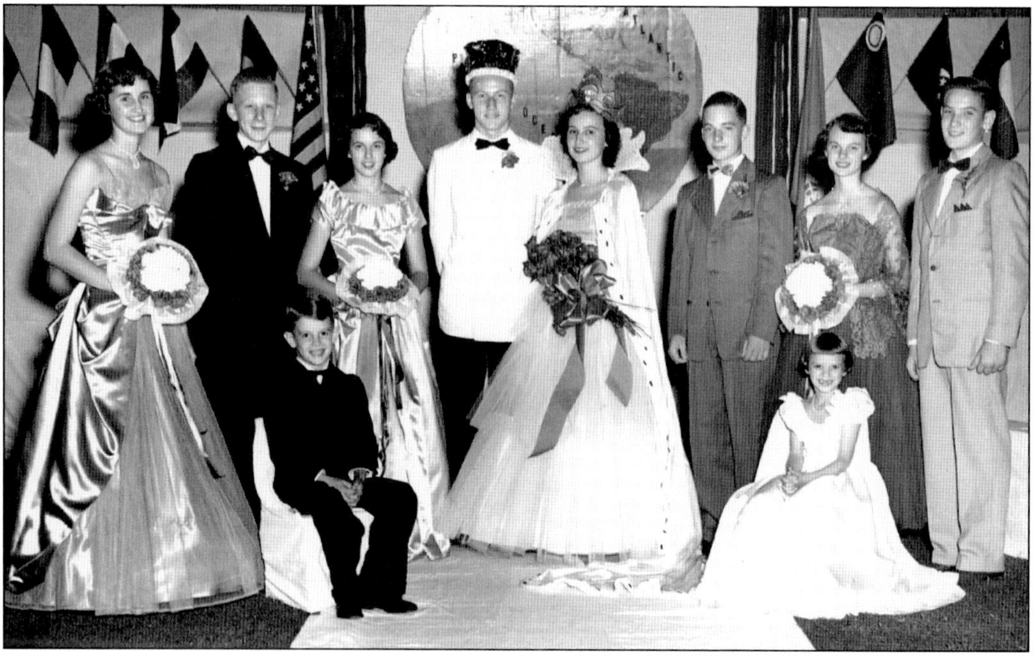

The king and queen and their court reigned over the Halloween Carnival in 1950 at Statesboro schools (both grammar school and high school). The Grady Street gym was transformed into a carnival. Winners, from left to right, are Betty Womack and Frank Williams (junior class); Lynn Smith (freshman); king of the carnival C.P. Claxton and the queen Ann Evans; Cliff Cannon (freshman); Jean Martin and Gilbert Cone (sophomores). The mascots, seated, left, are first graders Bobby Pound, and right, Dottie Donaldson.

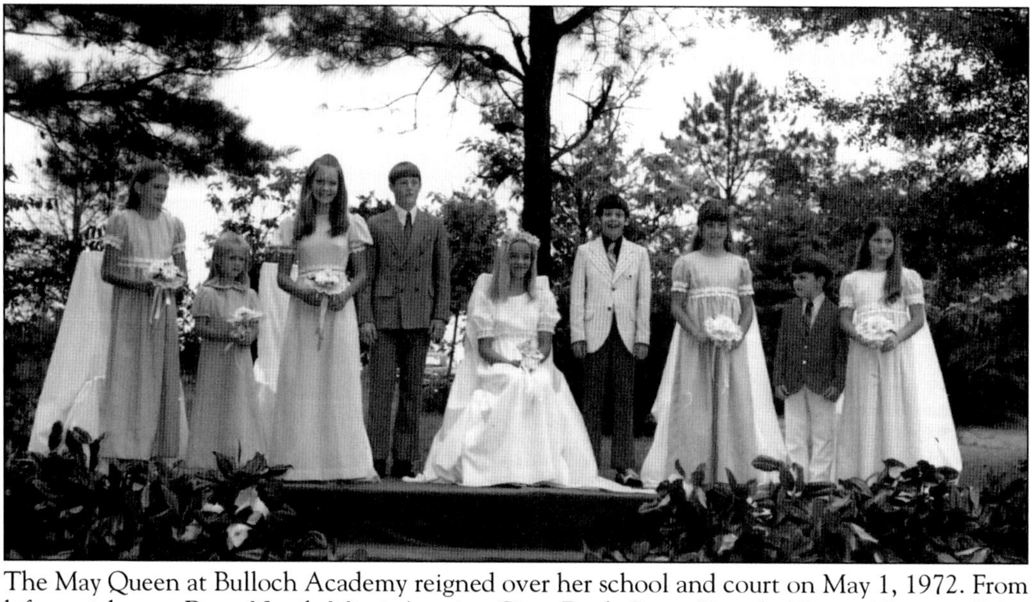

The May Queen at Bulloch Academy reigned over her school and court on May 1, 1972. From left to right are Dana Nevil, Mimi Averitt, Gina Deal, Scott Hosick, Nancy Newton (May Queen), Chuck Rockett, Connie Morris, John Hodges, and Susan Blitch. The school opened its doors in the fall of 1971, serving grades one through six. In 2003 the school offers classes for pre-kindergarten through twelfth grade for over 500 students.

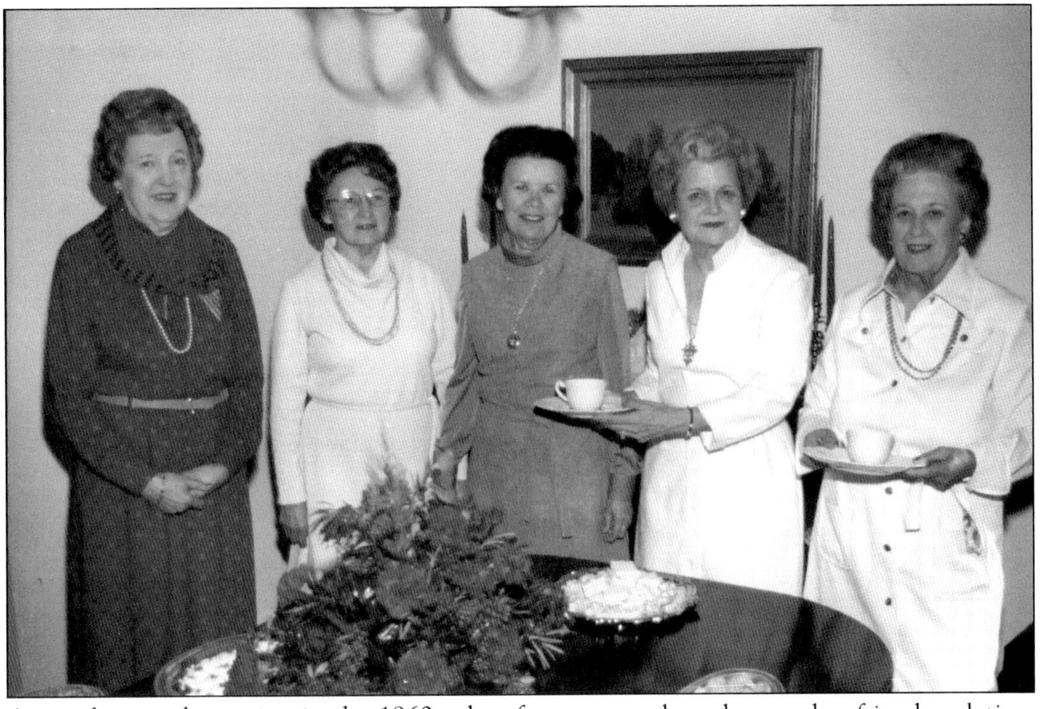

A popular social occasion in the 1960s, the afternoon tea brought together friends, relatives and, sometimes, out-of-town guests. Shown here are hostesses for a tea (from left to right) Leona Newton, an unidentified honoree, Lucy Donaldson, Lavinia Floyd, and Elizabeth Sorrier.

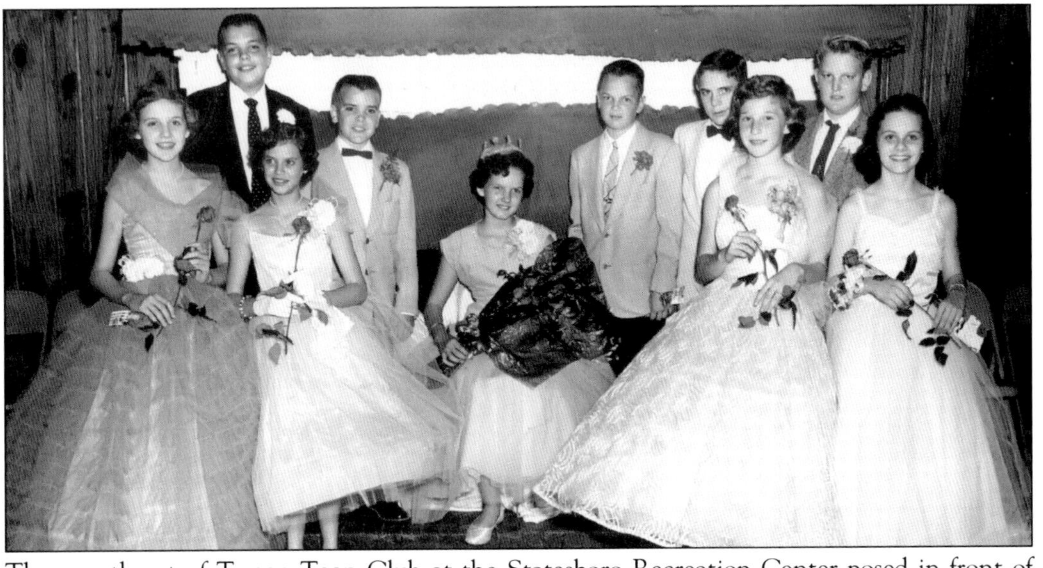

The sweetheart of Tween Teen Club at the Statesboro Recreation Center posed in front of the gigantic fireplace in what once was the Woman's Club building in 1957. This club was designed for grades 8 and 9, and its membership was 120. After completing the annual awards ceremony, participants and guests enjoyed dancing to music provided by Emma Kelly and her combo. From left to right, in the front row, are Mary Emmye Johnston, Dottie Donaldson, Ellen McElveen (Sweetheart), Donna Minkovitz, and Gloria Lane. In the back row are Nat Allen, Johnny Martin, Ed Ellis, Jimmy Scearce, and Bucky Crockett.

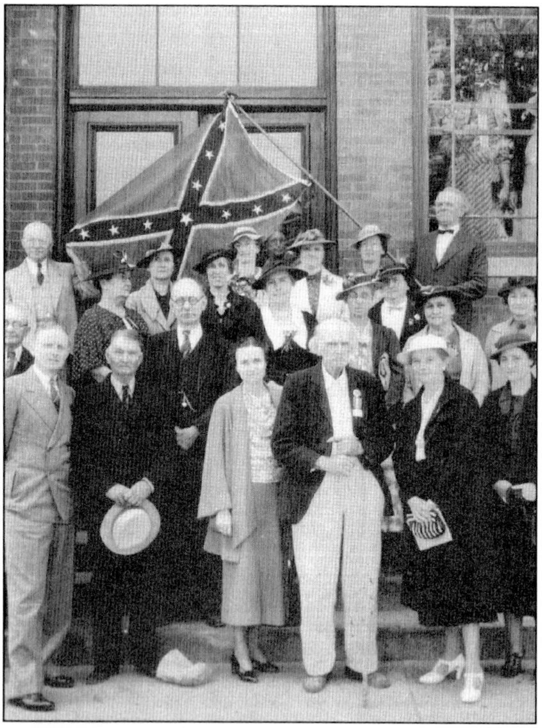

William Jasper Brown, center, in 1937 was the only surviving Confederate veteran in Bulloch County. He is shown at the courthouse on April 22, 1937, following a Confederate Memorial Day service in which he was honored. Included from left to right are (first row) John B. Spivey of Swainsboro, Memorial Day speaker; Elbert Bird of Metter; Miss Hattie Powell; Mr. Brown; Mrs. Julian C. Lane; and Mrs. Lawton Brannen; (second row) Walter Roundtree of Summit; D.B. Turner; Mrs. W.H. Blitch, president Bulloch County Chapter of the United Daughters of Confederacy; Mrs. J.J. Zetterower; Mrs. Charles E. Cone; and Miss Anna Bird; (third row) Mrs. C.M. Cummings; Mrs. Inman M. Foy; and Mrs. R.J.H. DeLoach; (fourth row) R.J.H. DeLoach; Mrs. Fred T. Lanier; Mrs. Ralph Moore; Mrs. Frank Smith; Mrs. W.E. Smith; Mrs. W.E. Simmons, and Col. A.M. Deal. Mr. DeLoach and Mr. Deal are holding the Confederate flag.

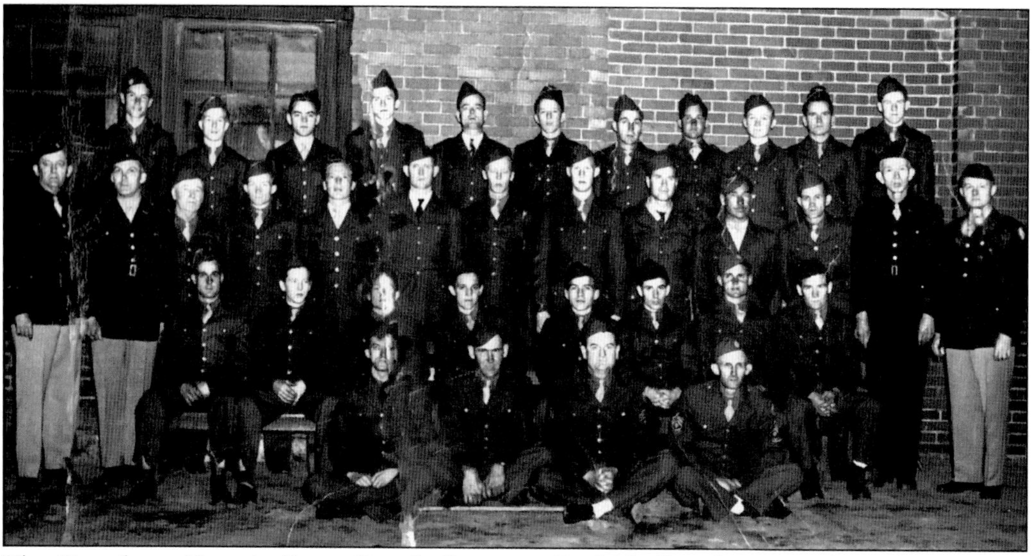

The Statesboro Georgia State Guard, Company B, 14th Battalion, stands in front of the Statesboro Armory located on East Vine Street in the early 1940s. In the first row, from left to right, are Sgt. F.S. Pruitt, Sgt. Roy E. Allen, Sgt. Farley Haygood, and Sgt. C.O. Bohler. In the second row, from left to right, are Carl Brown, Billy Riggs, two unidentified, ? Clark, two unidentified, and Bert Barlow. In the third row, from left to right, are Capt. M.E. Alderman, Lt. Kermitt Carr, W.W. Jones, three unidentified, Sidney Beeland, Mr. Suddath, unidentified, Sgt. M.F. Butler, Cpl. Homer Simmons, Lt. Dan McCormick, and Lt. Sidney Lanier. In the fourth row, from left to right, are two unidentified, Roy McClain, unidentified, Rufus Anderson; Jerry W. Howard; J.R. Kelly, three unidentified, and Ben Robert Nessmith.

One of Statesboro's earliest motorcycle policemen was Clinton Tucker, affectionately known as "Tuck," shown here on duty in the 1950s. Highly regarded by citizens from all walks of life, he dispensed justice, including occasional traffic tickets, as he patrolled the highways and streets when Statesboro was on the main route from Northern states to Florida. After suffering injuries from several accidents, he was assigned to monitor parking meters and to direct traffic on downtown streets. Citizens enjoyed seeing the cheerful "Tuck" as he went about his daily routine.

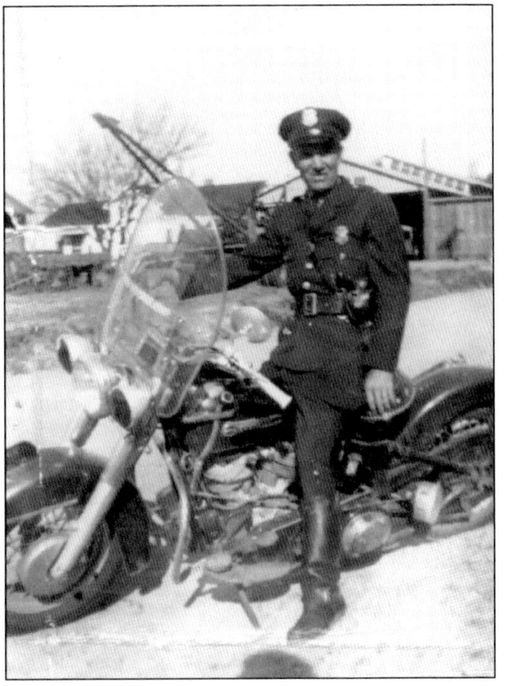

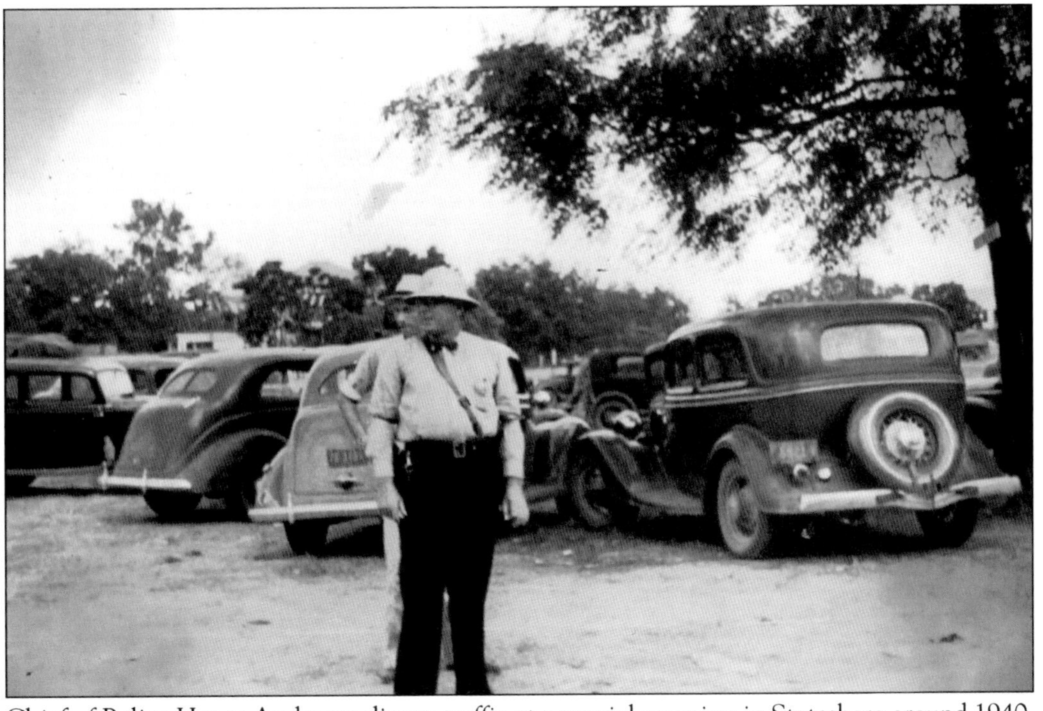

Chief of Police Henry Anderson directs traffic at a special occasion in Statesboro around 1940. For many years he was a senior policeman. Respected widely by citizens, he served for several decades as a faithful guardian of the city's streets and public places. His trademarks were his pith helmet and leather bow tie. Toward the end of his long career he was honored as Georgia's Policeman of the Year.

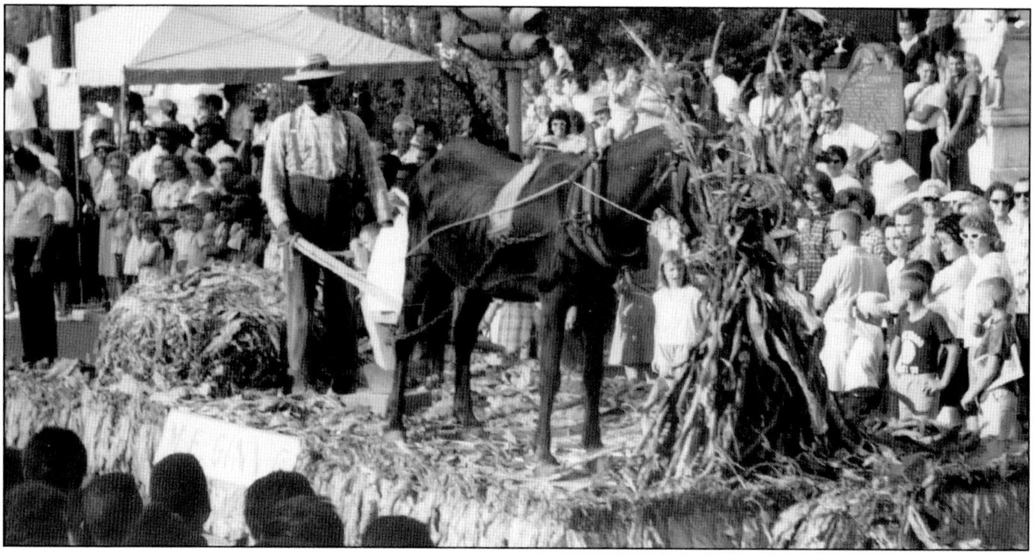

In the 1960s local merchants sponsored the annual Tobacco Festival parade each July. The parade featured floats decorated with tobacco and laden with beauty queens. Cars filled with dignitaries joined the parade, along with local high school bands. Local politicians were featured guests. This particular float pays tribute to old-time tobacco farmers who used mule power to plant and harvest their crops. Everyone who saw this parade was astonished to see a live mule stand still on the float for the duration of the event.

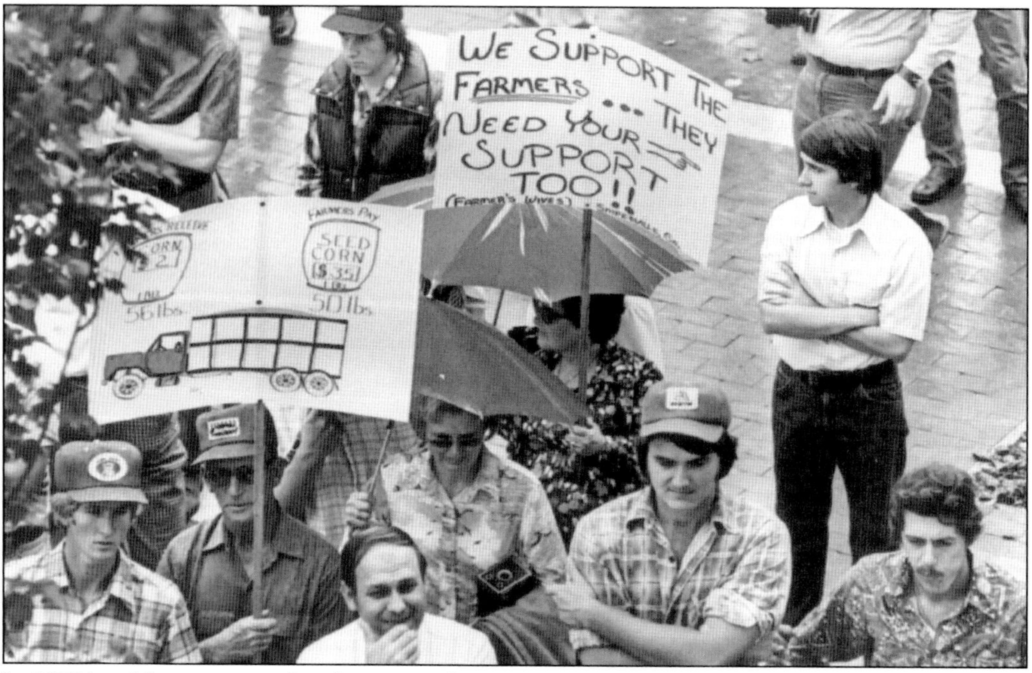

In 1977 local farmers joined in the national protest against rising production costs and decreasing profits. Many small farmers were unable to compete and were forced into bankruptcy. This event took place after a series of disastrous droughts dried up local harvests. Tractors and trucks lined up for several miles as they made a journey through Statesboro to demonstrate their concerns in Washington, D.C.

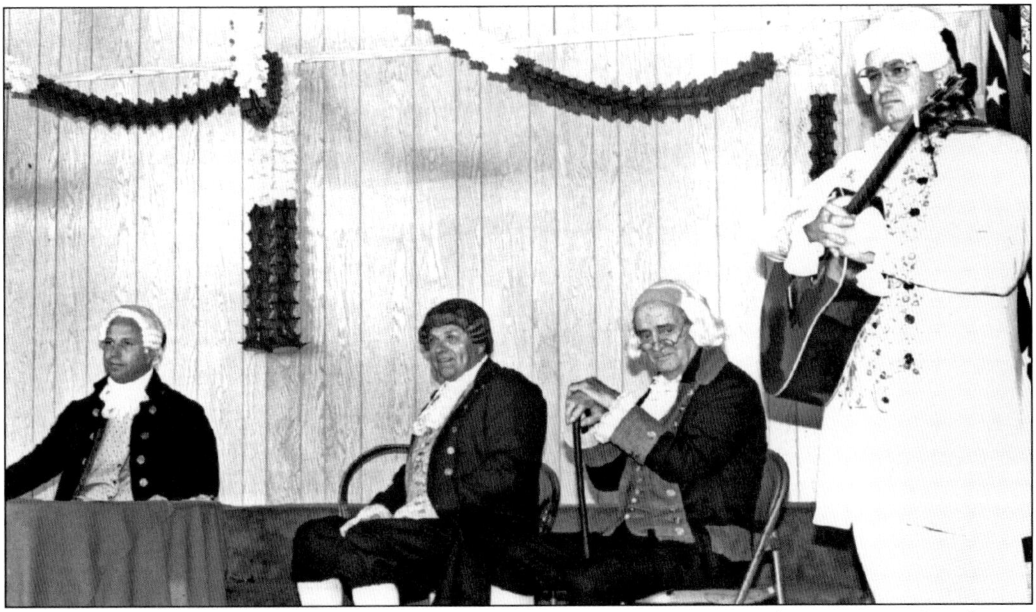

Local citizens joined in the American Bicentennial celebration in 1976 by portraying key figures of 1776. This drama presented at Sallie Zetterower Elementary School featured (left to right) Gilbert Groover (George Washington), Wallace Spivey (Abraham Baldwin), Dr. Fielding Russell (Benjamin Franklin), and Johnny Hathcock (James Madison).

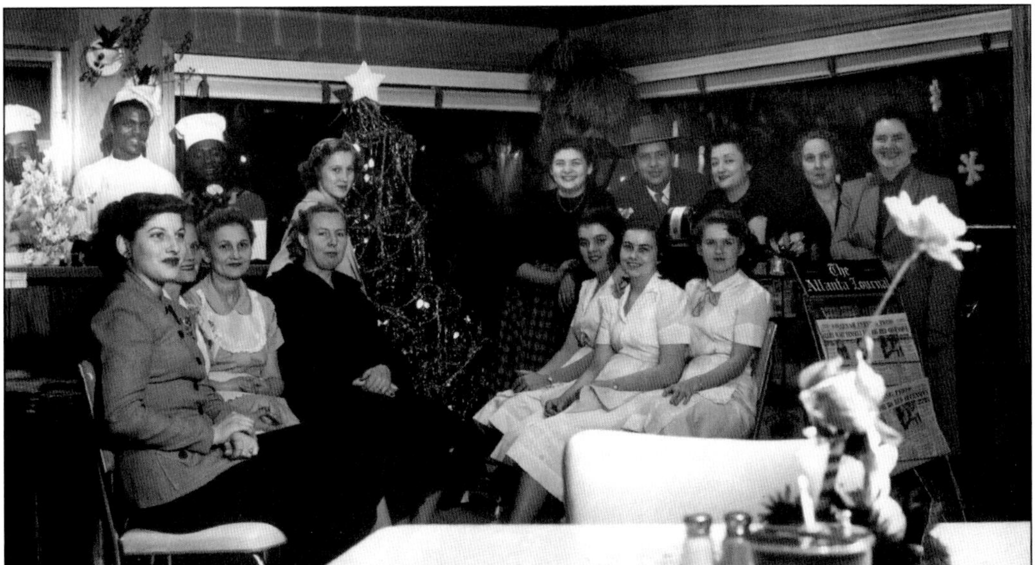

On February 12, 1950, the *Bulloch Times* announced a new restaurant would open on South Main in the Andersonville area. Mrs. Bryant's Kitchen, owned and managed by Marguerite and Charles Bryant, honored their staff at a Christmas party in December of 1950. From left to right in the front row are Dewetta Wallace, Sarah Nell Cannon (Burke), Letha Anderson, Louise Brown, unidentified, Carolyn Bunce, and Margie Brinson; (back row) Chefs Robert Wilbourn, Calvin Mincey, and Harvey Burnes; Villette Hursey, Lavinia Bryant, Charles Bryant, Marguerite H. Bryant, Iris Hursey, and Eleanor Akins. For several decades the restaurant had an excellent reputation among both national travelers and local citizens.

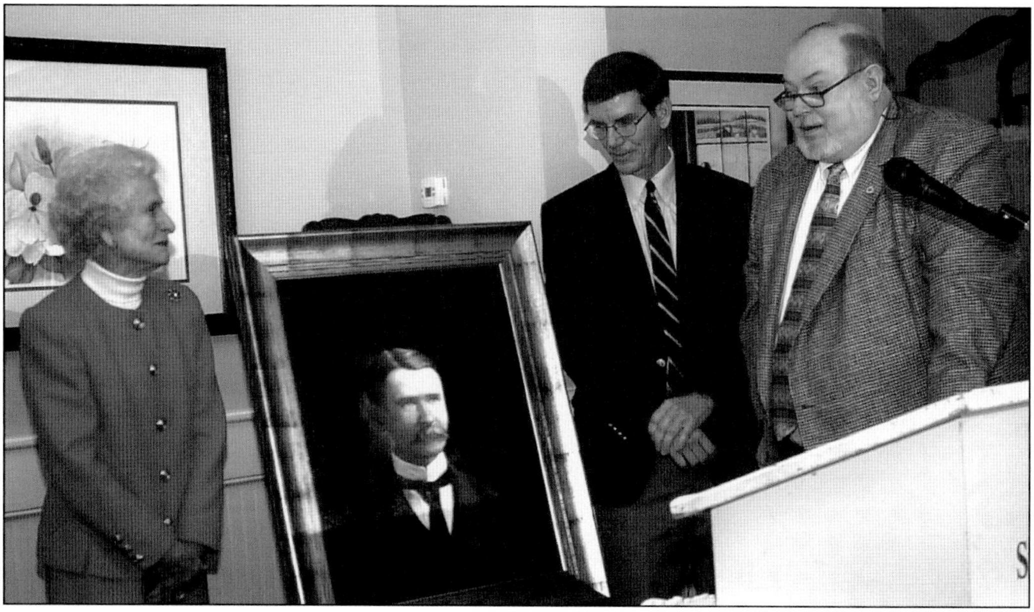

On January 16, 2003, Statesboro observed the first official bicentennial event at a Founder's Day Luncheon held at the Statesboro Inn, which attracted over 160 participants. A featured attraction was the unveiling of a portrait of the city's first mayor, the Hon. James A. "Lonnie" Brannen. From left to right are Mrs. Claude (Cecile Brannen) Howard, the mayor's granddaughter; Cecil Brannen Howard, great-grandson and donor of the portrait; and Smith C. Banks, co-chair of the history committee of the bicentennial committee. The portrait now hangs in the lobby of the Statesboro City Hall.

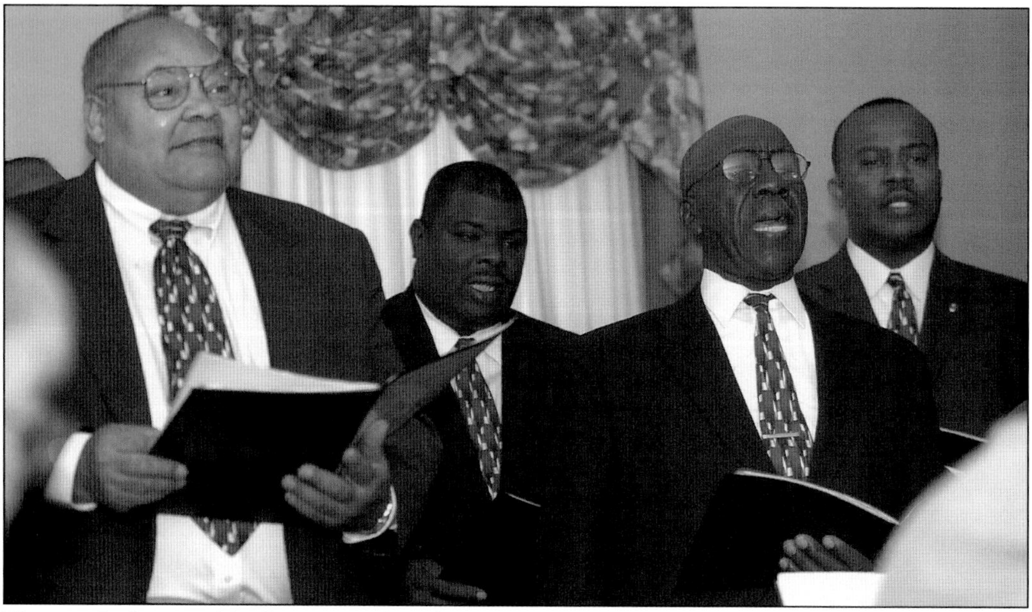

The men's chorus of the Brannen Chapel United Methodist Church performed at the Founder's Day luncheon. Directed by Wimberly Ponder, the choir sang "O Statesboro, Where the Sun Smiles," composed by Mr. Ponder for the occasion. From left to right are Gordon Alston, Gregory McBride, Quinton Mincey, and Cleve White.

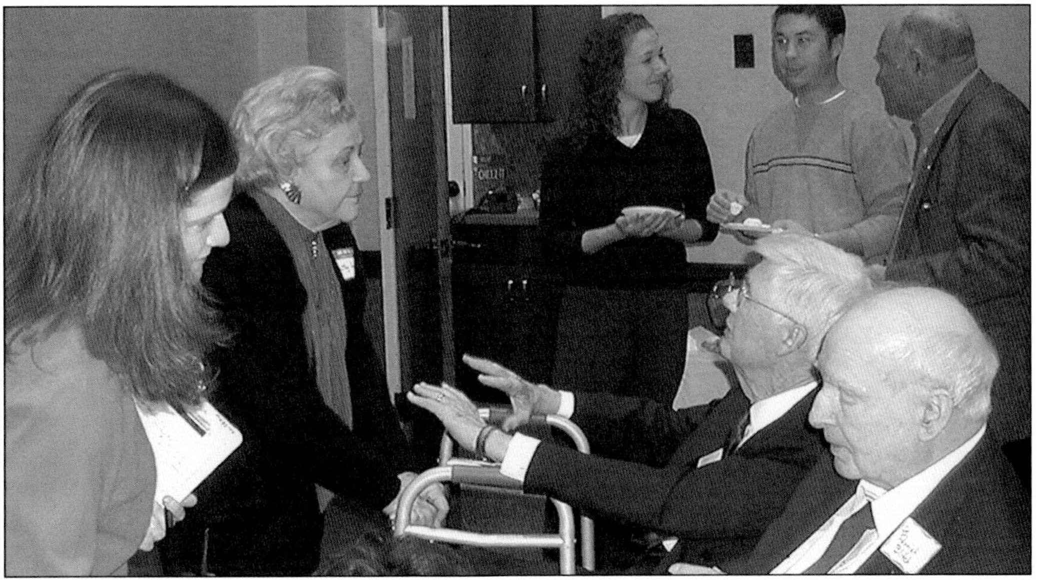

On January 24, 2003, the Statesboro Regional Library sponsored a genealogy workshop, an official bicentennial event. Featured speakers were senior historians and lifelong local citizens. Dr. Betty Lane speaks with historian Dr. Jack N. Averitt, who sits next to his boyhood friend, Dr. Parrish Blitch. Dr. Averitt gave a colorful "lecture-walk" through downtown Statesboro focusing on the year 1893. Dr. Blitch presented a unique history of the three Statesboro courthouse buildings. Afterwards the audience asked questions and enjoyed refreshments.

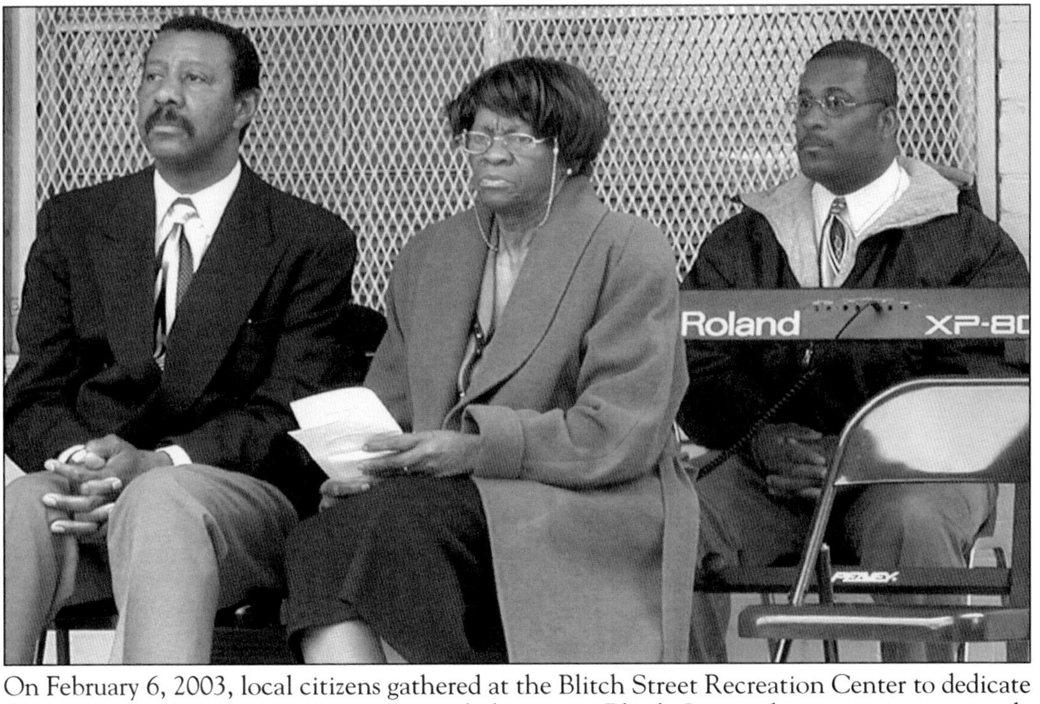

On February 6, 2003, local citizens gathered at the Blitch Street Recreation Center to dedicate the Martin Luther King Jr. Drive. Formerly known as Blitch Street, the new name was made possible by grass-roots efforts of city councilman Gary Lewis (left). The master of ceremonies was Alethia Lewis (middle). Rev. Allen Webb, at the keyboard, provided special music.

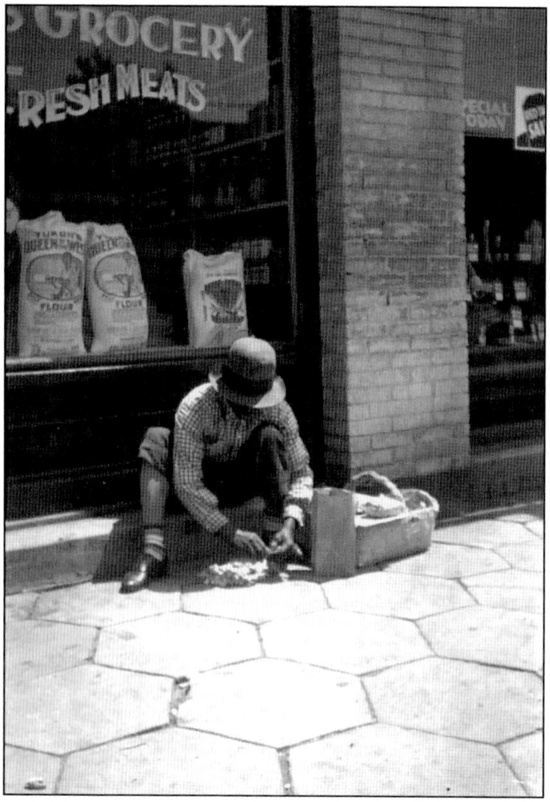

Taken in the 1940s, this photograph captures an often overlooked part of local history. Bub Beal peddled peanuts and other goodies on the streets of Statesboro. His basket always seemed to be full. He was regarded as a local character and curiosity. Notice the hexagonal blocks that once paved the sidewalks of Statesboro. Local citizens were concerned to discover that, after a long absence from the streets of Statesboro, Bub Beal's body was discovered, apparently a victim of robbery and homicide. The case was never solved.

A landmark since 1927, Triangle Park is located at the intersection of Savannah Avenue and East Main Street. In earlier years the pool held goldfish. For generations people enjoyed driving by the fountain during winter months. The frozen fountain appeared to be a cascade of ice. This is the site of the original Statesboro Waterworks built in 1904. Originally a well supplied the water for the city.

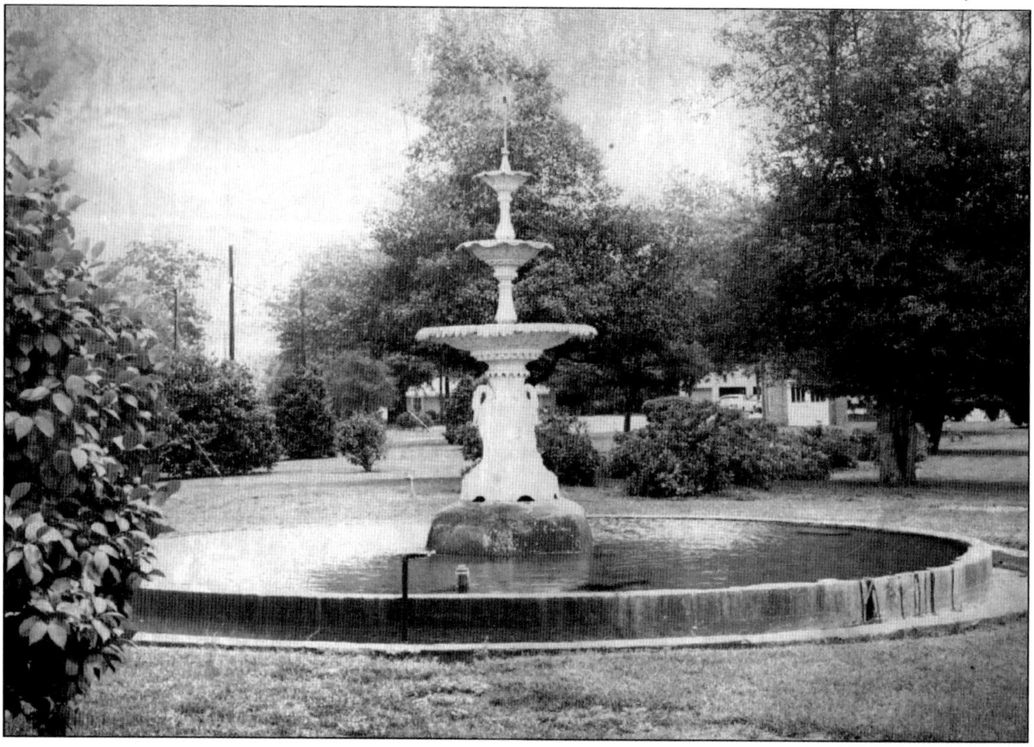

Two

Uptown for Business

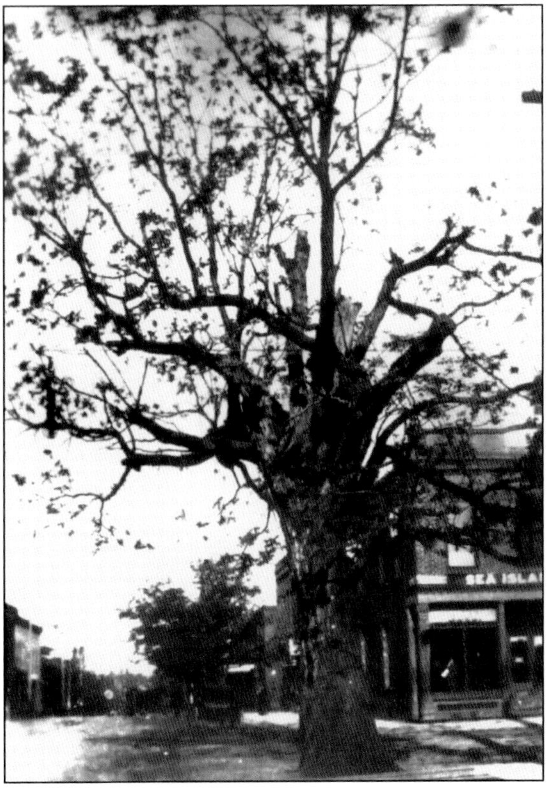

Statesboro's most famous landmark, although it was removed in 1917, remains the old walnut tree that stood on the northeast corner of the intersection of the Main Streets in the center of town. A few feet from the curbing around the Court House Square, the tree was probably present when the city was organized in 1803. Early courts held sessions there, and officials posted notices on the trunk. Its removal prompted a wave of protests, especially among the youth. Sea Island Bank, shown in the background, was located on the northwest corner of the Main Streets, diagonally across from the bank's location in 2003.

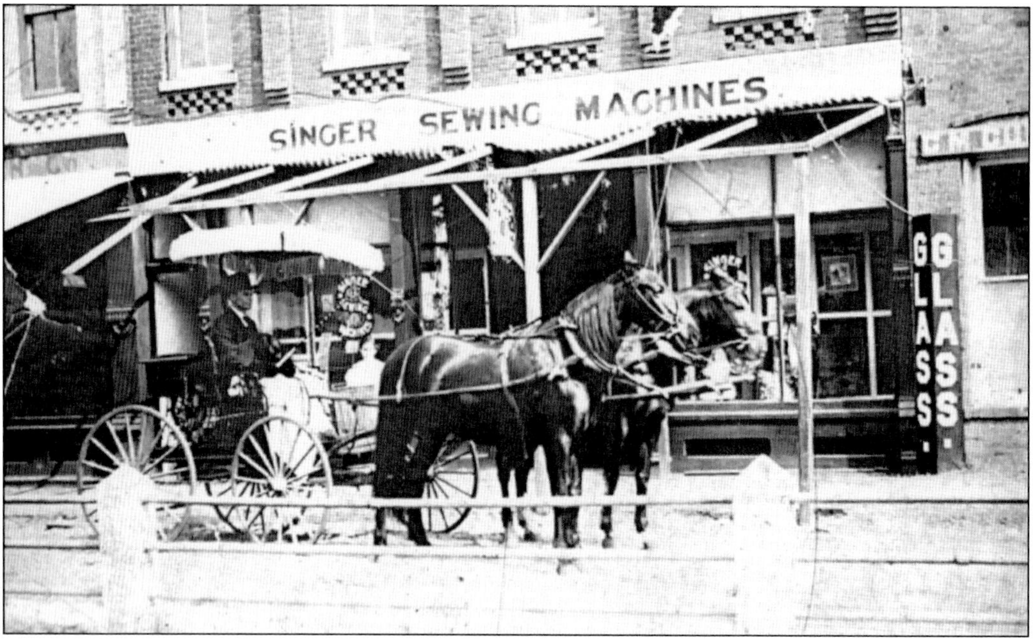

Mr. John Everett Parker sits in his buggy outside his store on Courtland Street, located next door to the Buggy and Wagon Company. He traveled in rural areas, selling and repairing one of the essential objects in many household—the sewing machine. Women usually used the Singer to make family clothing and home furnishings. At this time, in the early 1900s, the "Singer" was powered manually by a foot treadle.

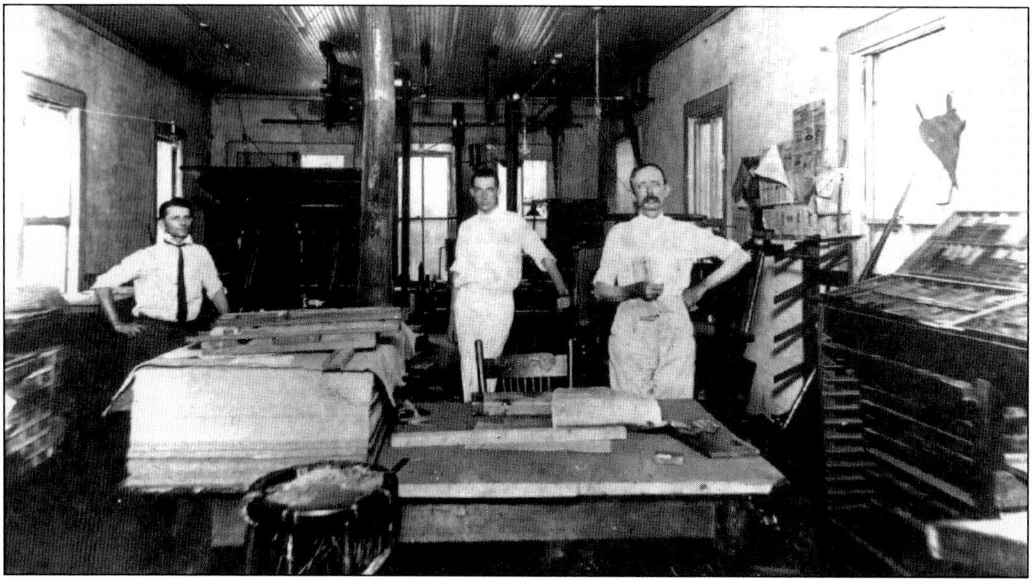

Mr. Dave Turner (far right), publisher and editor of the *Bulloch Times*, is shown in his printing office around 1900. Originally located on West Main Street, the newspaper office eventually was moved near the corner of East Main and Railroad Streets, adjacent to Mr. Turner's home. He was widely regarded as the dean of Georgia newspapermen. Known affectionately as "Uncle Dave," he wrote humorous columns as well as penetrating editorials. He began his newspaper career in 1893 in Statesboro and continued through the first half of the 20th century.

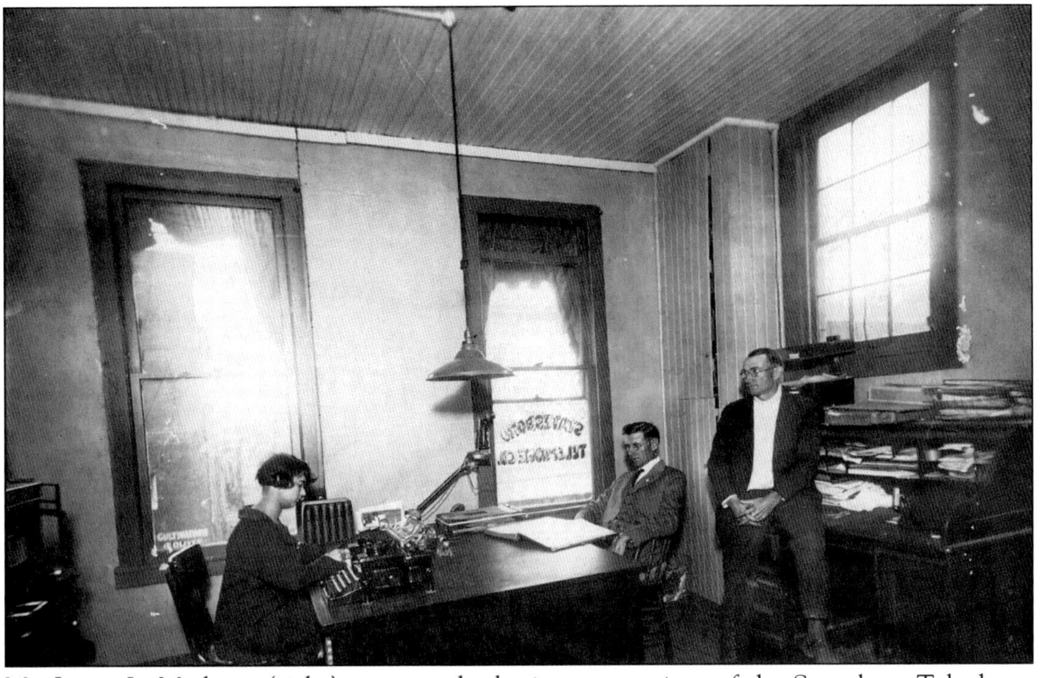

Mr. James L. Mathews (right) oversees the business operations of the Statesboro Telephone Company, located in an upstairs office at 9 South Main Street. The telephone came to Statesboro in 1901, and it remained a local, independent company until the 1990s.

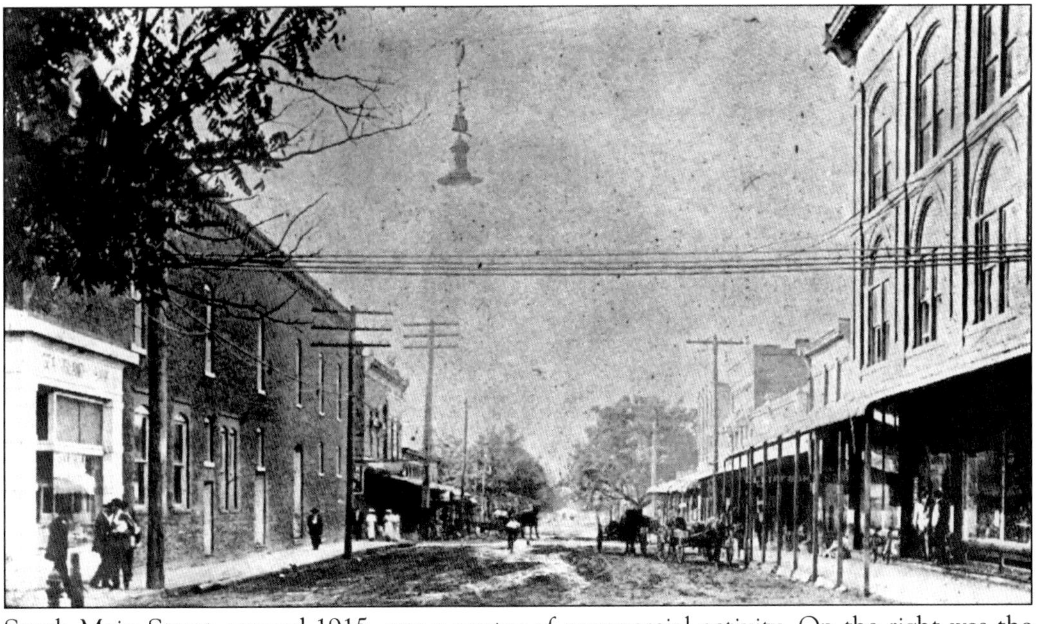

South Main Street, around 1915, was a center of commercial activity. On the right was the R. Simmons company, which later became Jake Fine's, then H. Minkovitz. Sea Island Bank, on the left, moved to this location in 1913, after earlier operating on the northwest corner of Main Streets. Note that sidewalks are made of wooden boards, and streets are unpaved. Metal canopies cover some sidewalks. In the left foreground are leaves and branches of the famous walnut tree. In the center of the picture, a typical street light provides illumination.

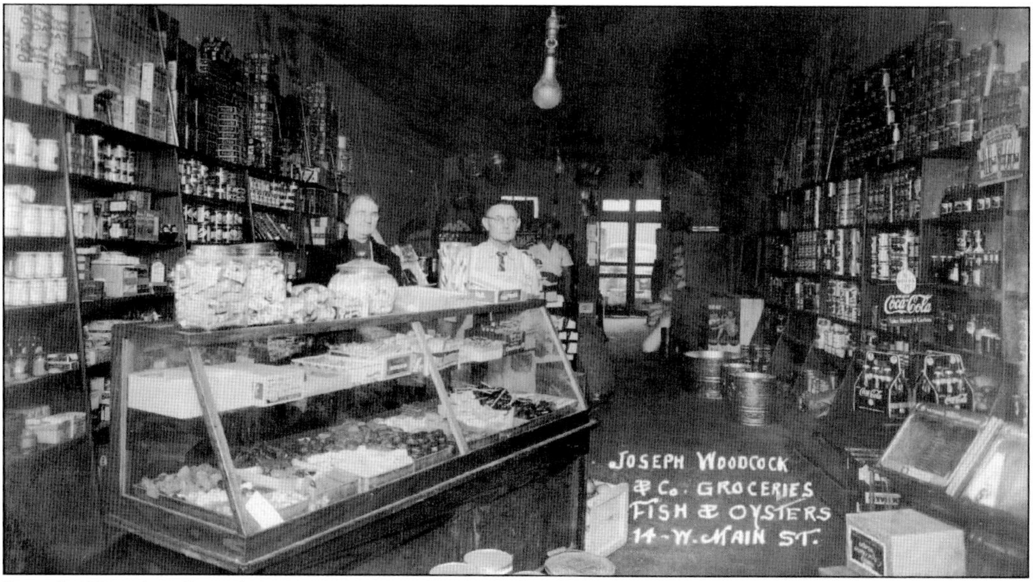

Joseph Woodcock and Company at 14 West Main Street featured groceries, fish, and oysters. Mr. and Mrs. Woodcock stand behind the candy counter in the 1930s. This is a typical "Mom and Pop" grocery store of the period. They parked their vehicle in the alley behind the store, and the auto can be seen through the screen door. Note in the right foreground the cookie display and a selection of the popular soft drink, Coca-Cola. A light bulb suspended from the ceiling provided sufficient light for the small store.

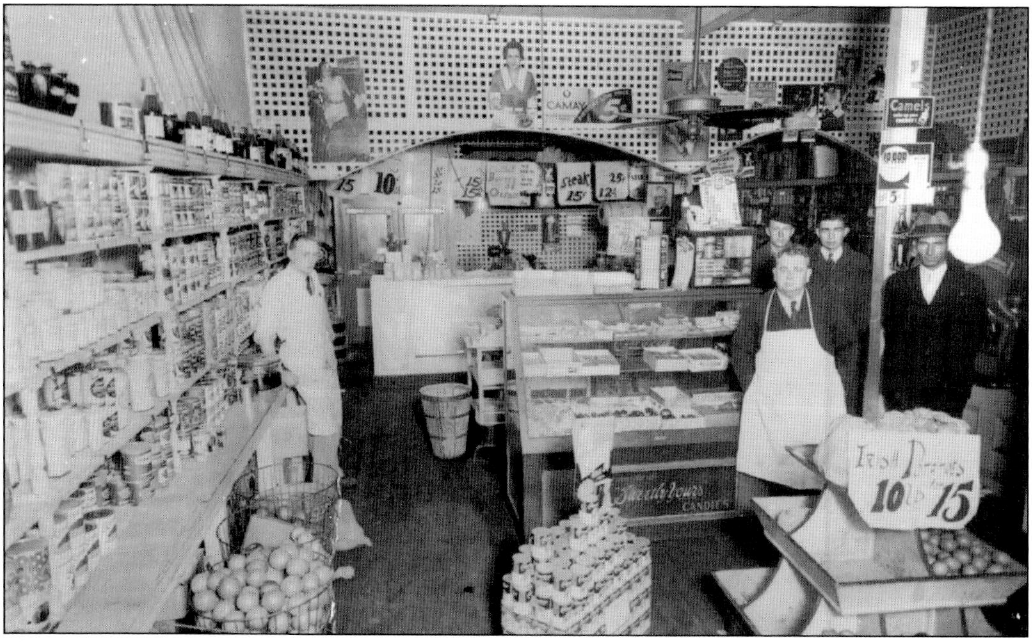

This is the interior of the Cail and Donaldson Grocery Store on South Main Street in the 1930s, on the site of what became H.W. Smith Jewelers. At far left is J.D. Allen. Continuing from left to right are Mr. C.B. Cail (with apron), Marvin Thompson (with hat), Harold Beasley, and Willie Fred Hodges (with hat). Irish potatoes sold at 15¢ for 10 pounds. On the back wall, advertising special prices, is a portrait of President Franklin D. Roosevelt.

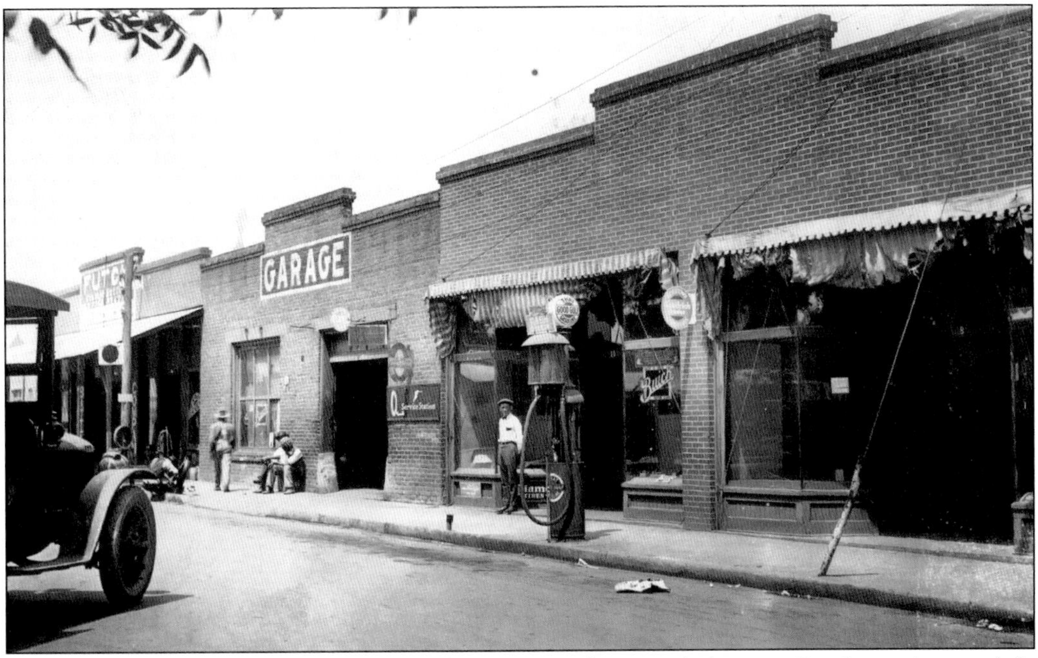

Siebald Street, across from the courthouse, was home of Averitt Brothers Automobile Company in the 1920s. Percy and Barney Averitt began selling automobiles as early as 1908. Percy was the first citizen of Statesboro to drive an auto into town. In the right foreground was Statesboro City Hall, across the alley from the Bank of Statesboro building. Averitt Brothers sold General Motors cars (note the Buick sign in the window). The gasoline pump was hand powered.

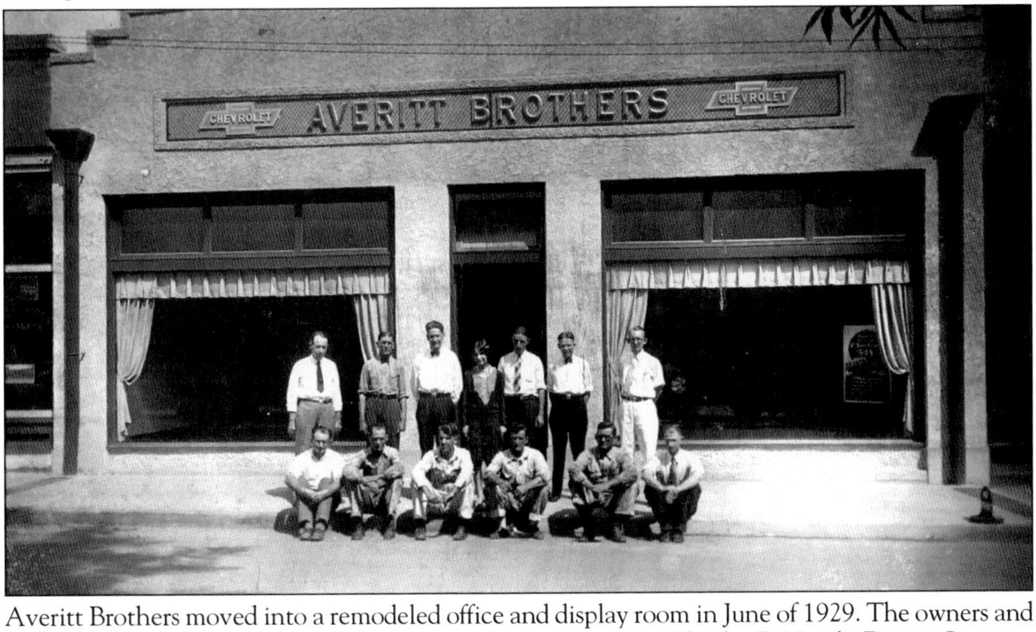

Averitt Brothers moved into a remodeled office and display room in June of 1929. The owners and employees, from left to right, are (front row) Harvey Brannen, Charles E. Nevils, Dewey Cannon, and three unidentified; (back row) Jeff E. Bedenbaugh, D. Percy Averitt, James B. Averitt, Lilla Mae Oglesby (secretary), Dan T. Lingo, Harold W. Averitt, and O. Carl Franklin.

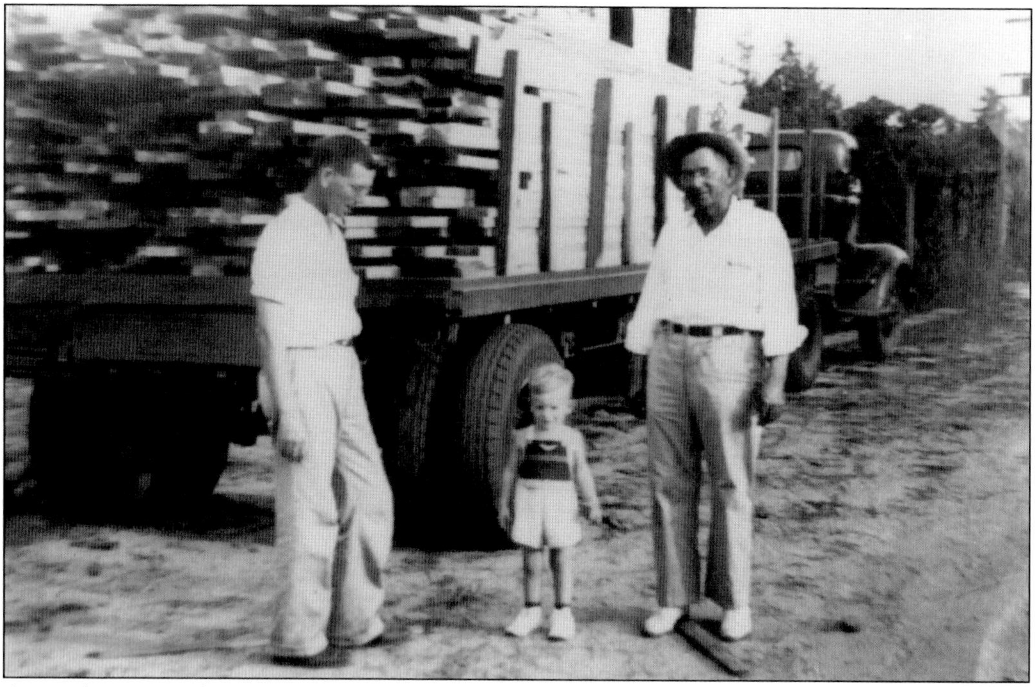

Around 1898 Arthur Howard and his brothers moved their portable saw mill from Wrens, Georgia to Bulloch County. In 1920 Mr. Howard located his mill on Mulberry Street, north of Hill Street. He operated at this location until 1956. In 1946 his son, Claude, established a saw mill on the Central of Georgia Railroad at the end of Park Avenue. Pictured from left to right are Claude Howard, his young son, Arthur, and Claude's father, Arthur Howard. Four generations of Howards have been in the lumber business in Bulloch County for over 100 years.

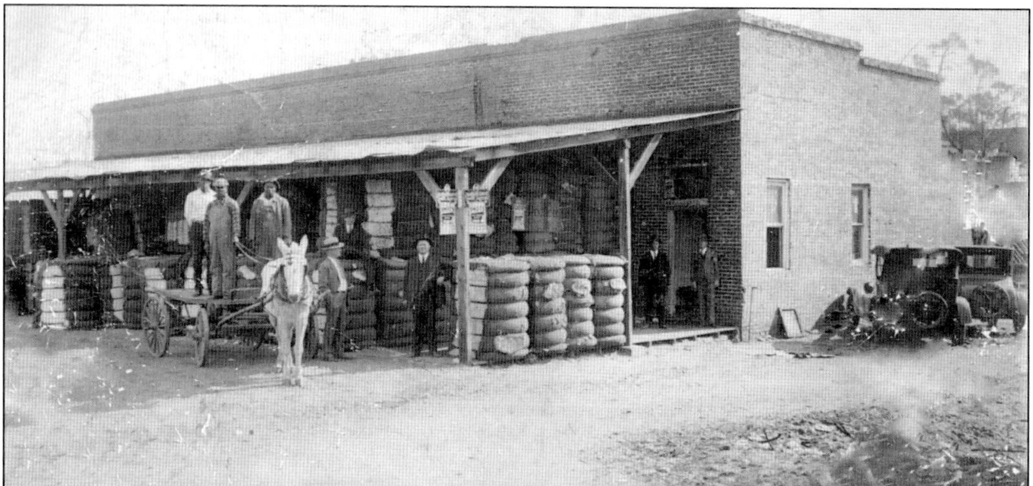

The cotton warehouse on East Vine Street served the needs of farmers and brokers in Statesboro in the 1920s. After brokers purchased the cotton, they stored the bales in this dry place until it could be shipped to destinations throughout the world. From the early 20th century Statesboro was a leading market for cotton, particularly Sea Island or long staple (black seed) cotton. This building stands virtually unchanged in 2003, without benefit of the mule, wagon, cotton bales, and period automobiles.

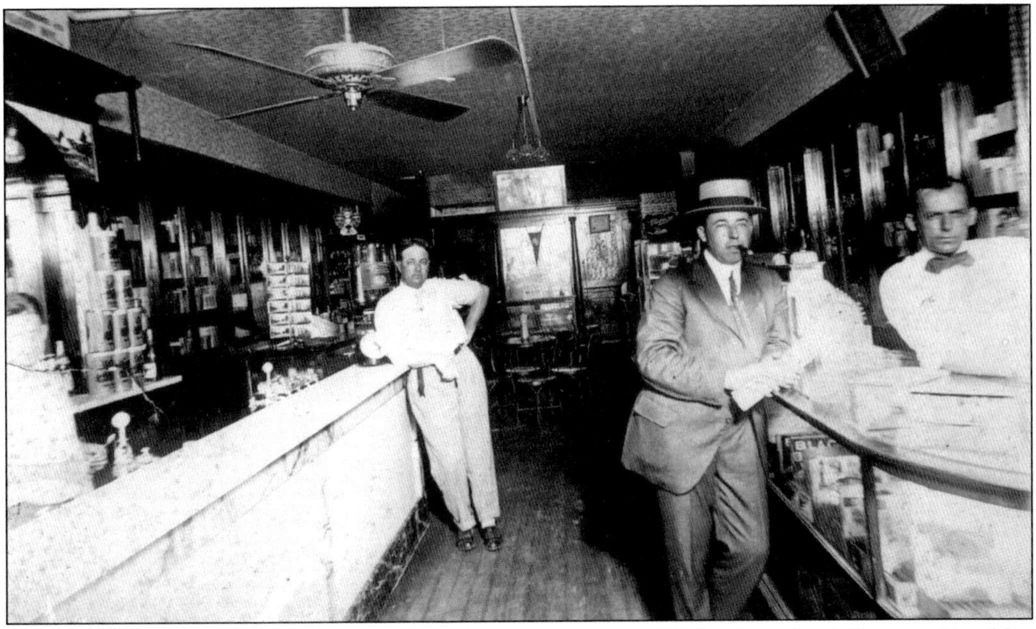

Franklin Drug Stores began serving Statesboro in the year 1908, when Paul Gustave Franklin Sr., and E.A. Brannen assumed charge of the Crouch Drug Store. Paul Franklin Jr., pharmacist, continued the drug business until his retirement in the 1978. Franklin's featured a full-service soda fountain, and the "soda jerk" can barely be seen in the left foreground. Paul Sr. is on the far right, as if speaking with his friend, Dr. Norris.

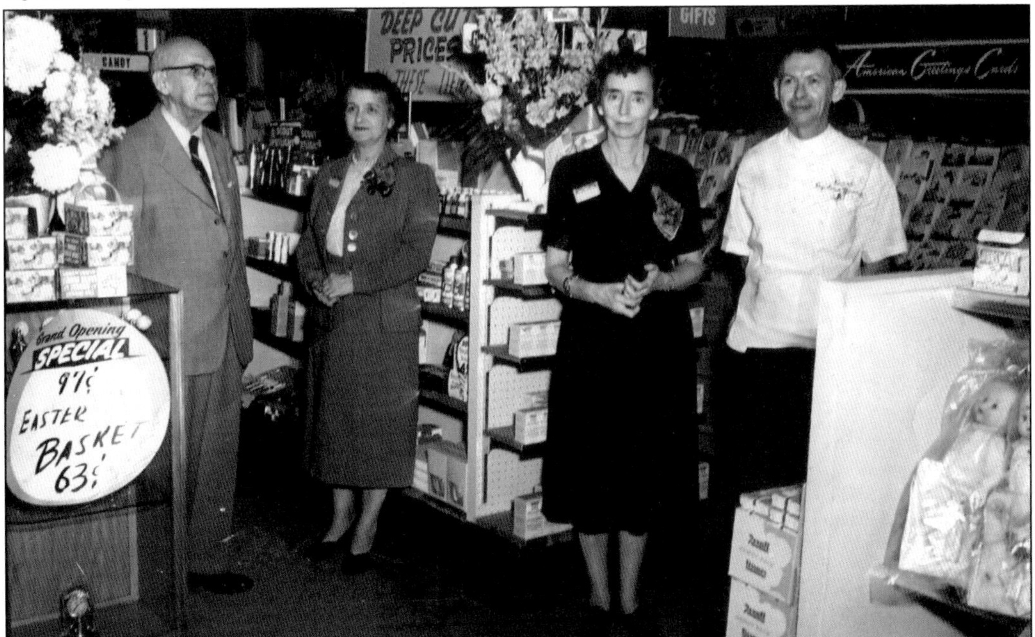

In November of 1955, Franklin Drug Store moved from 10 East Main Street to 29 North Main Street at the entrance to the Simmons Shopping Center. Pictured here, from left to right, are Mr. Paul G. Franklin Sr.; Mrs. Fred B. Hartley; Henrietta Parrish, longtime clerk; and Paul G. Franklin Jr. Compare some of the prices with those of today.

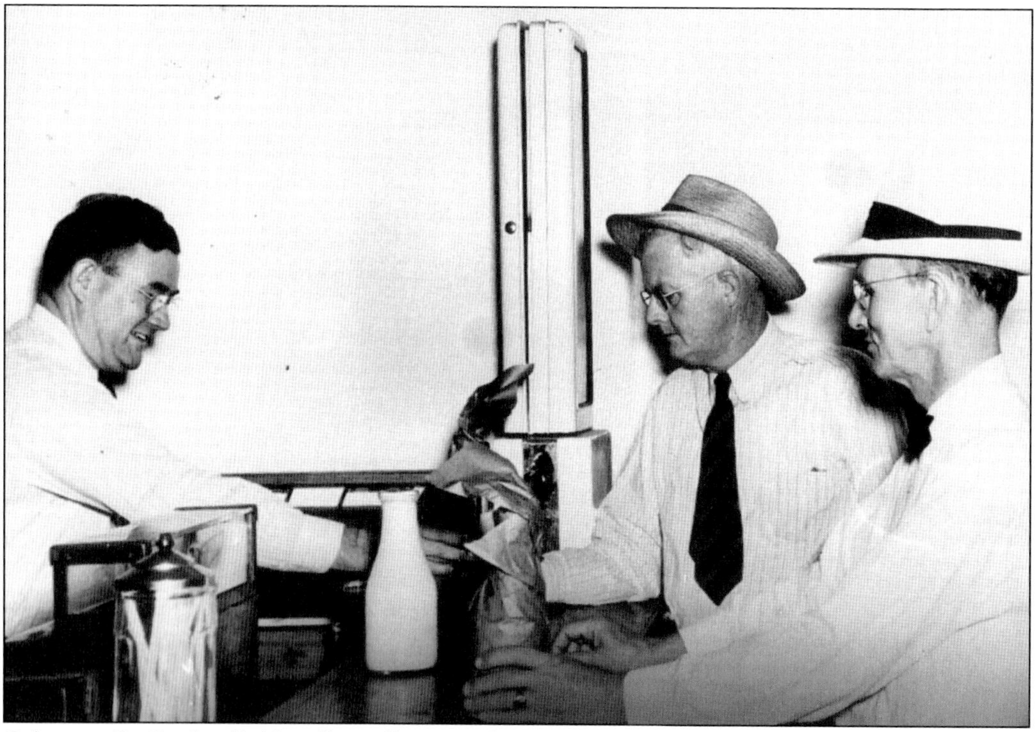

Osborne C. Banks (left) sells milk to Josh T. Nessmith, manager of Production Credit Association in Statesboro, and Tom Rouse of the Federal Land Bank. The City Dairy Company, Statesboro's only dairy processing plant, in 1943 sold ice cream and milk products at their store on West Main Street. The tall contraption in the center is an ice cream cone dispenser for double-dip cones. The company's mascot was a cow named "Molly Moo."

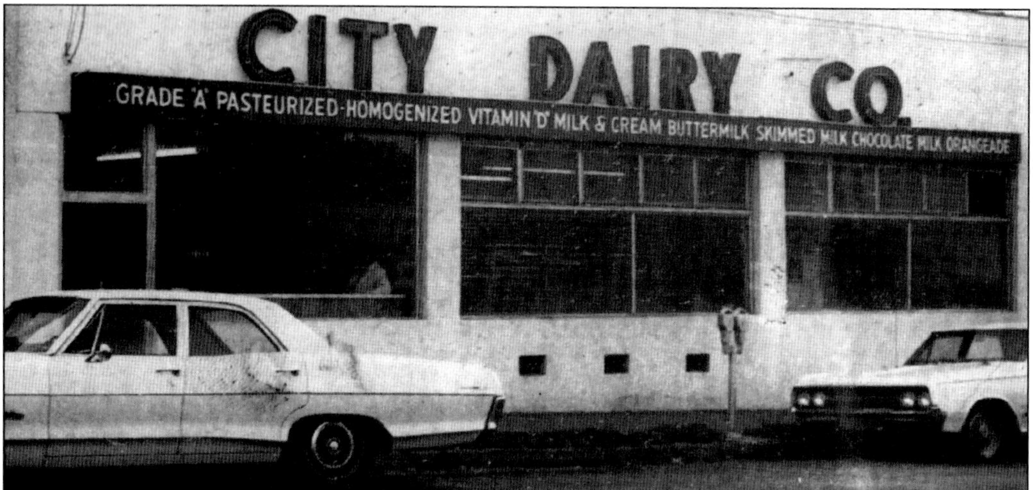

The City Dairy on West Main Street in 1962 processed, sold, and delivered milk to homes and stores in Bulloch and surrounding counties. Founded in 1931 by Osborne C. Banks and his father, the elder David C. Banks, the company delivered milk in both morning and evenings, because most homes did not have refrigerators then. In 1974 the company was sold to Coble Dairies Co-op, and in 2002 the property was sold to the City of Statesboro for a parking lot.

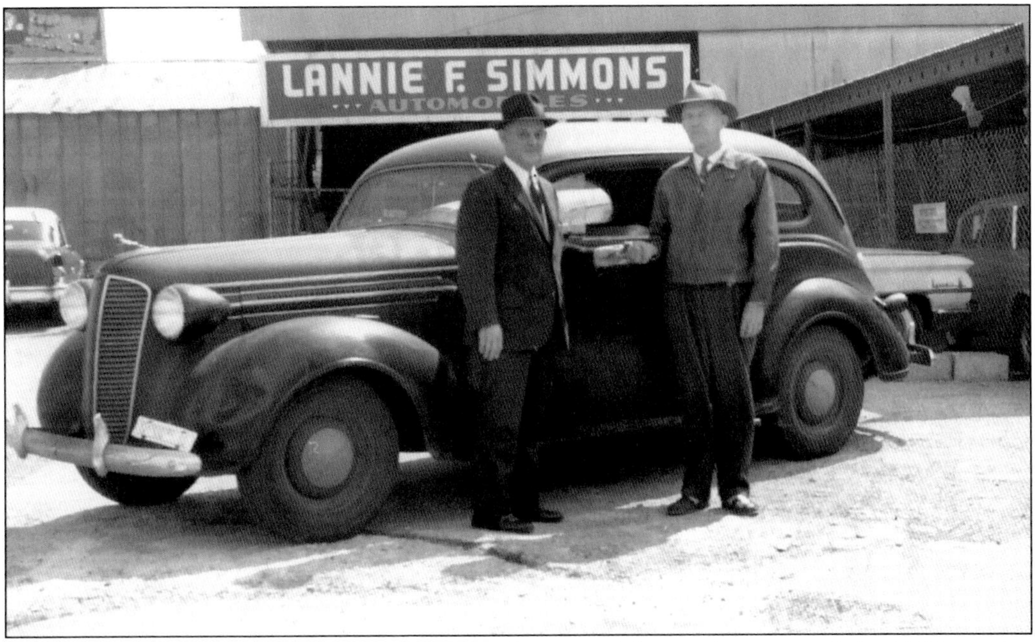

In March of 1962 Lannie F. Simmons (left) is shown with Remer Proctor and the 1937 car that Judge Proctor, Remer's father, bought that year. After 25 years the car was in perfect running order with just over 16,000 miles on the speedometer. Mr. Simmons was widely regarded as a master salesman. In his earlier years he owned and operated a grocery store. From the 1930s until 1960s he sold automobiles, especially Dodge, GMC, and Studebaker. He was an expert horseman and one of the town's early pilots.

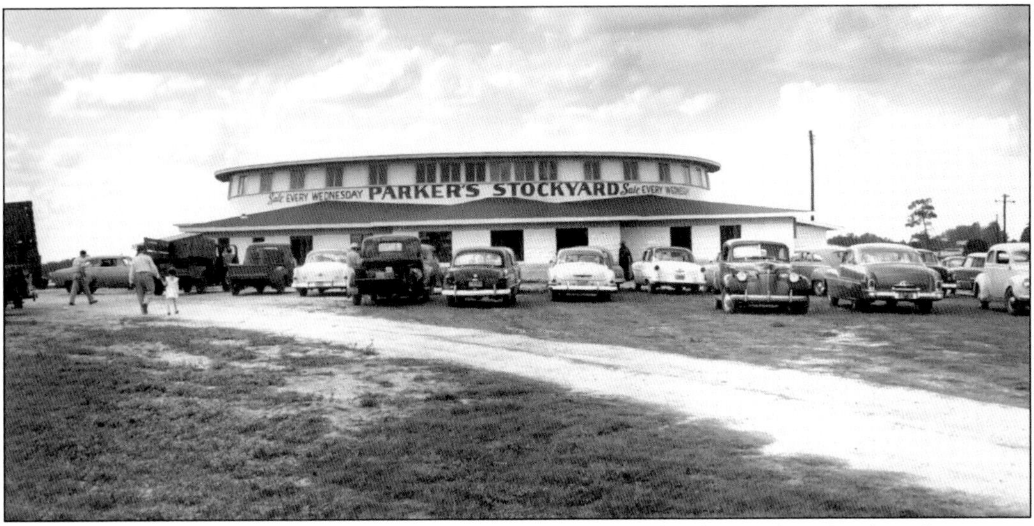

A well-known structure on Williams and Stockyard Roads, the Parker Stockyard was one of two active stock auction houses, the other being Bulloch Stockyard. The markets in Statesboro led the region in auction activity. Out-of-state buyers were regulars, and many world-famous Smithfield hams came from Bulloch County hogs. Each Wednesday auctions were held at Parker Stockyard, and radio station WWNS regularly broadcast the event as it happened. A popular attraction at Parker's was their excellent café, which served home-cooked meals on sale days.

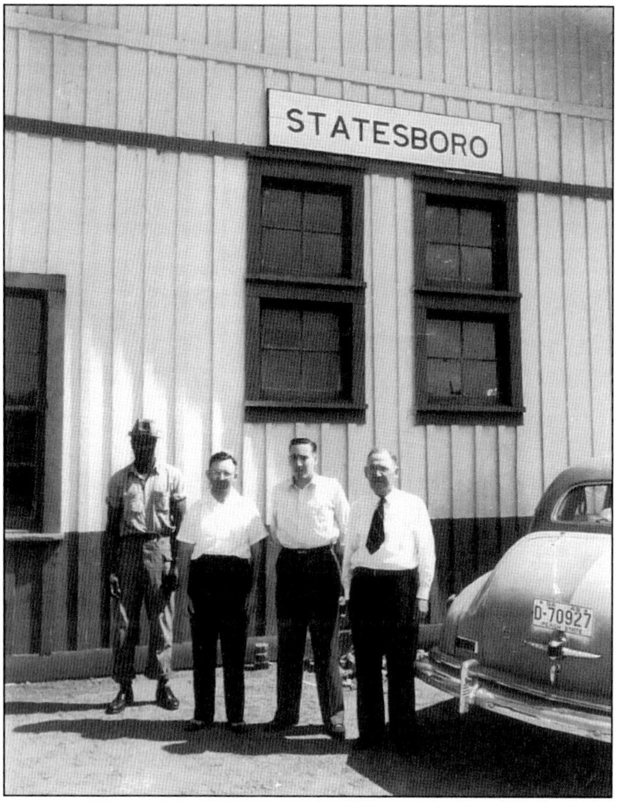

This is Statesboro's Central of Georgia Depot on East Main Street and Savannah Avenue, as it looked around 1949 (note year of auto tag on right). This station is on the site of the original depot of the Dover and Statesboro Railroad that was completed in 1889. With the completion of this line, local farmers and merchants obtained an outlet to state and national markets. Passenger service also made it possible for residents and visitors to travel to Savannah, Macon, Atlanta, and thence to national destinations. A freight handler named Jake; Doy Akins, telegrapher; unidentified; and George Bean, station agent, are pictured from left to right.

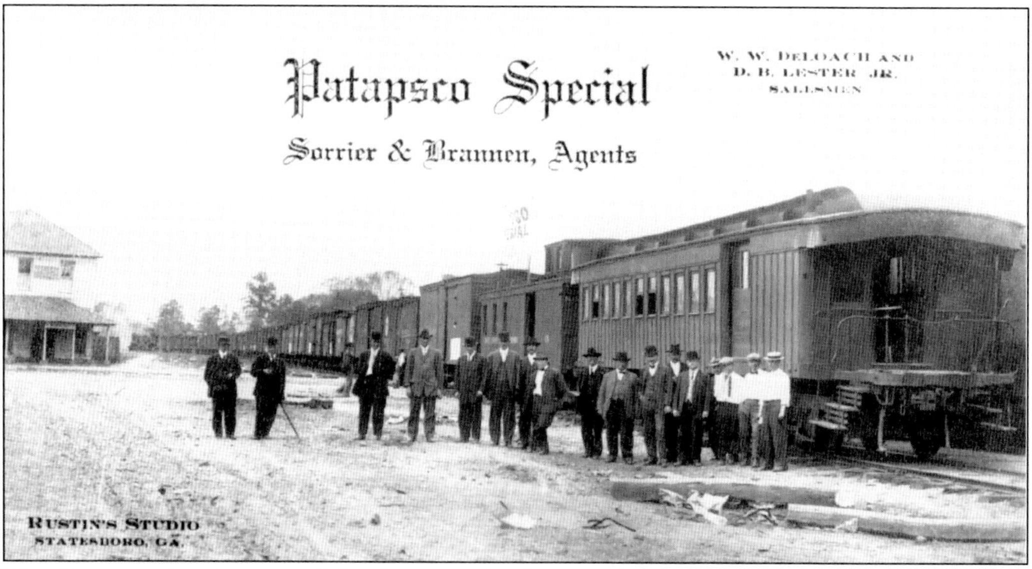

The Patapsco Special carried fertilizer for the business of Sorrier and Brannen in the early 1900s. Patapsco Guano Company, named for a river in Maryland, operated out of Baltimore. W.W. DeLoach and D.B. Lester Jr. were salesmen for this company. The setting is the Central of Georgia Depot at East Main and Savannah Avenue. On the far left is the two-story Preetorius building, which stood for many years on the northeast corner of East Main and Railroad Streets.

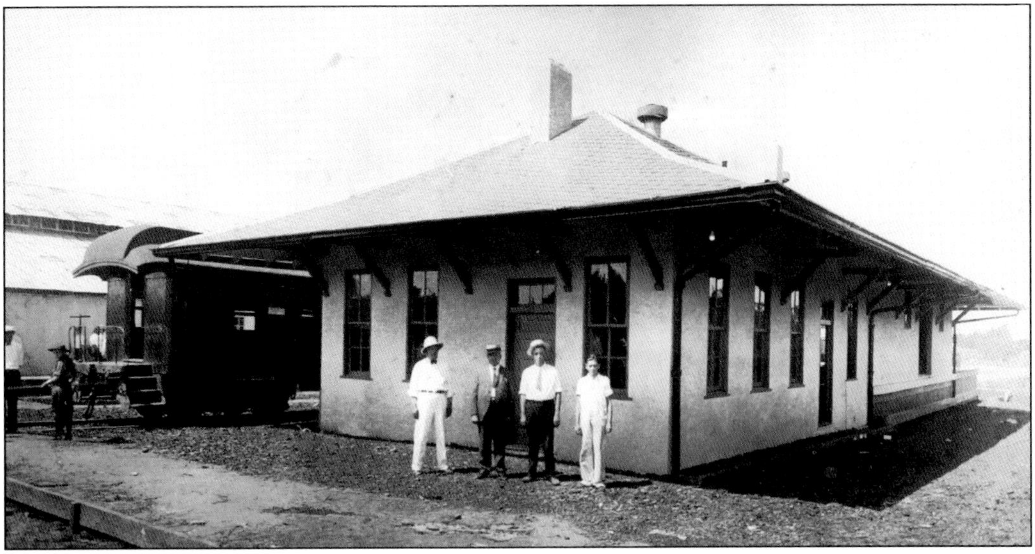

The Midland Railroad began serving the region in 1915. It became the Statesboro Northern Railroad after the Georgia & Florida Railroad purchased the company in 1924. The line linked Statesboro's tobacco market with national companies. Cobb and Foxall tobacco warehouse is on the far left. When railroad president J.P. Williams stayed at his mansion on South Main Street, he parked his luxurious private railroad coach at the depot on South College Street near Vine Street. The new depot opened on August 1, 1928. From left to right are J.A. Bennett, commercial agent from Savannah; Col. Hinton Booth, director; T.D. Julian, agent; and Frank C. Parker Jr., clerk.

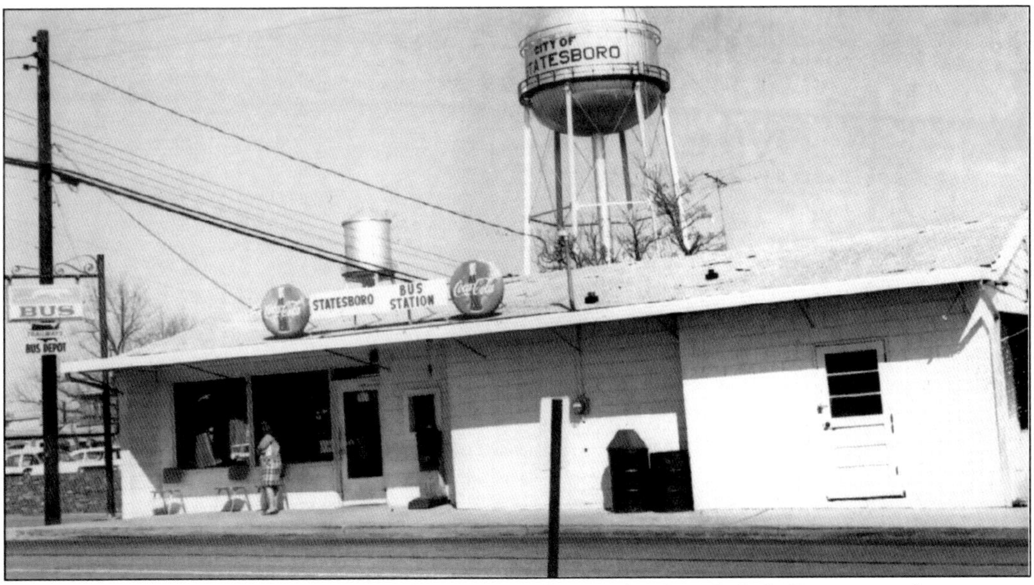

Statesboro's bus station, located at the corner of Courtland and Oak Streets, is shown as it looked in the 1970s. The first bus station in 1937 was located in the Preetorius Building (built in 1911) on the corner of Railroad and North Main Streets, shown in the picture on page 50. Bus service began before 1926, and passengers from Statesboro were able to board Greyhound or Trailways buses to major destinations in the United States The station had a small food service counter. In the 1970s a newer and smaller bus station appeared on North Zetterower Avenue.

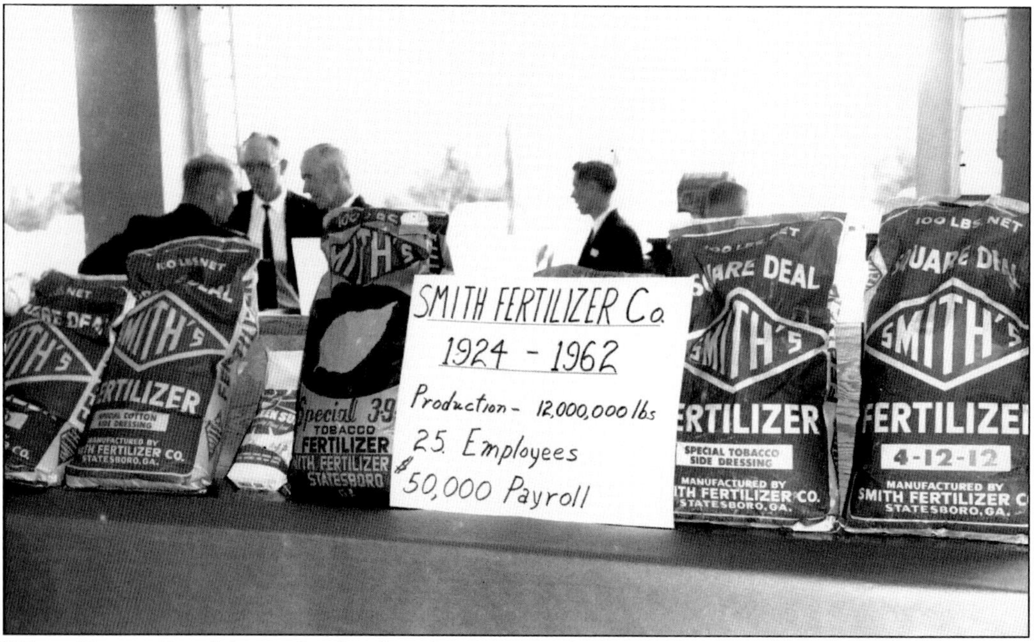

When Horace Smith began his fertilizer business on the north side of East Cherry Street in 1924, he hired 20 men to mix the fertilizer by hand. Farmers used his products, and soon he added a machine-driven mixer. Instead of faltering during the Great Depression, Smith Fertilizer built a new plant on the south side of Cherry. By 1953 new equipment turned out over 100 tons of fertilizer a day.

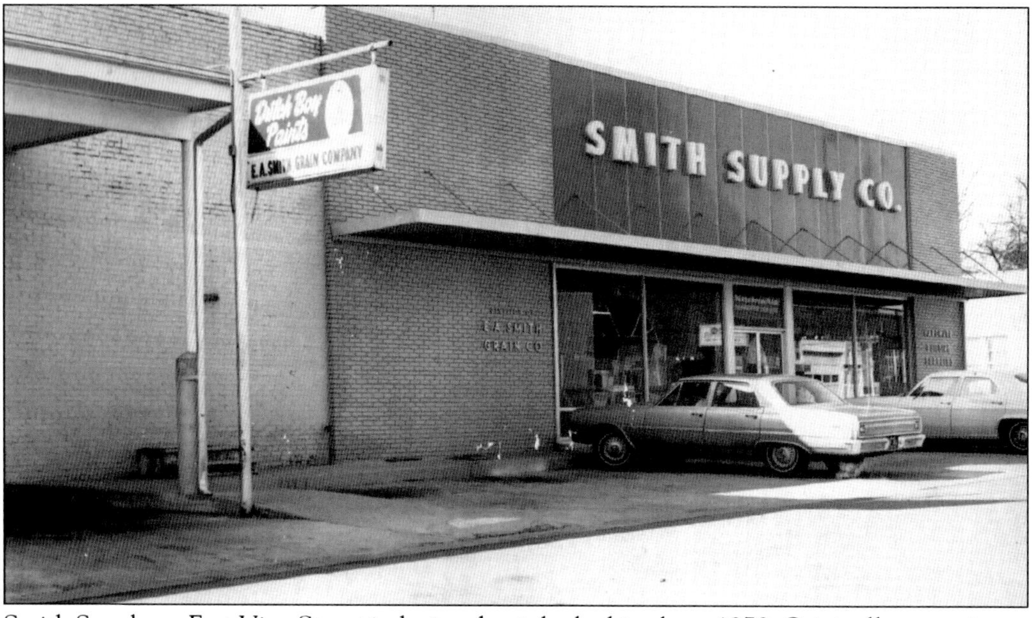

Smith Supply on East Vine Street is depicted as it looked in about 1970. Originally operating as E.A. Smith Grain Company, it was founded in 1911. Three main divisions operated successfully in Statesboro: Smith Supply Co.; Smith Cotton Co.; and Smith Fertilizer Co. After Mr. E.A. Smith's death, the businesses were operated by Horace Z. Smith Sr., Horace Zack Smith Jr., and W.R. "Bobby" Smith. Smith Supply later was sold and became Howard Hardware, Inc.

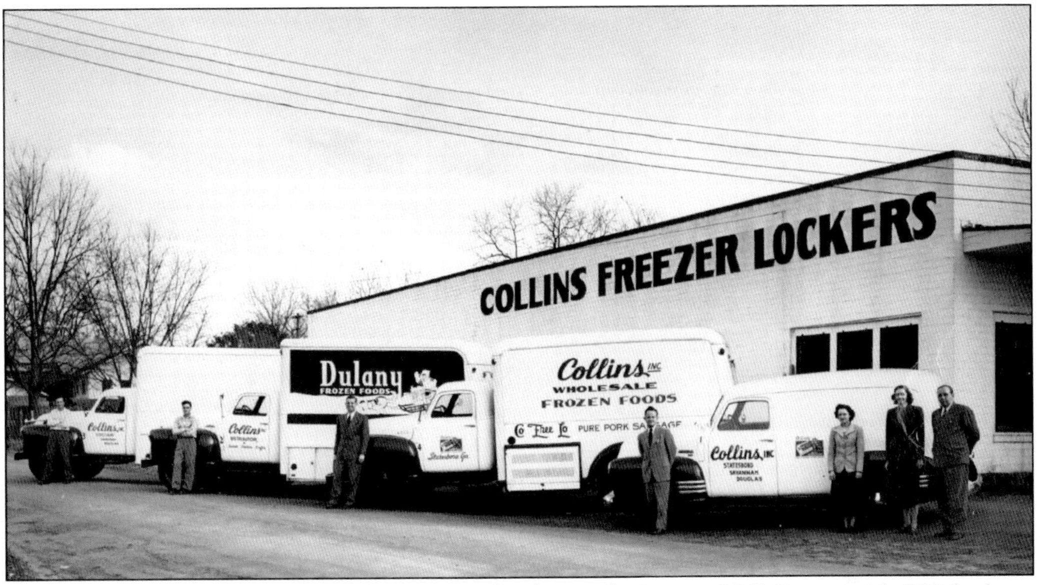

In 1944 Mr. and Mrs. Jimmy Collins opened a freezer locker on Hill Street with 370 lockers. Within a year local demand required him to double the number of lockers. In 1957 Collins Frozen Foods, Inc. began distributing portion-sized frozen meat products to colleges, hospitals, and other institutions. In the late 1960s the company operated a fleet of refrigerated trucks serving a long list of customers in the southeastern United States. Shown in the photograph are Mr. and Mrs. Collins (far right) and other employees.

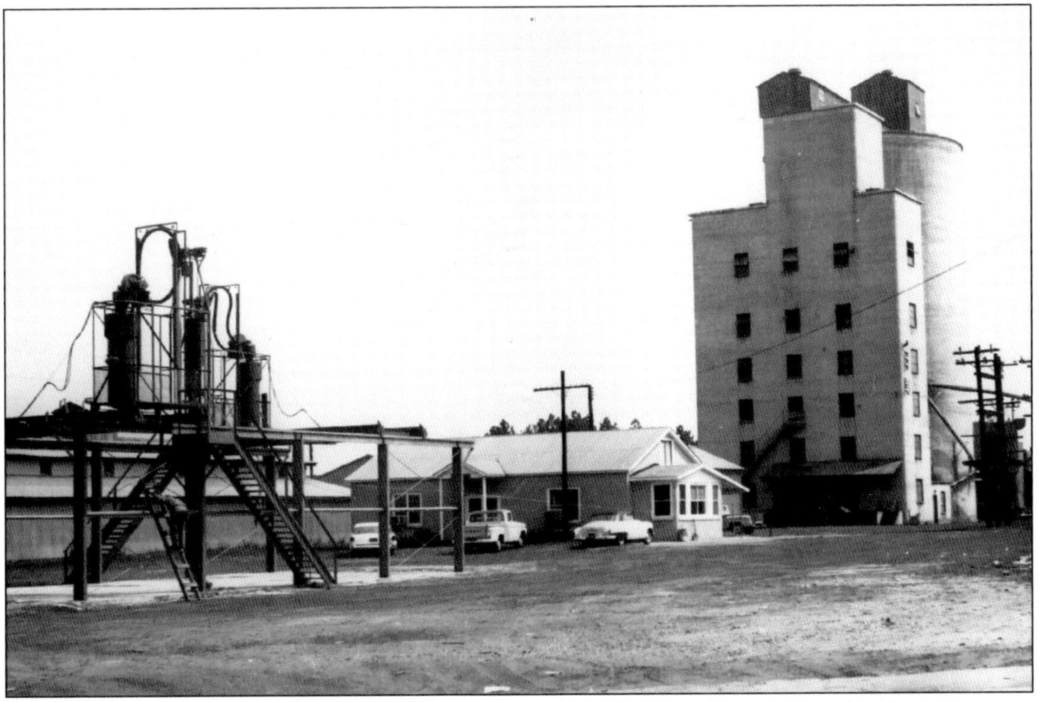

The East Georgia Peanut Company was organized in 1945 by Homer Ray, S. Dew Groover, and Horace Z. Smith Sr. One year later the company built what everyone considered to be the tallest building in the county. The business is now owned by Gold Kist.

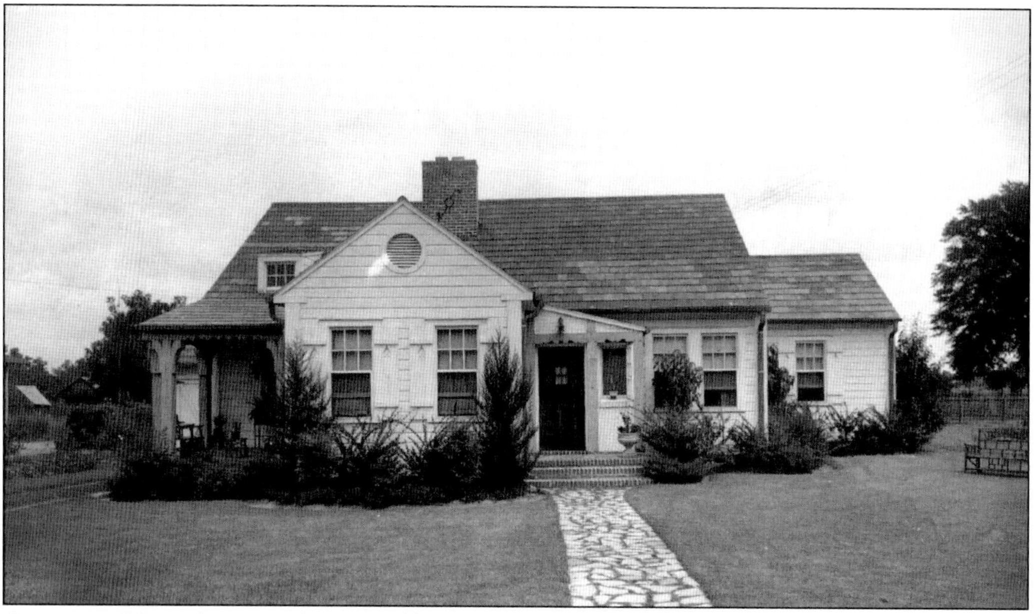

A native of Statesboro, Walter H. Aldred graduated from Georgia Tech in 1927 with a degree in architecture. After gaining experience in Atlanta, he returned home in the early 1930s. He designed and built many homes and buildings in Statesboro. Both architect and contractor, he was eager to build structures of any size. This home on Savannah Avenue was designed for the family of Mr. and Mrs. Glenn S. Jennings around 1940. Even though relatively small, the home featured genuine architectural touches—ornate pillars and a flagstone sidewalk. The home in 2003 is an office for a brokerage firm, and the exterior has been covered with brick.

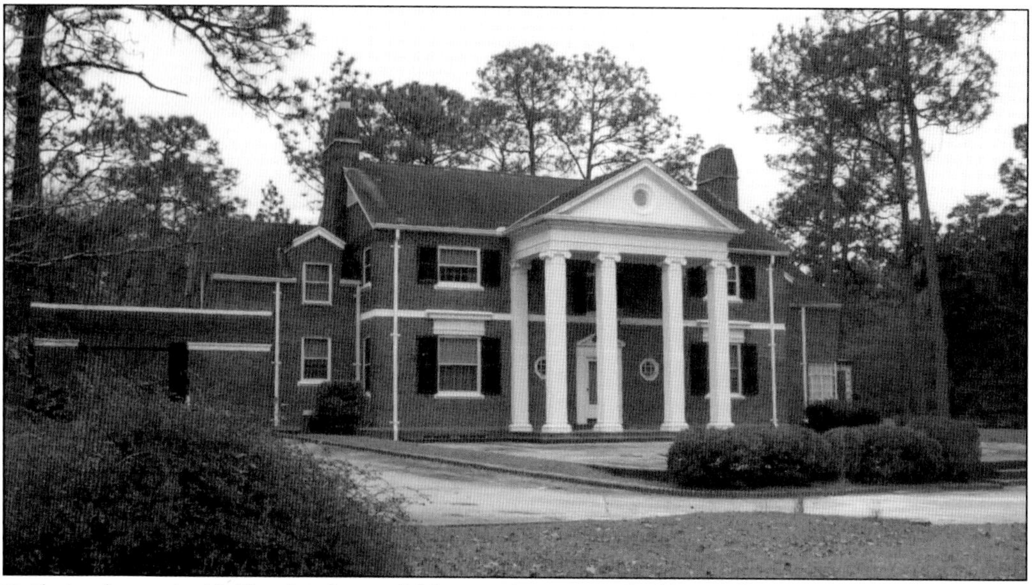

Built in the early 1940s, this beautiful home, known as Biddie Hill, is located at 500 North Main Street. Designed and built by Walter H. Aldred, it served as a residence for his family. The name refers to Mrs. Aldred, formerly Vivian Matthews, whose nickname was Biddie. The structure is situated on a spacious lawn, landscaped in tall pines with azaleas and other beautiful shrubs. In 2003 it is the home of the Aldreds's daughter, her husband, and family.

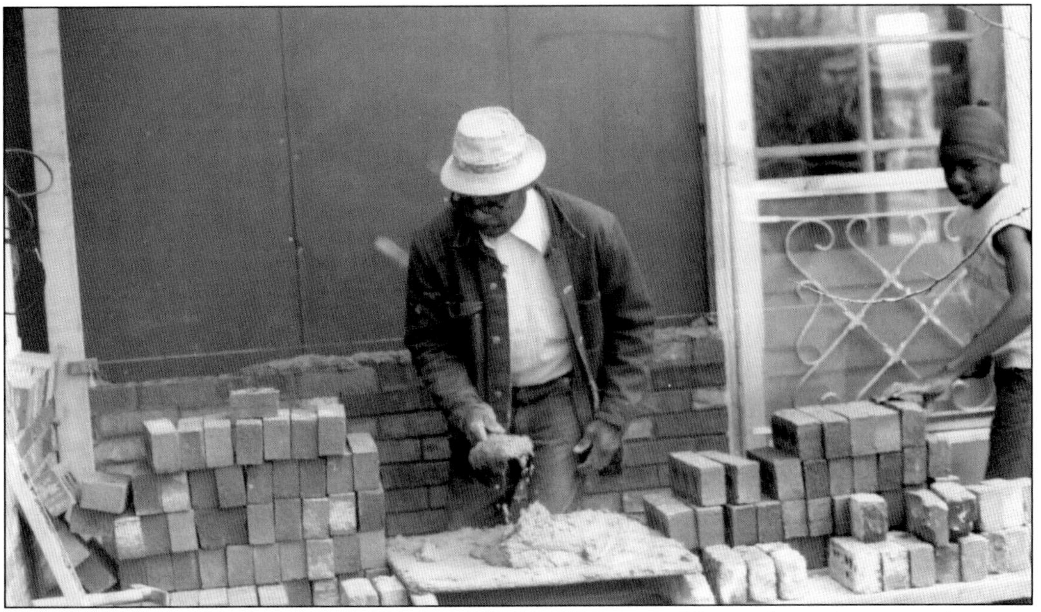

Jesse Moore was one of Statesboro's most skilled brick masons. His work can be seen in business districts and neighborhoods. He usually preferred to work alone with just one helper. He is shown on the job in 1979 with young Vincent Moore who keeps his bricks and mortar handy.

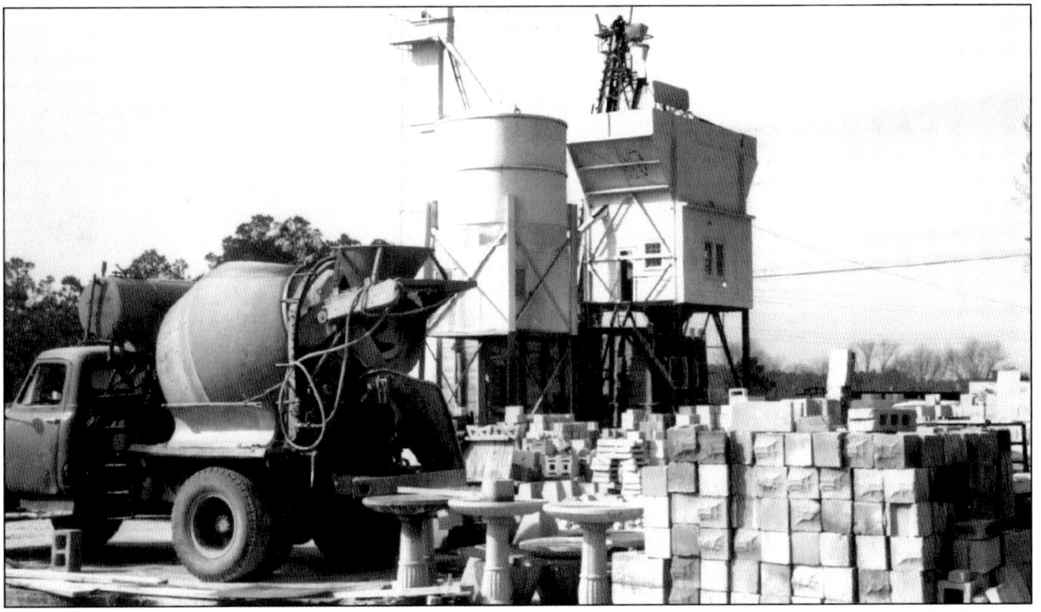

Founded in 1945 by Statesboro native R.J. Kennedy Jr., this business was originally known as Concrete Products Company. He built his plant on the site of the railroad shops of the old Savannah and Statesboro Railroad on South Zetterower Avenue. In 1949 he added ready-mix concrete trucks, the first to be offered in any city between Macon and Savannah. From the beginning Mr. Kennedy manufactured concrete blocks (called "Ken-blocks") that supplied thousands of building projects in Statesboro and at Georgia Southern University. In 2003 the Kennedy name survives in the Ken Brick company, operated by his son, Mike Kennedy, and Kennedy Trucking, managed by his grandson, Reid Kennedy.

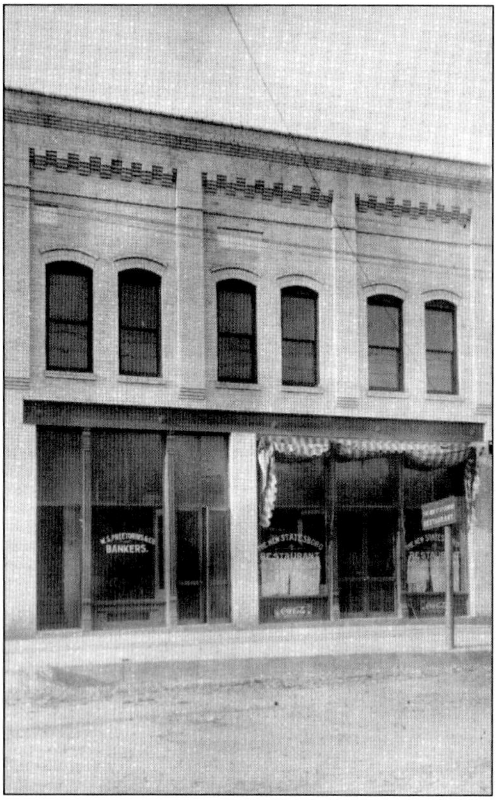

One of Statesboro's earliest businessmen was W.S. Preetorius, whose father, Charles Preetorius, had been appointed a commissioner for the town of Statesboro in the year 1866. Charles immigrated from Mainz, Germany. In 1910 his son organized the W.S. Preetorius and Company Bankers and built the building on the north side of East Main Street, across the alley from the later site of the Georgia Theater. Note that the bank is on the left, and the business on the right is the New Statesboro Restaurant. A radio station is located in this building in 2003.

Located on North Main Street at the corner of Hill Street, the Bulloch County Bank moved into an attractive modern building in 1966. Chartered in 1934, it first occupied the building of the old First National Bank on the corner of North and West Main Streets. Note that the clock was a landmark that had been moved from the old location. Other buildings housed active businesses in downtown Statesboro. In 2003 this bank is known as BB&T.

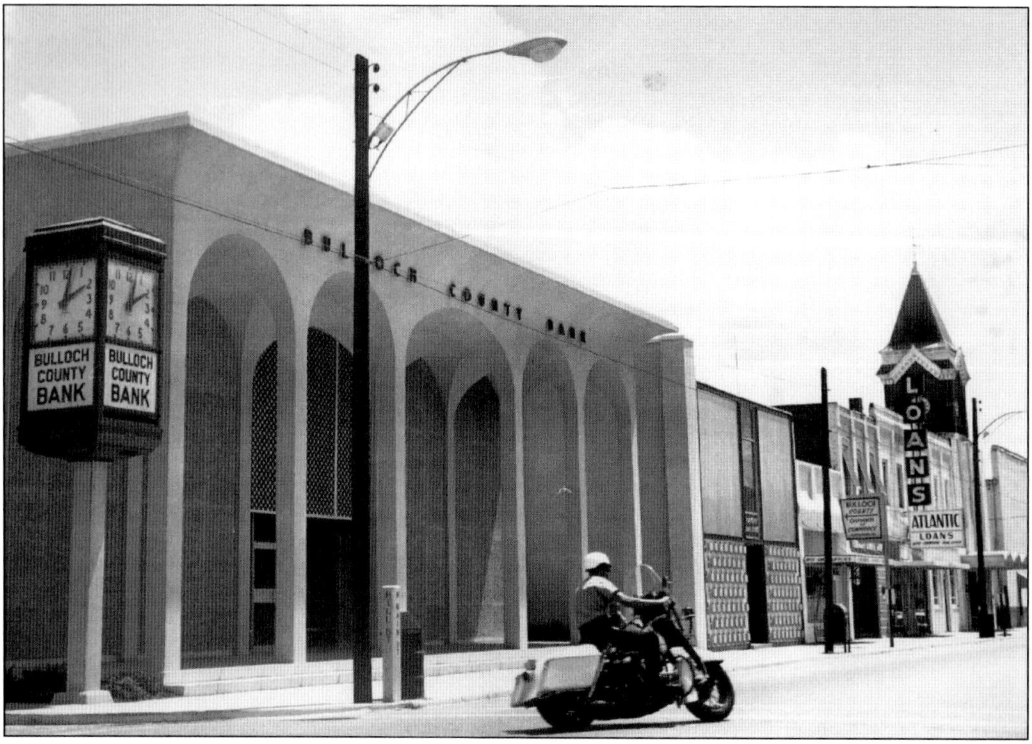

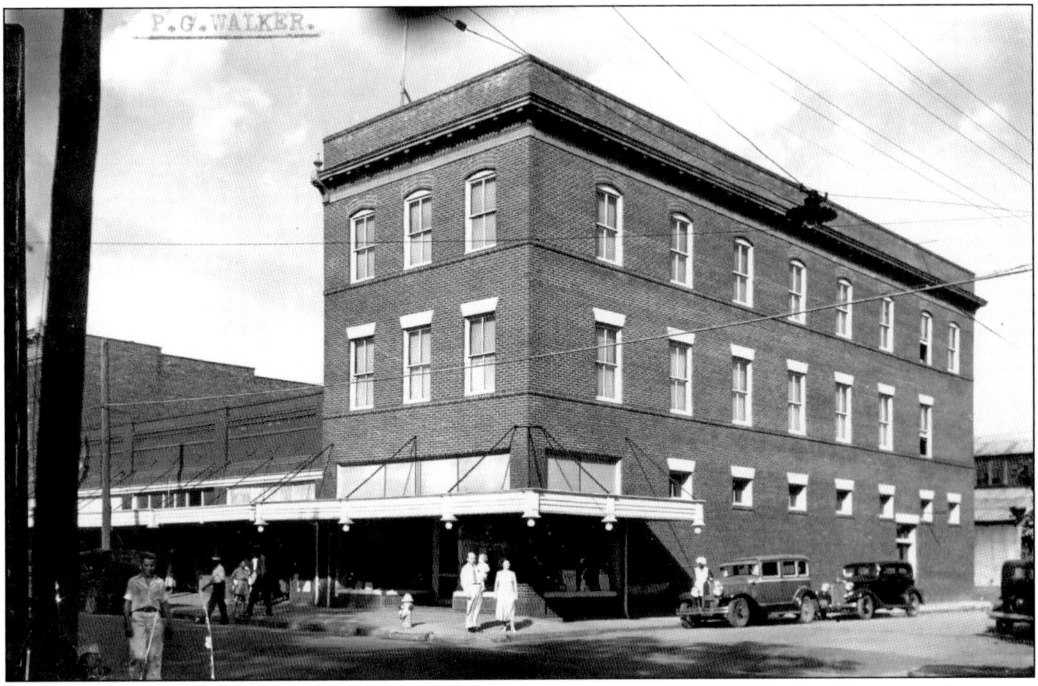

Brooks Simmons, son of Rafe Simmons, built this attractive three-story building as a furniture store before 1920. He sold the building to Anderson, Waters, and Brett Furniture in the 1920s. In the 1930s and 1940s, P.G. Walker owned the furniture store. In recent years it has been used temporarily as a bank and as a loan office. Note the interesting design of the canopy, which extends north toward the middle of town.

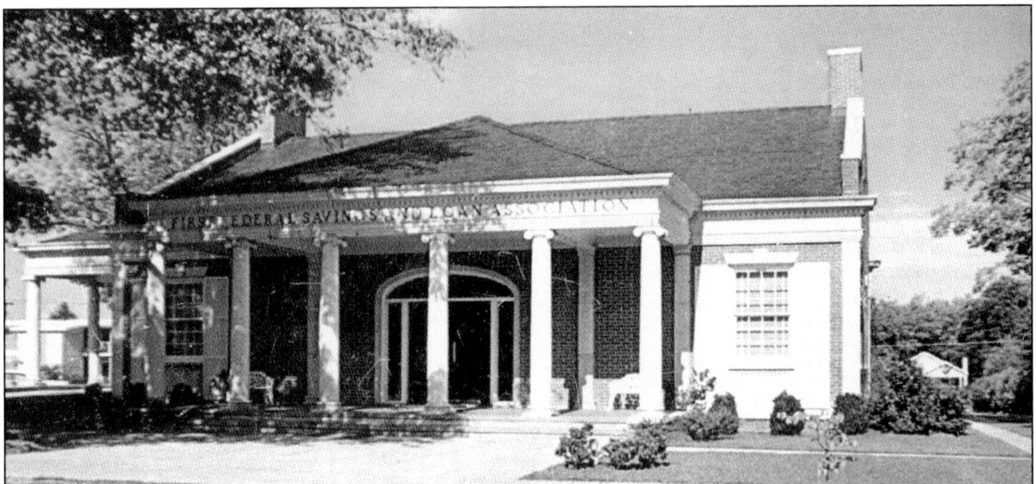

First Federal Savings and Loan Association of Statesboro began operating in 1936 with assets of $25,000. Its mission was to provide financing for home construction—a service not provided by Statesboro's two local banks. The company originally operated on Siebald Street near the old Bank of Statesboro and later moved to a building on Courtland. In 1957 the company moved into its elegant new headquarters on 115–117 North Main Street. In the 1970s the structure on North Main doubled in size. In 2003 it is the Bulloch County Court House Annex, housing county offices.

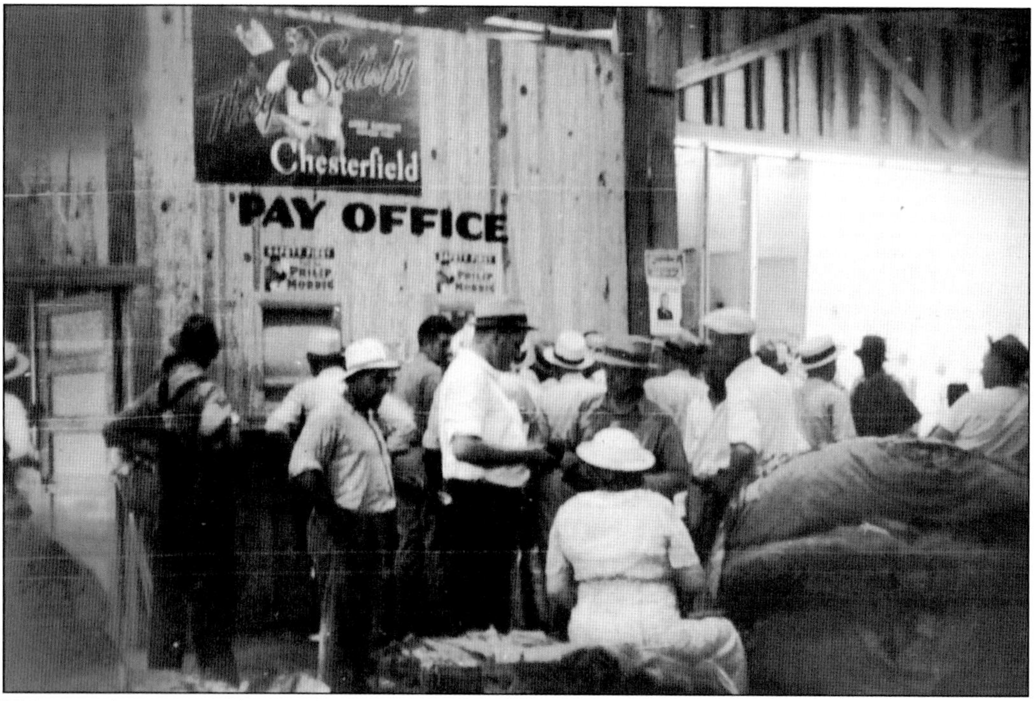

Tobacco farmers in the 1950s were eager to receive payment for a major cash crop. The transition from cotton to tobacco as the main crop allowed this community to recover from the Great Depression quicker than most. By 1953 over 20 million pounds of tobacco passed through tobacco warehouses in Statesboro annually, making it the largest market in the "Bright Tobacco Belt" spanning Georgia and Florida.

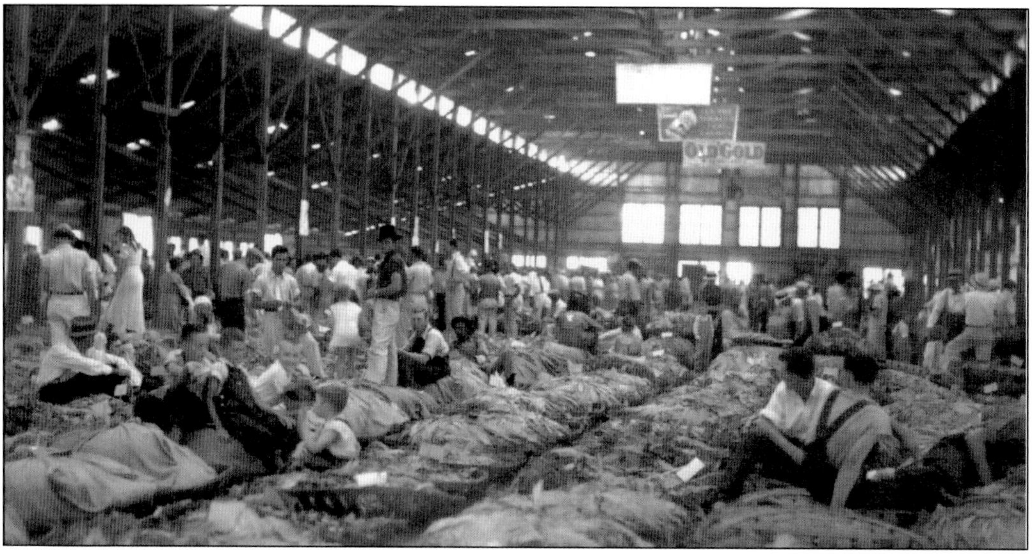

Cobb and Foxhall Warehouse was located at the corner of Cherry and South College Streets. The owners were Willis E. Cobb and H.P. Foxhall. The picture reveals that farmers were quite interested in the auction, which often provided cash for farm operations. On the north side of this warehouse a boardwalk connected to their second warehouse. The Georgia and Florida Railroad track was adjacent to the warehouse.

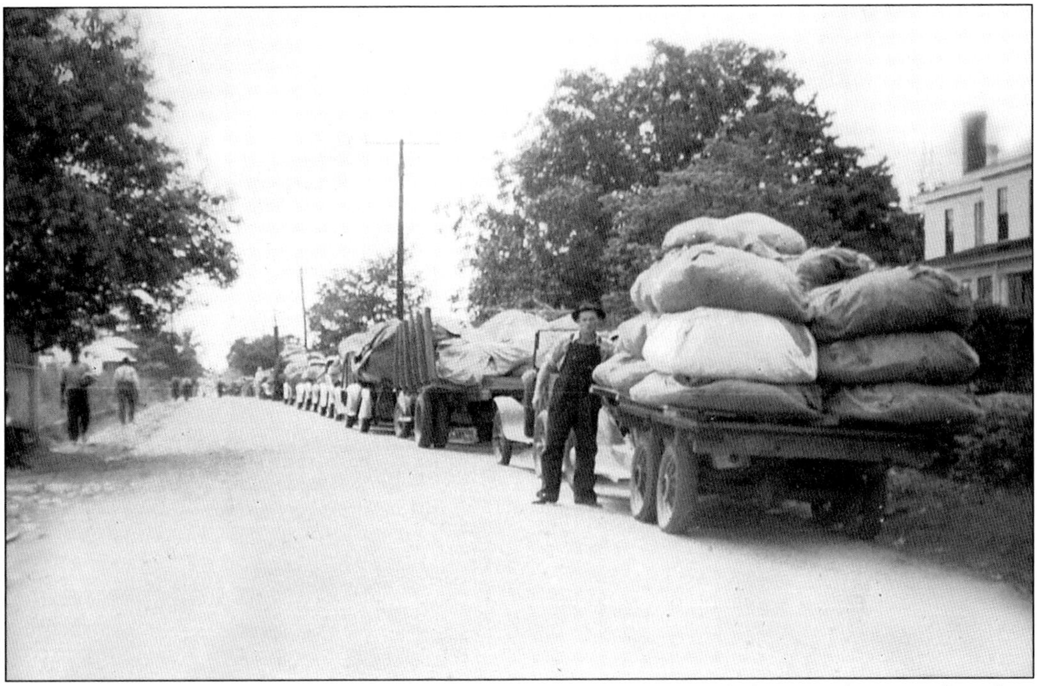

In the 1940s and 1950s, farmers throughout south Georgia and the Carolinas preferred to sell their tobacco to the warehousemen of Statesboro. The local market had the reputation of providing the best prices. Bumper-to-bumper vehicles lined up on South College Street to weigh in at their favorite warehouse. They used any conveyance possible—from huge trucks to pickups and even passenger cars.

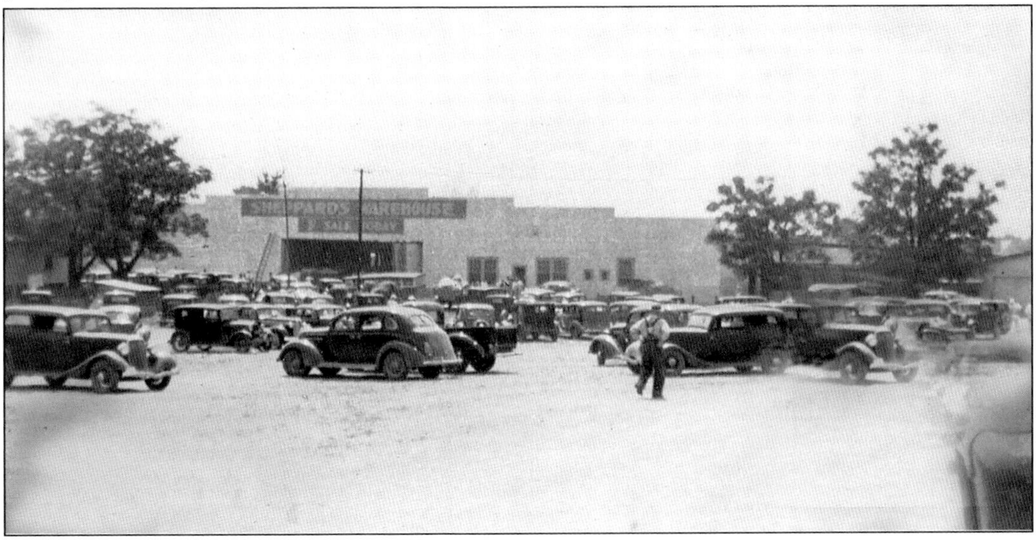

In 1933 R.E. "Bob" Sheppard came from North Carolina to operate a tobacco warehouse in Statesboro. Shown here in the 1940s is his large warehouse on the corner of Bulloch and South College Streets. The cars and trucks were parked in the open field across the street. Aulbert Brannen Sr. of Statesboro later became a partner of Mr. Sheppard; they built a second and third warehouse on South Zetterower and Packinghouse Road at Highway 301. In later years Mr. Brannen became sole owner and his sons, Aulbert Jr. and Bob, joined him in the business.

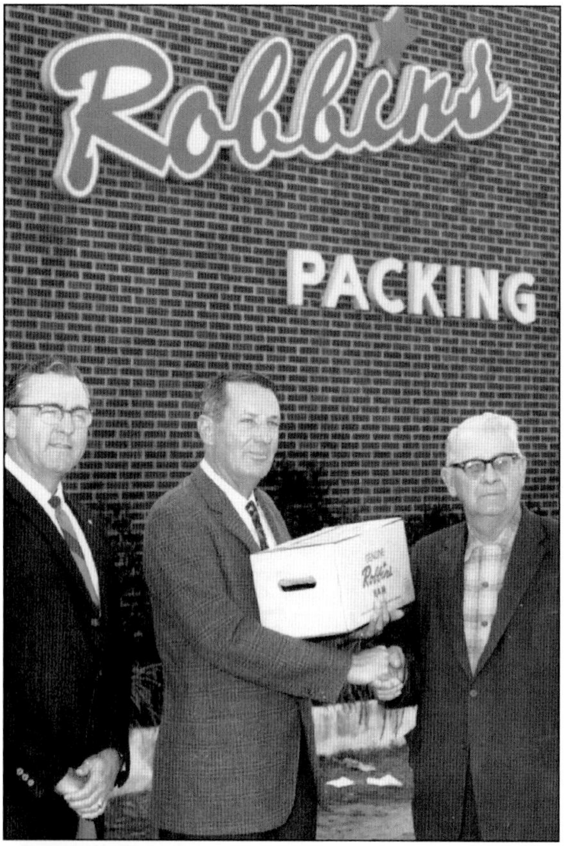

In 1949 the Robbins Packing Company opened its business on Stockyard Road. They processed meat products, both pork and beef. By 1952 the plant doubled in size, and in the late 1960s the company's revenues were over $2 million a year. The company was a leader in community development and sponsored an annual fishing rodeo. In this photograph, mayor of Statesboro Bill Bowen receives a Robbins ham from C.M. Robbins Sr. (right) and C.M. "Chollie" Robbins Jr. (left).

In 1962 the *Bulloch Herald* celebrated its 25th anniversary and honored its staff. From left to right are (front row) Mrs. Jim Rowe, Mrs. W.H. Morris, Mrs. Ernest Brannen, Miss Ann Hendrix, and Mrs. E.F. Tucker; (middle row) Miss Ann Evans, Mrs. H.H. Zetterower, Mrs. Eubie B. Riggs, and Mrs. Fielding Russell; (back row) Dr. John Mooney, Leodel Coleman (co-publisher and editor), Mrs. G.C. Coleman Jr., G.C. Coleman Jr. (co-publisher and managing editor), Mahlon Jones, and Max Lockwood.

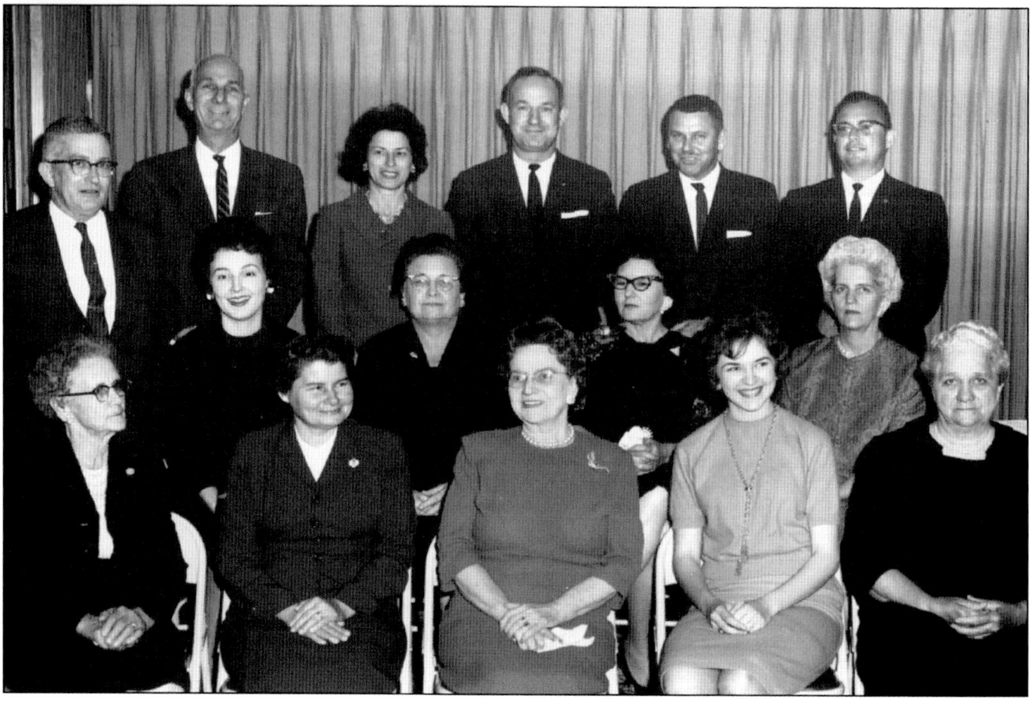

The Statesboro Telephone Company opened its new building on the south side of East Grady at Mulberry Street in 1954. The building was constructed to house the equipment for the new dial telephone system. The following are owners and managers of the company: (from left to right) J.L. Mathews, Mrs. J.L. Mathews, Mrs. Charlie Joe Mathews, Charlie Joe Mathews, and Mrs. C.B. Mathews. The company was one of the oldest continuous businesses in Statesboro when it was sold in the 1990s to the Rochester Telephone Company. In 2003 the company is owned and operated by Frontier Communications, Inc.

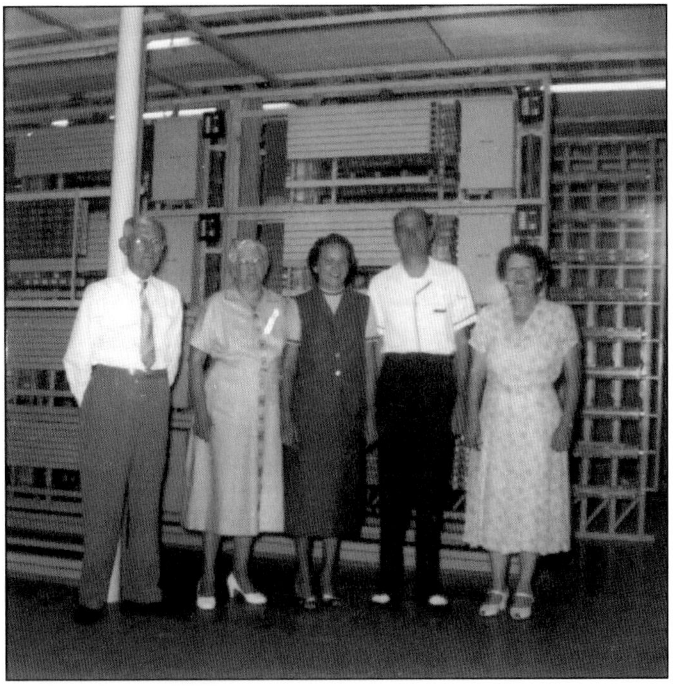

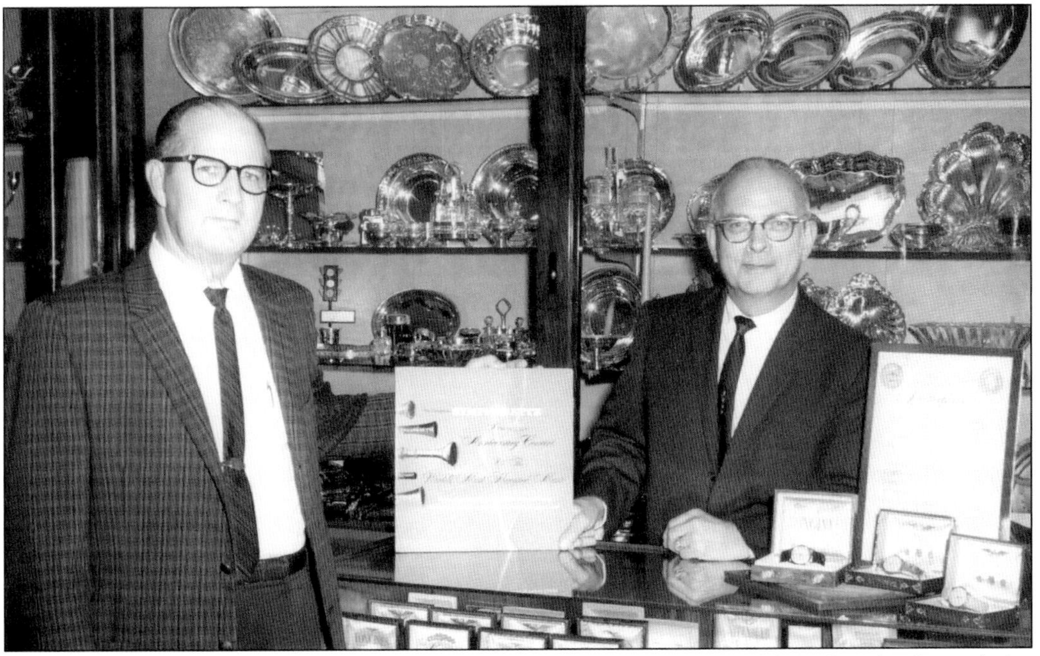

Harry W. Smith, jeweler, established his business in 1919. In 1966 Mr. Smith claimed the distinction of operating the oldest business in Statesboro under its original name and by the owner who established it. In addition to being a well-known jeweler and expert watchmaker, he was especially known for his excellent taste and beautiful stock of chinaware, crystal, and silver. After Mr. Smith's retirement, his son-in-law, W.R. "Dub" Lovett, continued in the business until his retirement in the 1990s. The business still operates at 3 South Main Street in 2003. Mr. Smith stands behind the counter as he displays watches to Harry Johnson.

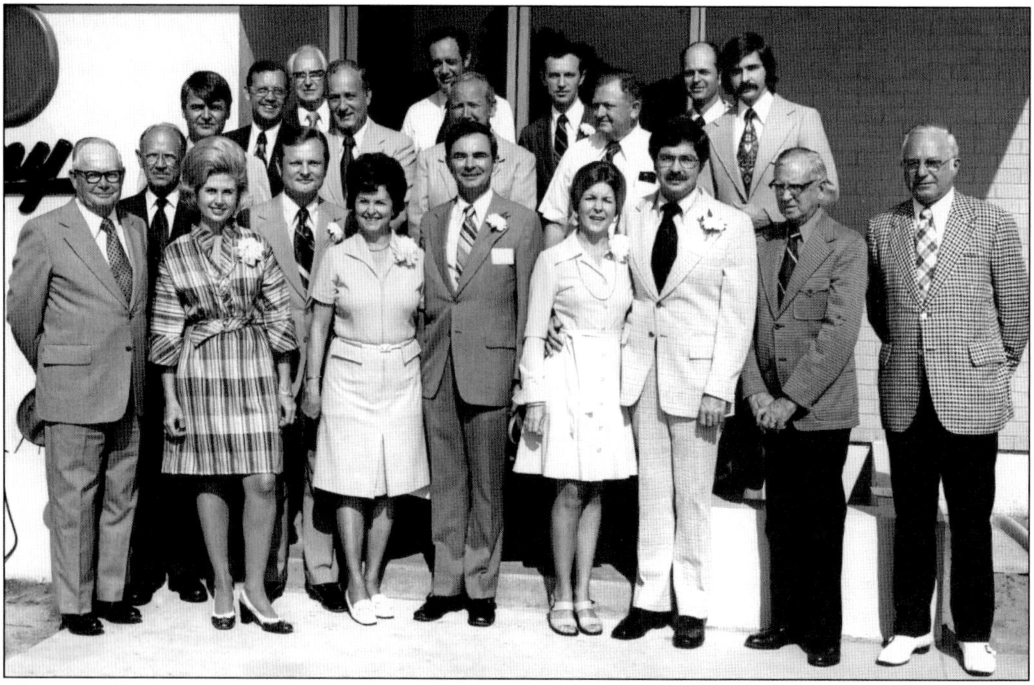

The grand opening of the new T.J. Morris Company warehouse and office building took place in 1975 on Highway 301 South. Mr. Morris established the company in 1920. Pictured from left to right are (front row) O.B. "Red" Bell, J.C. Williams, Mrs. T.J. Morris Jr., T.J. "Jimmy" Morris Jr., Mrs. Robert Morris, Robert F. Morris, Mrs. Phillip Morris, Phillip Morris, J. Robert Smith, and Everett Williams; (middle row) Hal Averitt, Ed Eckles, Thurmon Lanier, Don McDougald, Emit Deal, and Frank Morris; (back row) Virgil Donaldson, Joe Johnston, Edwin Akins, and unidentified.

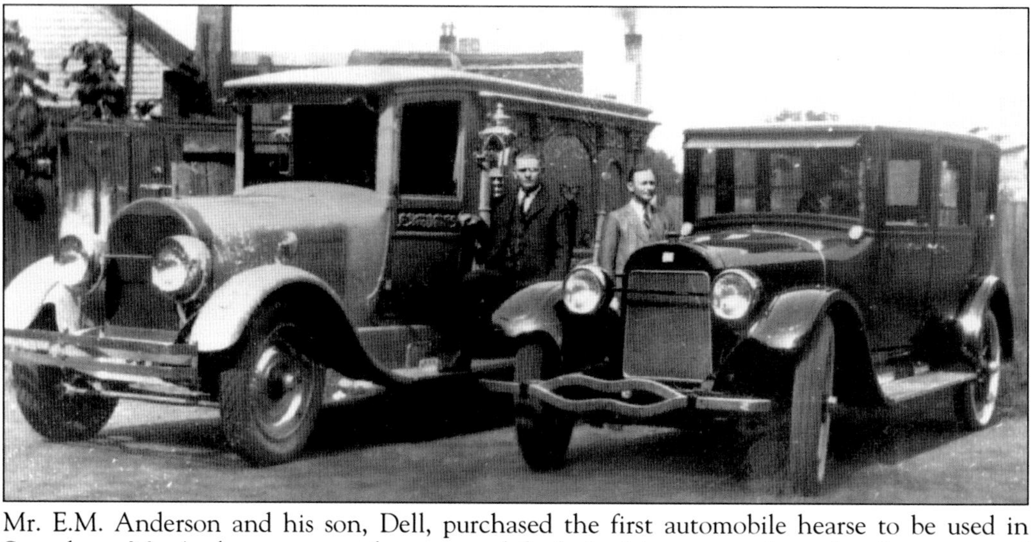

Mr. E.M. Anderson and his son, Dell, purchased the first automobile hearse to be used in Statesboro. Mr. Anderson operated an automobile dealership, a general merchandise store, and a funeral parlor. The hearse on the left was decorated with metal carving, and the car on the right was used to transport family members of the deceased. It is interesting to recall that many hardware dealers also operated funeral parlors in the early 20th century.

Three

THE BEST OF TIMES . . .

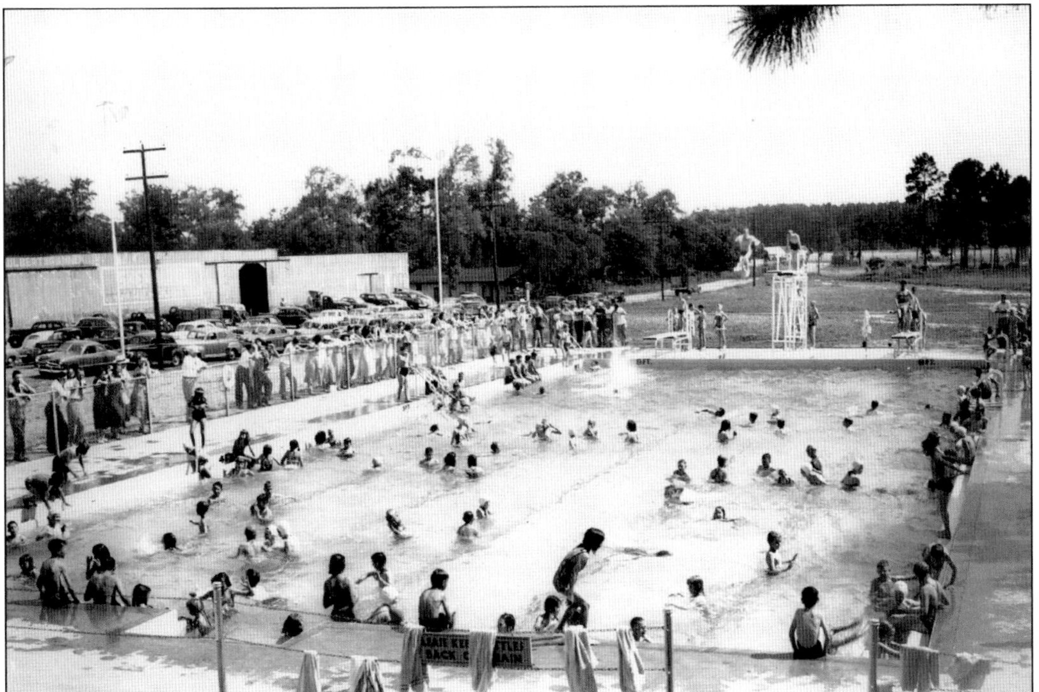

This scene is of a typical summer afternoon at the Statesboro Recreation Center swimming pool on South Zetterower Avenue, after the facility opened on June 1, 1949. Note the spectators lining the fence, the tobacco warehouses in the left background, and the absence of any commercial development near the pool.

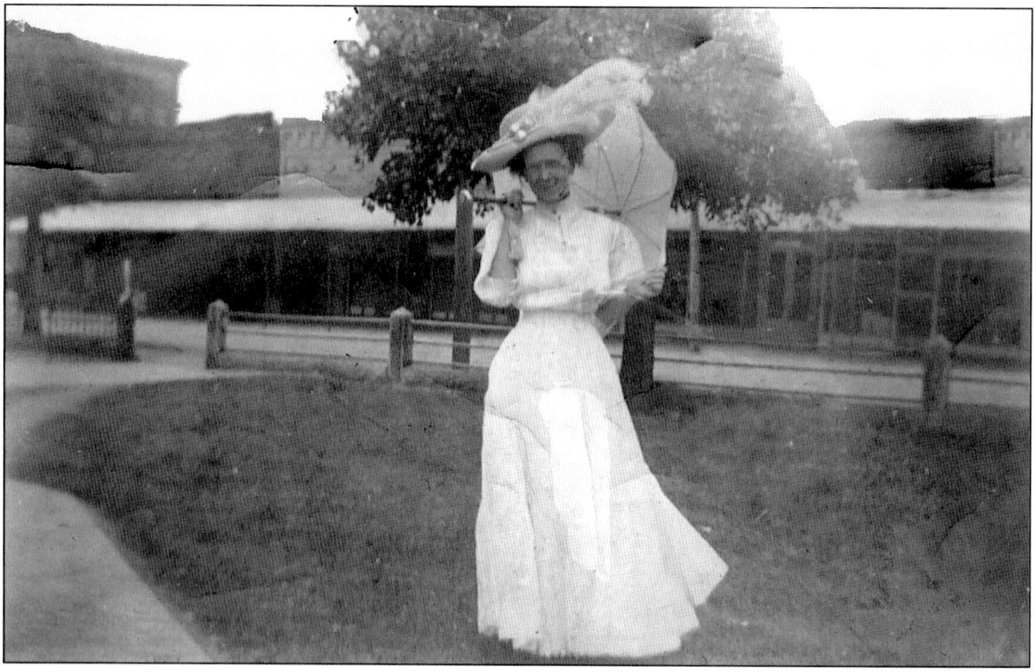

On Sunday afternoons in the early 1900s, young women enjoyed taking a stroll uptown, dressed in their stylish clothing. Mrs. W. Homer Simmons Sr. holds a parasol as she poses on the courthouse lawn with North Main Street in the background.

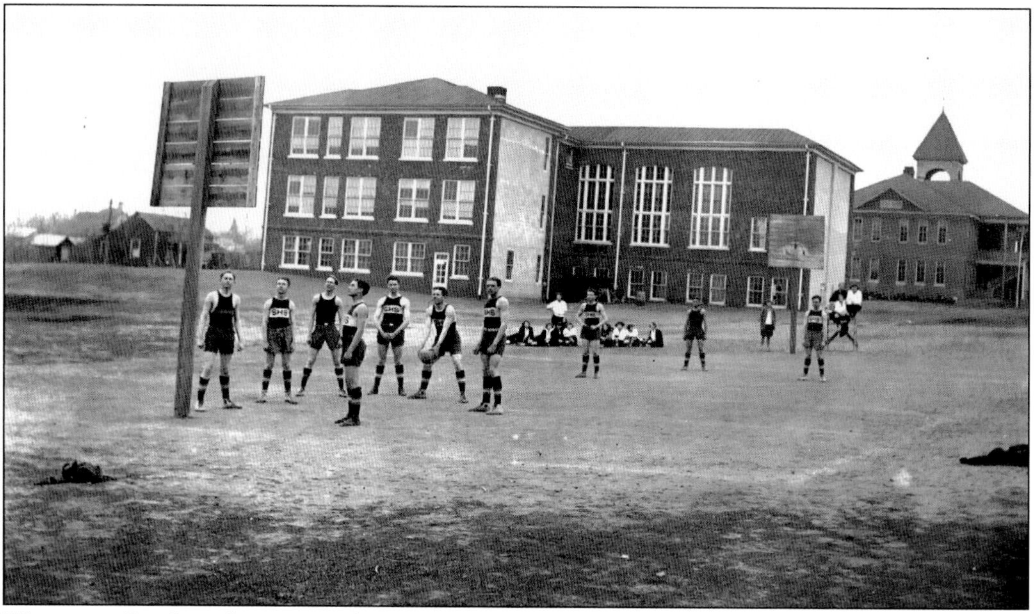

Wearing official uniforms, members of the Statesboro High School basketball team practice on their home court behind the high school building (completed in 1922). Notice the upper and lower porches as well as the steeple of the grammar school. The wing in the center of the photograph was the auditorium. The school lunchroom was in the basement underneath the auditorium. Statesboro High School was located on West Grady Street, the site of the fire department in 2003.

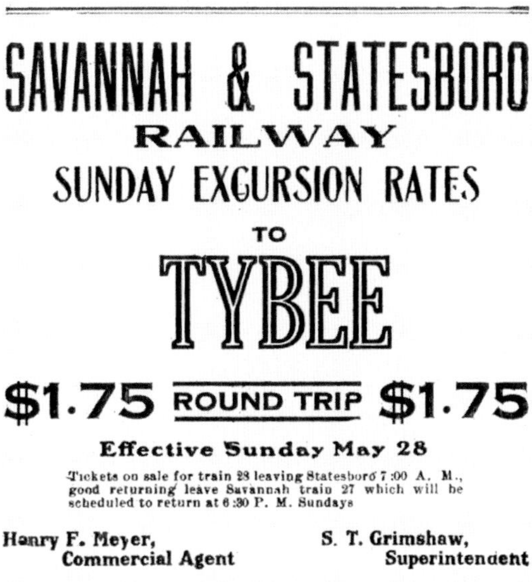

The Savannah and Statesboro Railway advertisement in the May 18, 1916, Bulloch Times featured the "cost".

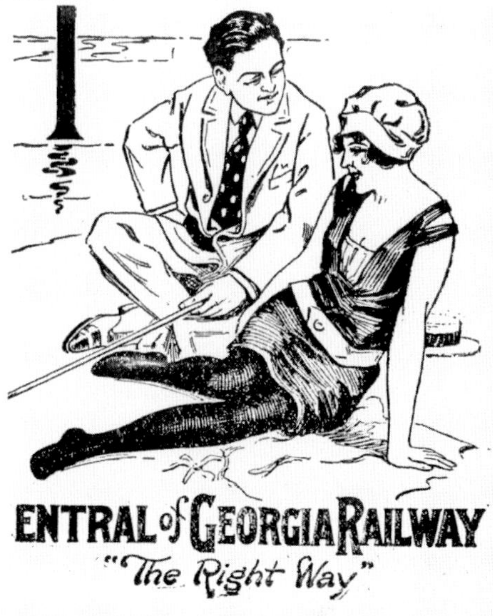

This Central of Georgia Railway during the summer of 1926, featured the "fun".

For many Statesboro residents in the early 1900s, the memorable summer activity was the Sunday School–sponsored excursions to Tybee. Often a group of 100 would board the Savannah and Statesboro Railroad Train at 6 a.m. Once in Savannah, they took horse-drawn hacks to the Tybee Railroad depot across town. Then they went to the Tybee pavilion for a picnic lunch. Afterwards everyone rented bathing suits and enjoyed a few hours in the sun. At 3 p.m. they boarded the train for a return trip home, arriving in the evening.

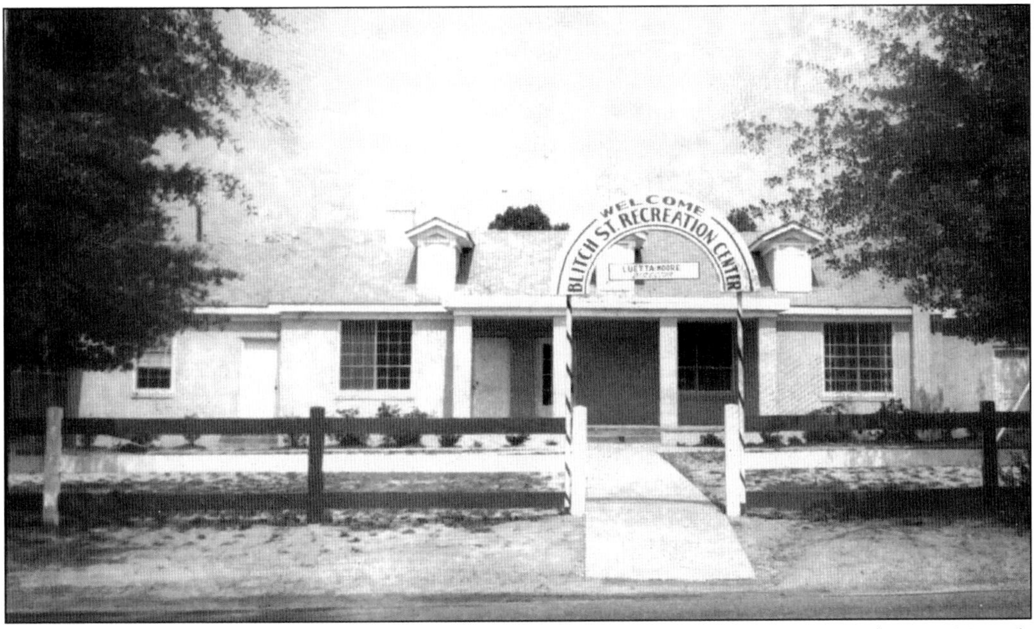

The Blitch Street Recreation center (now on MLK Jr. Drive) was inaugurated in 1956 with Mrs. Luetta Moore as its recreational supervisor. The center included the recreation building, a swimming pool, a dance pavilion, athletic fields, and a playground for younger children. In earlier years this was the site of the William James School complex.

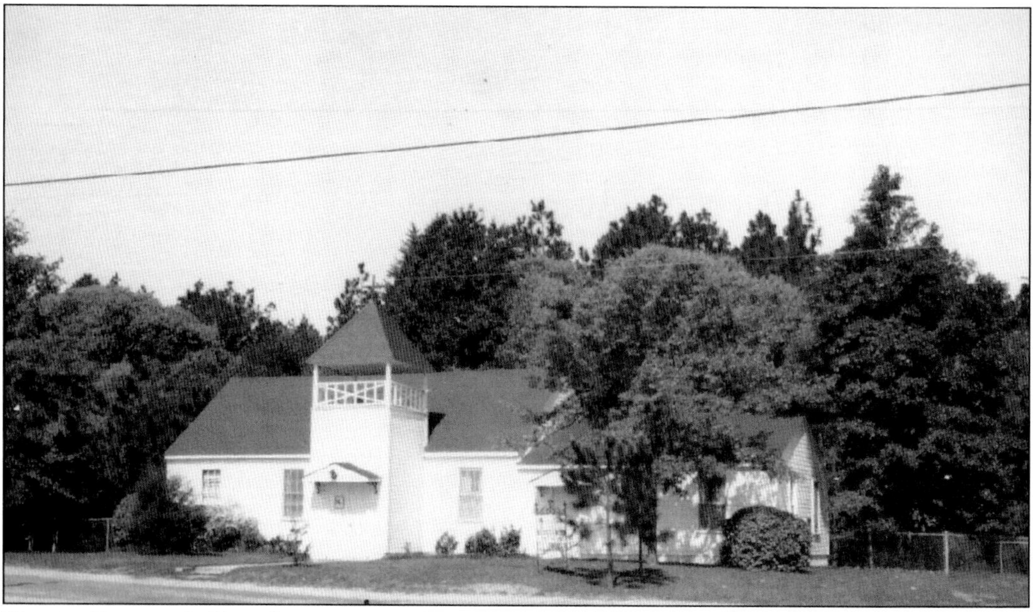

Trinity Episcopal Church, constructed in 1953 on the corner of Lee Street and Northside Drive, was the congregation's first permanent worship site. Later the building was sold to the Lower Mill Creek Primitive Baptist Church, which continued to use the facilities into the 21st century. The church built its second location on Chandler Road adjacent to Georgia Southern University in 1965. Today Trinity Episcopal Church has a beautiful new facility on the corner of Country Club Road and Veterans Memorial Parkway.

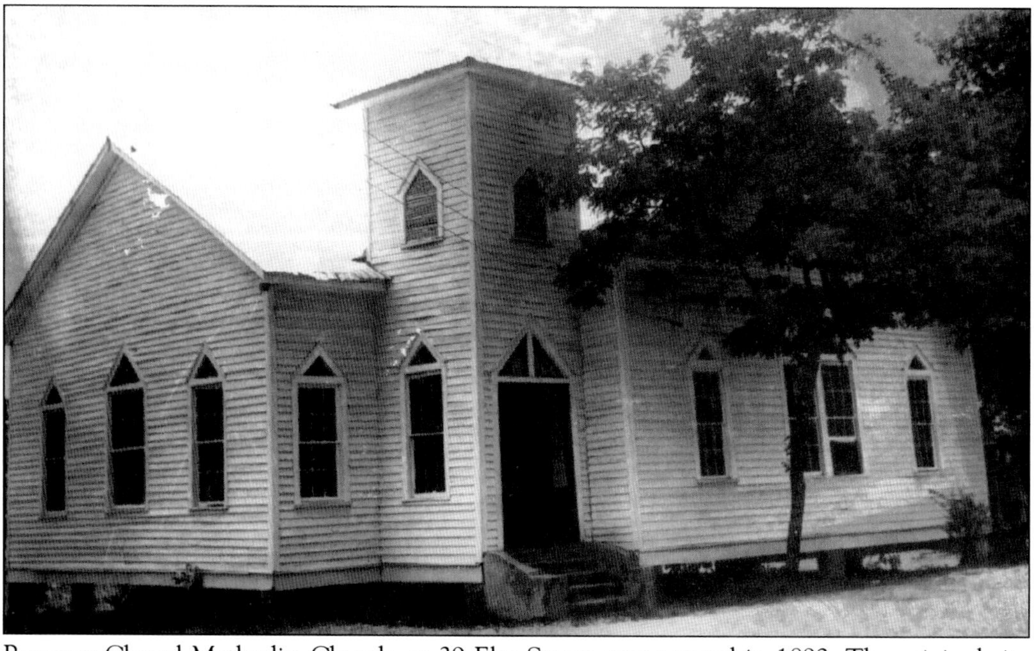

Brannen Chapel Methodist Church, at 39 Elm Street, was erected in 1892. The original site was on Proctor Street. The land on Elm Street was donated by J.A. "Lonnie" Brannen, in whose honor the church was named. In recent years the congregation built a modern brick facility on the north side of Elm Street.

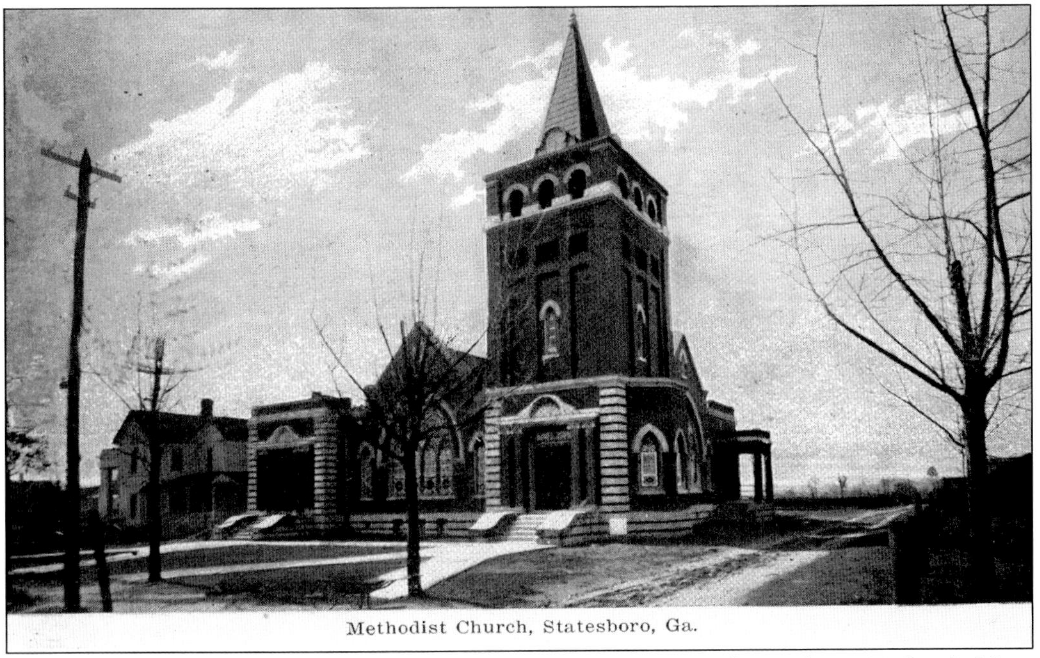

Statesboro Methodist Church, shown as it looked in 1910, was located at 101 South Main Street at the corner of Cherry Street. An earlier church was established on this same site in 1886. As shown the church was completed in 1903. Note that on the far right of the picture, the church has a side portico, and the fence across the street is for the Masonic Lodge. On the far left is the J.P. Williams mansion. In the 1950s the building was razed, and a new gothic structure, designed by architect Walter Aldred, was built dedicated in 1959.

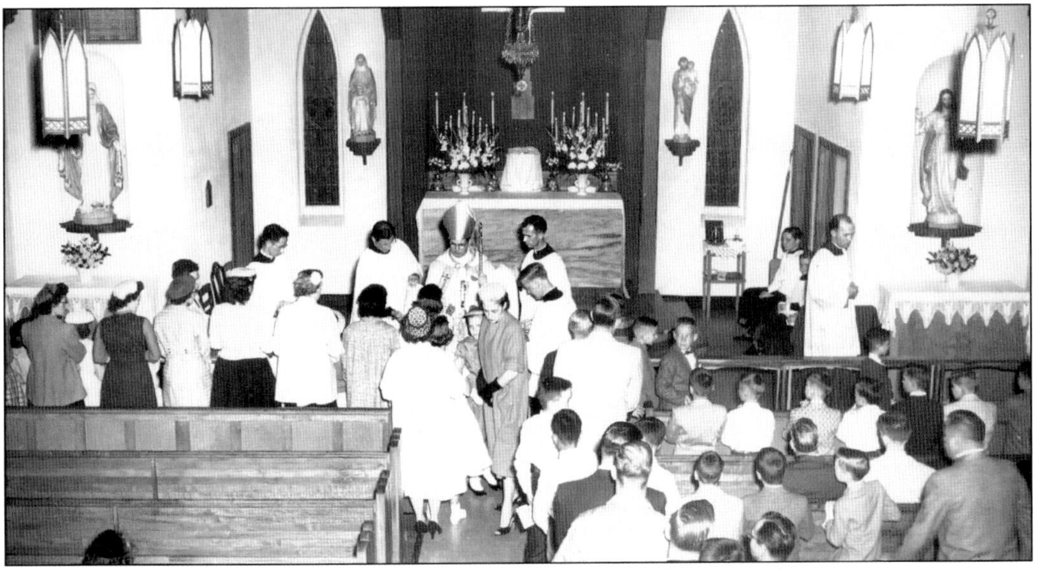

St. Matthew's Catholic Church was established in 1934. The original congregation met in a house on South Main Street, the site of Stiles Motel in 2003. Shown is the interior of the St. Matthew's Catholic Church, which was dedicated in February 1950 and was located on Northside Drive East. The building was razed in the 1980s when the congregation built a new church located on Gentilly Road.

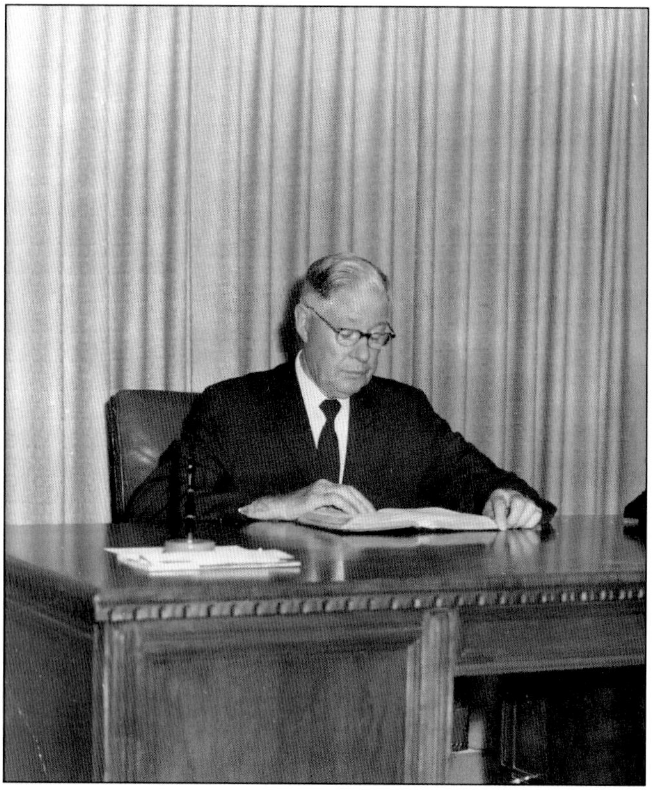

Elder V.F. Agan, ordained in 1913, was pastor of the Statesboro Primitive Baptist Church from 1934 until 1954. He was made pastor emeritus in 1962 and served the church in that capacity until his death in 1982. He was a minister in word and deed for 69 years. He is shown at his study around the time of his retirement.

The Pittman Park United Methodist Church was established in 1956, an outgrowth of the First Methodist Church. It is located on Fair Road in the Pittman Park subdivision. The land was a gift from Mrs. Marvin S. Pittman. A large educational and recreational annex was added in the 1990s.

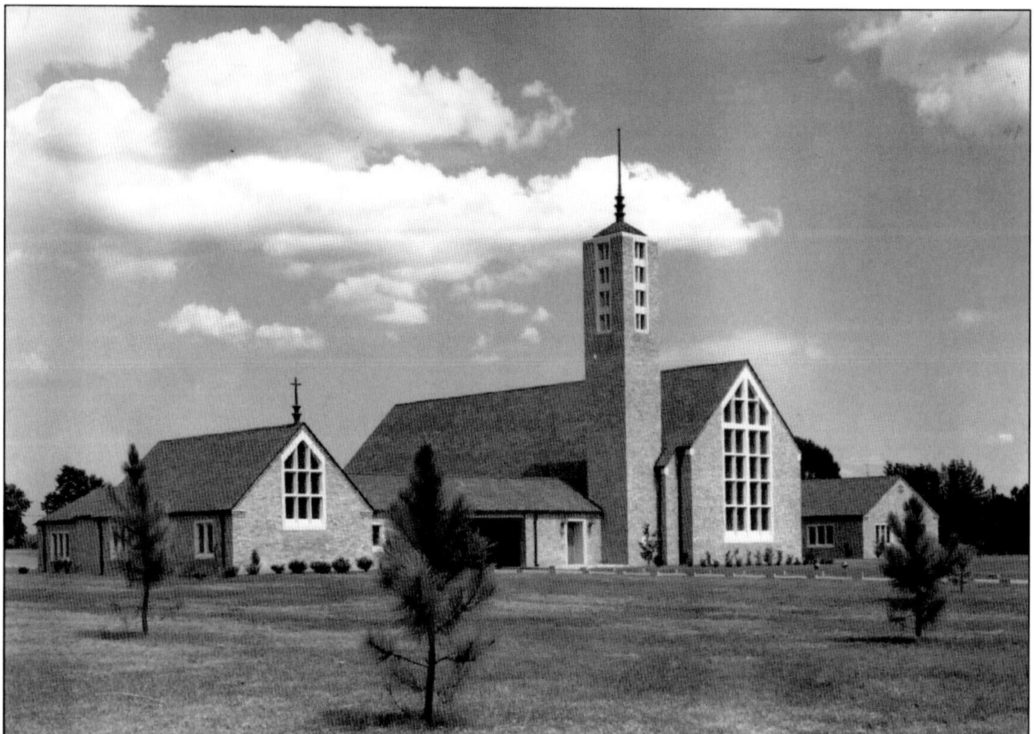

The Second St. John Missionary Baptist Church on Fair Road was established in 1896. Its first name was Rose Hill, and its pastor was Rev. A.C. Dunlap. During the pastorate of Rev. Charles Williams, the church increased in size and needed a larger facility. Mr. John McDougald, a Presbyterian elder, deeded a sizable plot of land adjacent to his turpentine distillery. In appreciation, the church re-named itself "Second St. John," out of appreciation to Mr. McDougald. The first St. John appears in the New Testament.

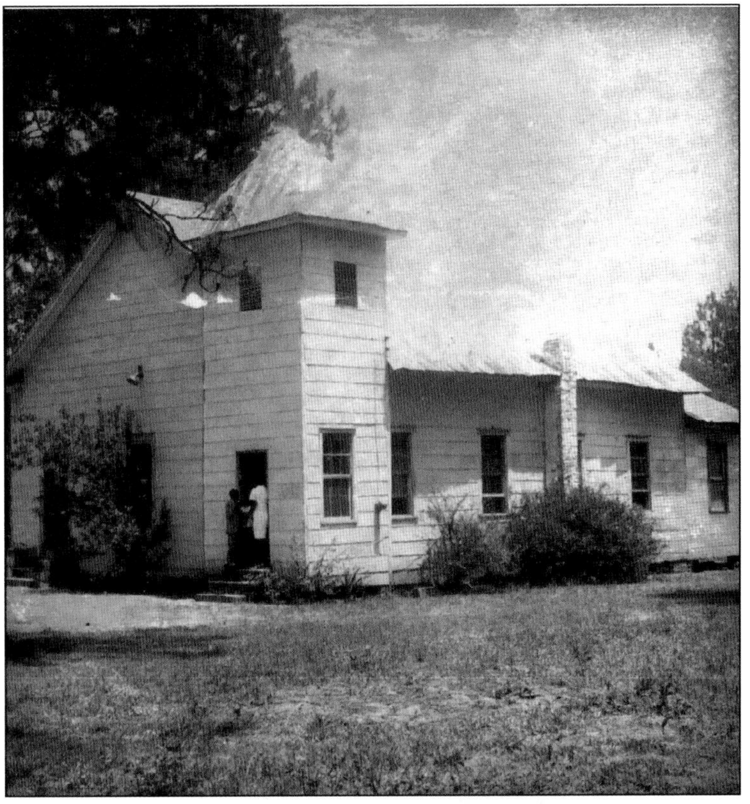

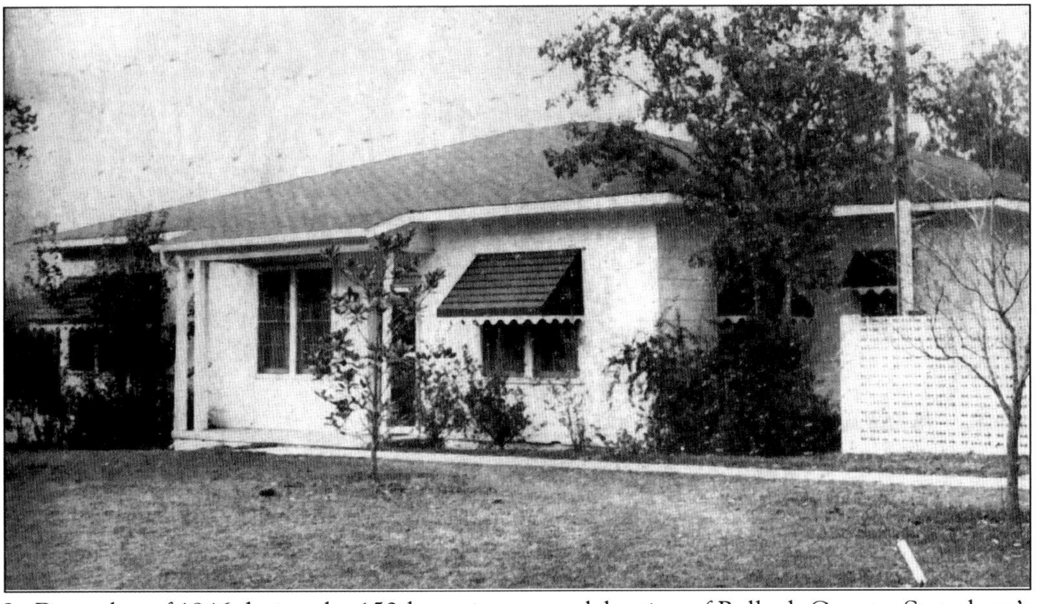

In December of 1946 during the 150th anniversary celebration of Bulloch County, Statesboro's first radio station came on the air. Its call letters, WWNS, stood for "Welcome, Where Nature Smiles." Shown here is the studio located on East Olliff Street. In 2003 the station still operated out of this building, entertaining and informing the citizens of Statesboro and surrounding areas.

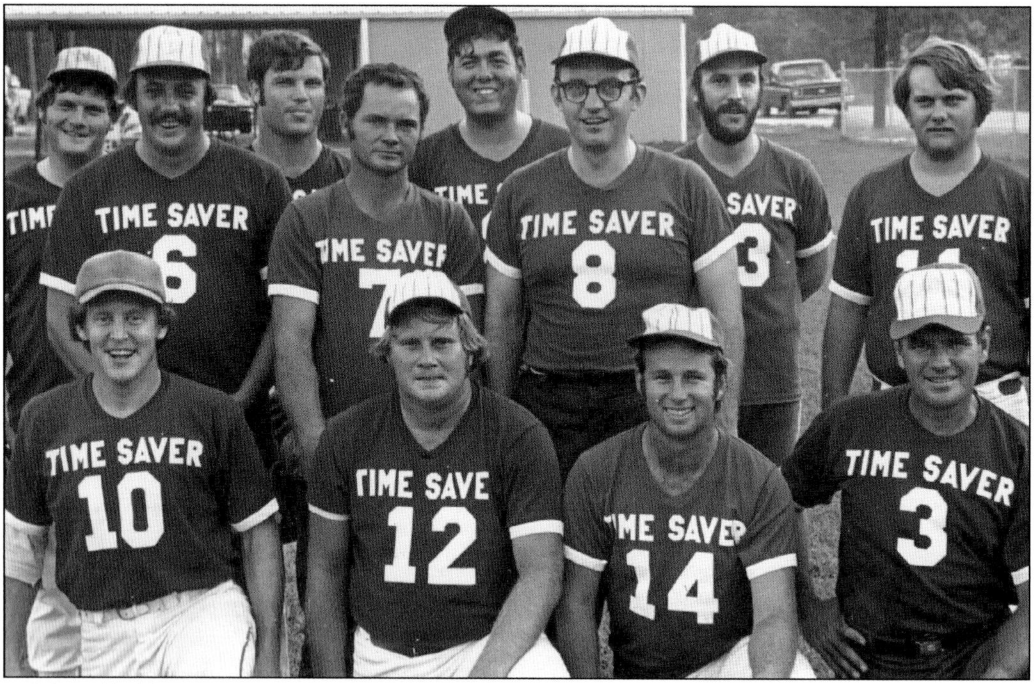

Adult softball teams provided many men and women with opportunities for competitive sports through the Statesboro Recreation Department. This team in the late 1970s won a regional championship; members appear both excited and exhausted. From left to right are (kneeling) Jim Davis, Romaine Bradford, Gary McCorkle, and Fred Shaver (coach); (standing) Charles Hunnicutt, two unidentified Larry Floyd, two unidentified, Raymond Poss, and Billy Lupton.

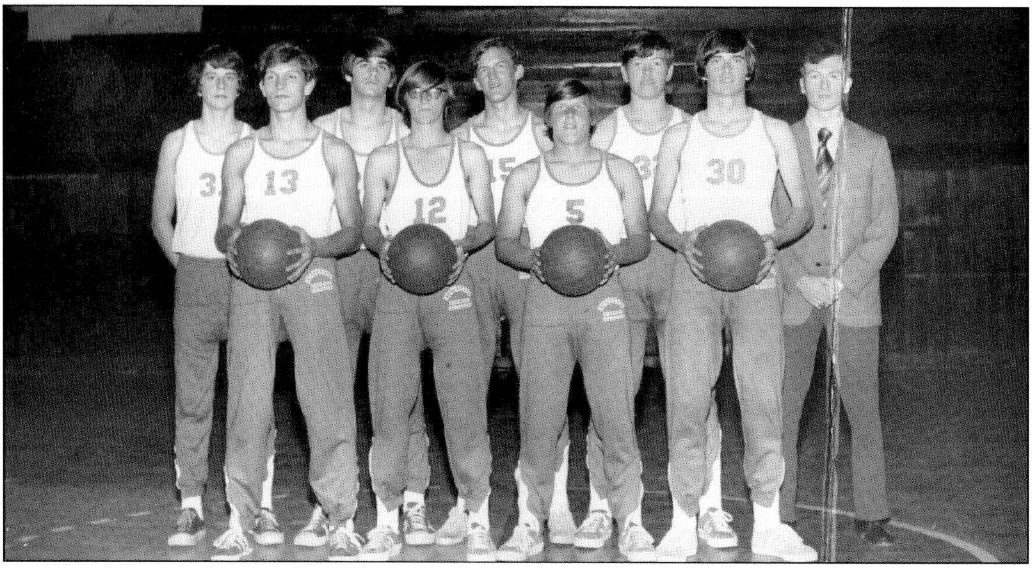

In 1971 the boys all-star basketball team of the Statesboro Recreation Department represented Statesboro in district competition. From left to right are (front row) Danny Woodard, Pratt Lockwood, Alan Tyson, and Gary Anderson; (back row) Marshall Spivey, Richard Mallard, Billie Joe Tillman, and Jack Webb. The coach, Charles Webb, was completing his first year as SRD sports director.

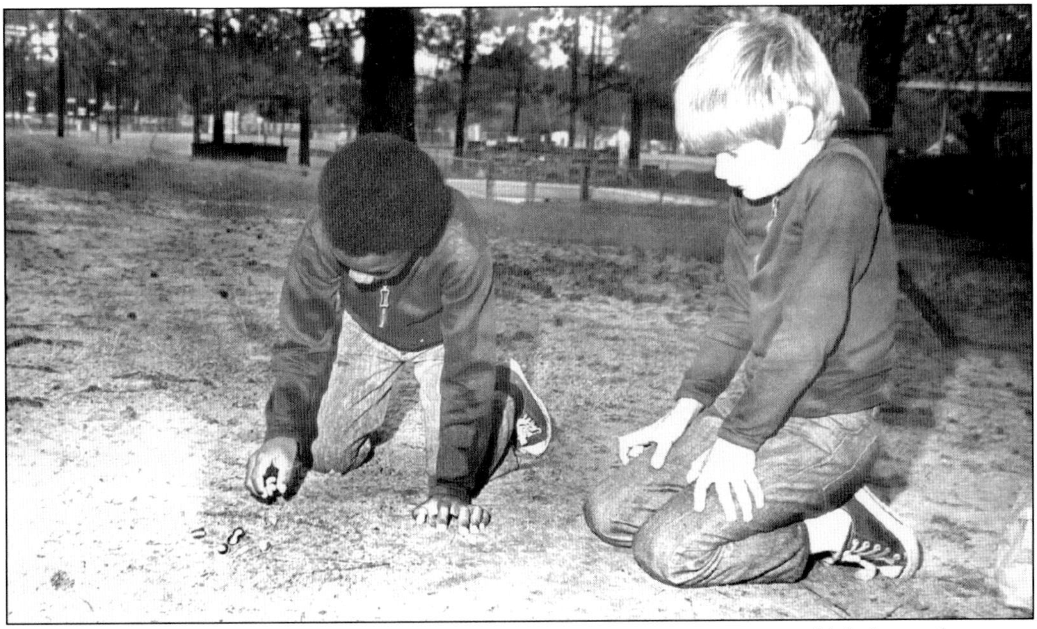

In an age of high-tech toys and games, these youngsters engage in an old-fashioned contest of marbles. On the sandy playground of the Statesboro Recreation Center on Fair Road, they draw a large circle and arrange their marbles within the boundary. Then each player uses his thumb to send a "shooter" into the clump of marbles, seeking to knock out more marbles than his opponent.

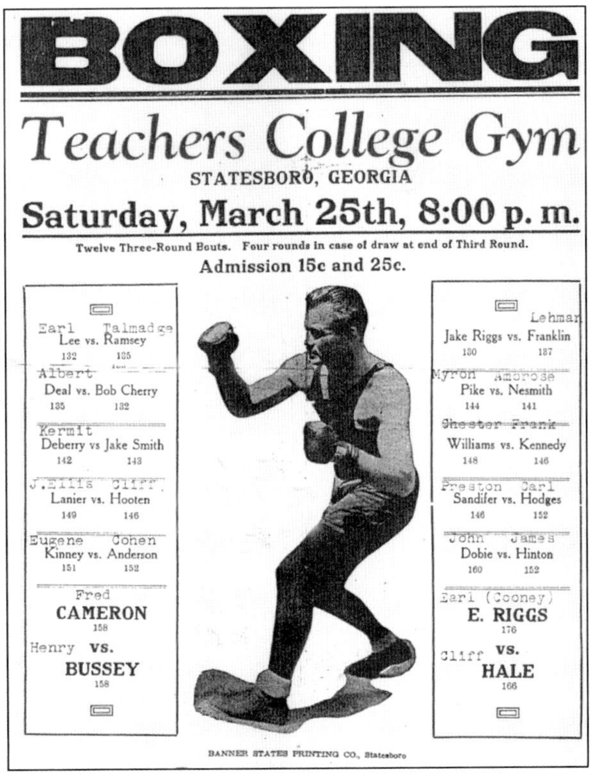

In the early 1930s boxing was a popular sport both at South Georgia Teachers College and in the community. Citizens preferred to see local athletes compete against each other, all honoring the rules of the Marquis of Queensbury. They competed according to their weight categories, as shown in the announcement. Note the names of local athletes on the poster. There are familiar names such as Lehman Franklin, Talmadge Ramsey, Earl Lee, Cohen Anderson, Albert Deal, Jake Smith, Carl Hodges, Cooney Riggs, and Chester Williams.

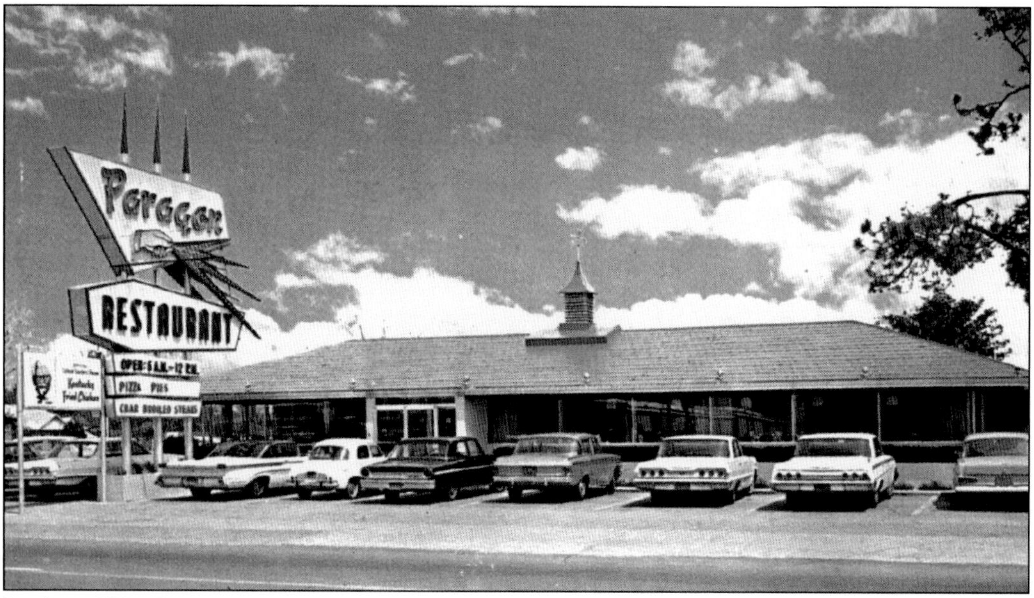

In the 1970s the Paragon Restaurant on the corner of South Main Street and Tillman Road, operated by Mr. and Mrs. Inman Hodges, was known for its variety of good food, especially its seafood buffet. The sign in front indicates its status as the first location of a Kentucky Fried Chicken franchise in town operating through a take-out window at the back. Eating establishments have been located on this site since the 1930s when Mr. and Mrs. Cecil Kennedy operated a small restaurant there. Later John Meyers ran the popular College Grill. Succeeding the Paragon Restaurant was Archibalds, honoring the namesake of Bulloch County, Archibald Bulloch.

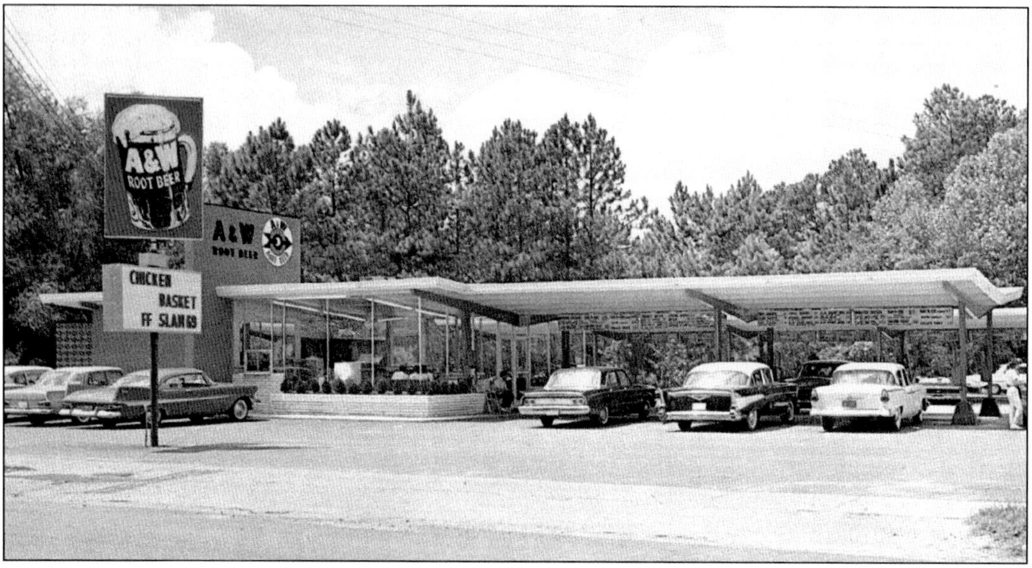

The popular drive-in restaurant, A&W Root Beer, is shown as it appeared in the 1960s. It was located on the west side of South Main Street in what once was known as Andersonville, near the "Big Ditch." The store offered dine-in and curb service. Each parking place was equipped with a speaker used by customers to place their orders. Popular items included the "Brown Cow," or root beer float, and cheeseburgers.

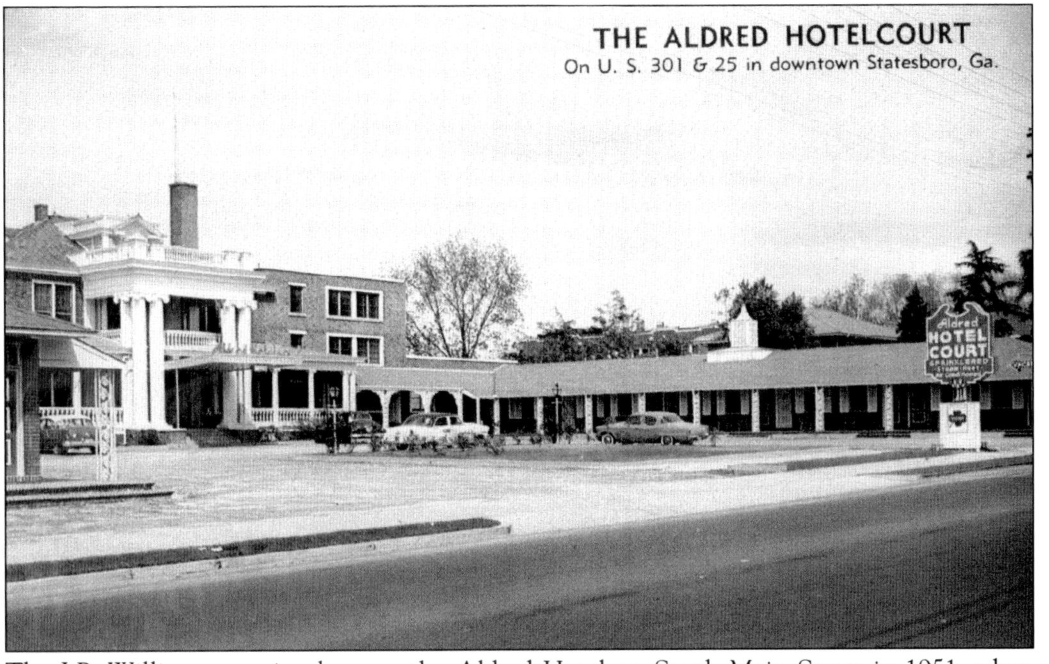

The J.P. Williams mansion became the Aldred Hotel on South Main Street in 1951, when Walter Aldred used his skills of architecture and construction to manage the transformation. Later he added motel rooms to the north and south sides of the building, and the Aldred Hotel became known as Aldred Hotel Court. It was popular not only with tourists, but with tobacco buyers as well. The hotel stood near the tobacco warehouses on South College Street.

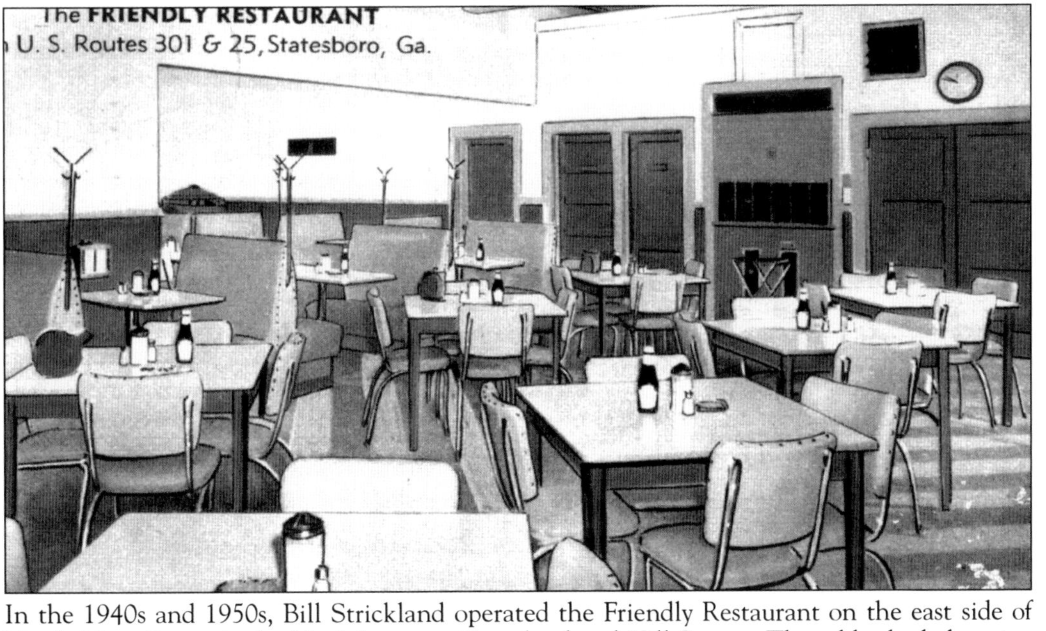

In the 1940s and 1950s, Bill Strickland operated the Friendly Restaurant on the east side of North Main Street in the block between Courtland and Hill Streets. The tables had gleaming formica tops. The chairs with chrome legs were covered with brightly colored plastic. A huge Carrier air conditioner, shown in the rear, kept the dining area cool and comfortable. The restaurant was known for home-cooked Southern meals.

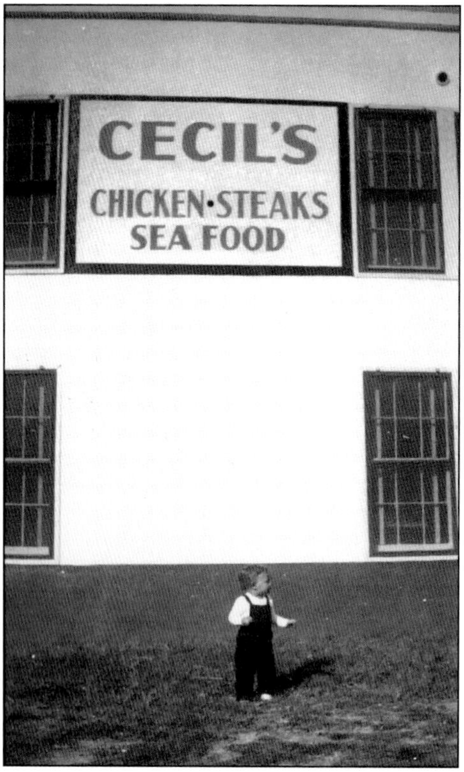

Toddler Holmes Ramsey is shown standing at the rear of Cecil's, a restaurant located at the corner of South Main and Tillman Streets. Mr. and Mrs. Cecil Kennedy built, owned, and operated the business. Diners enjoyed the excellent food and entertainment, including dancing. Waiters provided curb service in the rear of the restaurant. Mr. and Mrs. Kennedy ran the establishment from the mid-1930s until 1945, when they sold the business and opened a tourist home on 301 South.

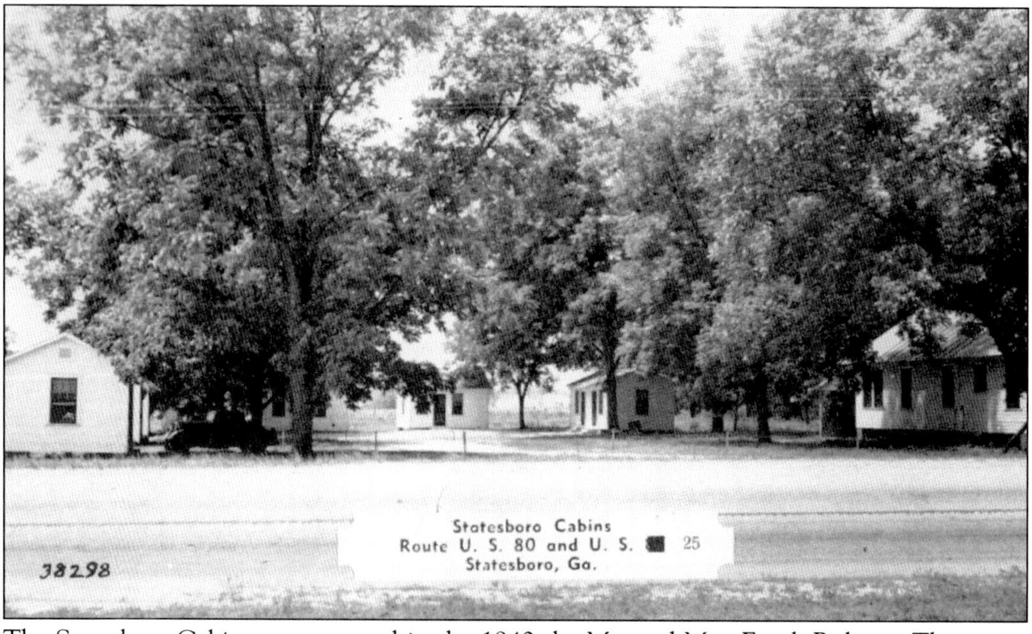

The Statesboro Cabins were opened in the 1940s by Mr. and Mrs. Frank Roberts. They were located on West Parrish Street near its intersection with what is now Martin Luther King Jr. Drive. It was one of the earliest establishments of this type devoted to serving the needs of travelers. The cabins were built before U.S. Highway 301 was completed and served travelers en route to Savannah via Highway 80 (West Parrish Street).

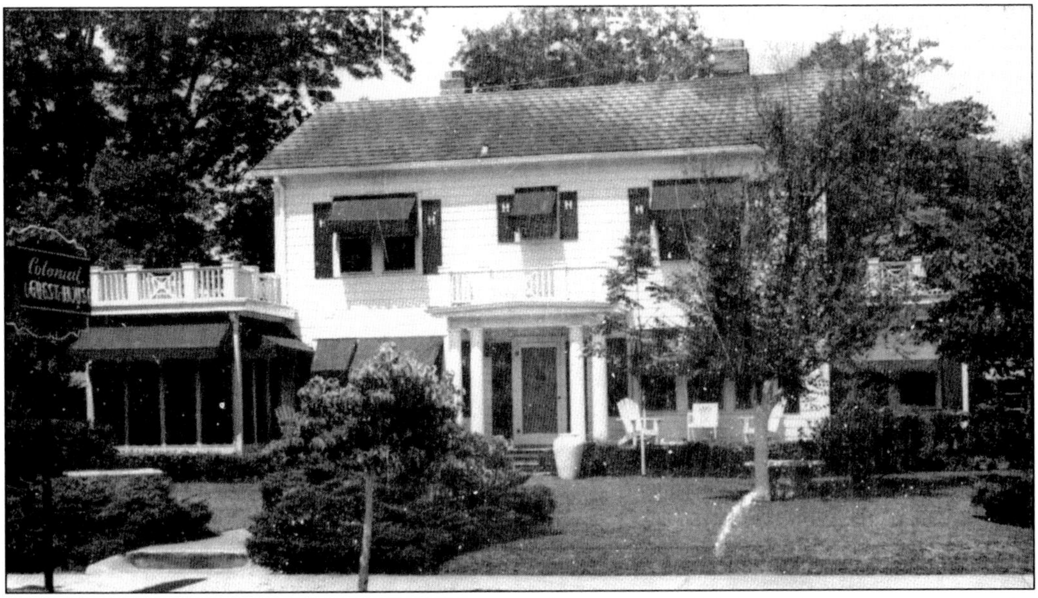

Mrs. H.F. Hook operated the Colonial Tourist Home in the 1950s, and it became a popular stop among travelers and tourists who passed through Statesboro. It was situated on the west side of South Main and Grady Streets. Locals called the attractive home "the house of mirrors and lamps." In 2003 the home was removed to Grady and Walnut Streets to accommodate Statesboro's newest bank, the First Southern National Bank.

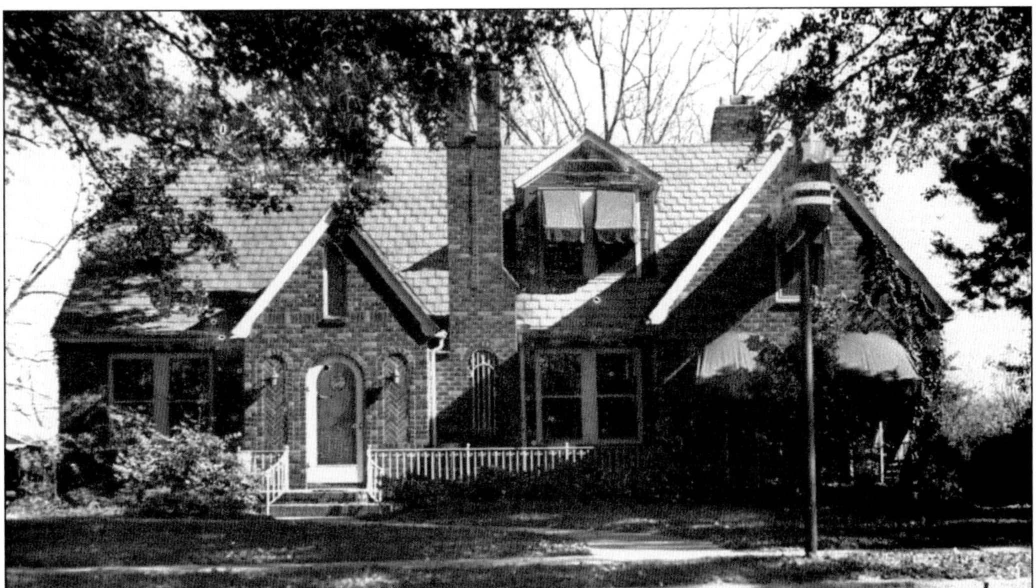

The residence of Mrs. Grady Johnston on North Main Street, near the intersection with East Olliff Street, became a tourist home in the late 1950s. She was among a number of homeowners along North and South Main Streets who converted their residences into tourist homes. The business helped alleviate the shortage of rooms for travelers, brought on by the popularity of U.S. 301.

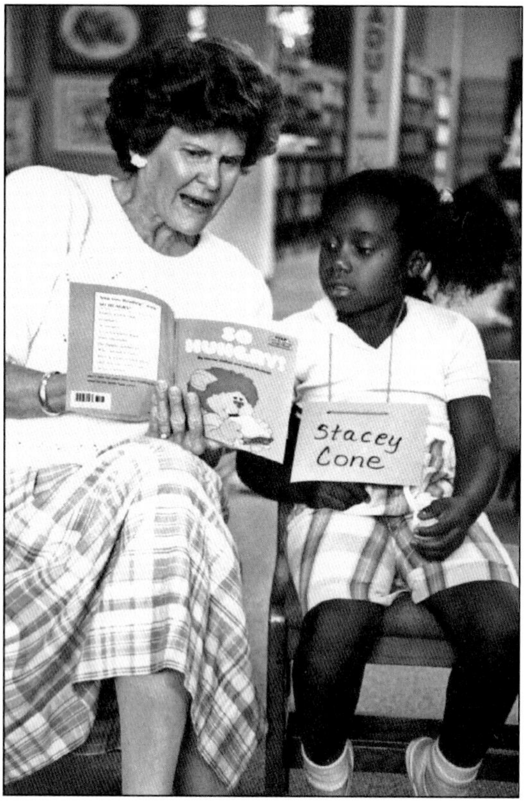

Mrs. Mary Jeanette Smith (known as Jenny) reads a book of stories for children to Stacey Cone at the Statesboro Regional Library in the 1980s. They are participating in the R.I.F. program (Reading is Fundamental) sponsored jointly by the Bulloch County Board of Education and the Statesboro Regional Library. The program, created in the latter half of the 20th century, encourages elementary students to enjoy reading.

The Skate-R-Bowl, located near the campus of Georgia Teachers College on U.S. 301 South, was a favorite gathering place for children and adults of Bulloch County in the 1940s and 1950s. The owner, Nathan Foss, rented skates to the young and old alike. He also rented bowling shoes. Many local bowling teams competed here for decades. Their snack bar served excellent hot dogs and milk shakes. A juke box provided music for young people who enjoyed dancing. In the 1980s Georgia Southern College purchased the property, which was razed for a parking lot and other uses.

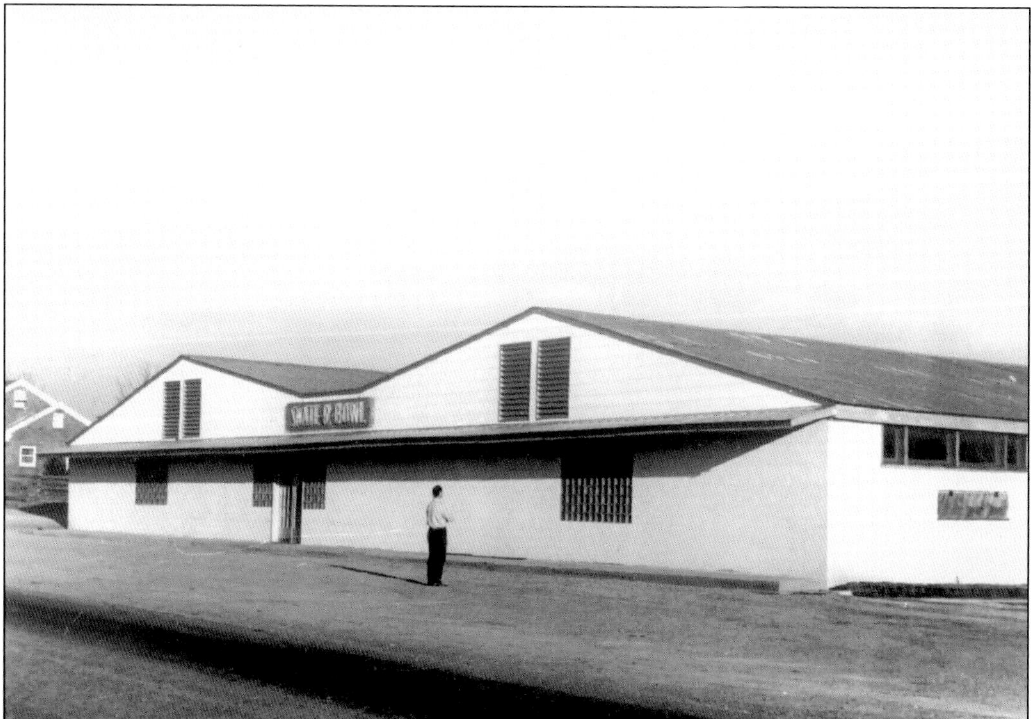

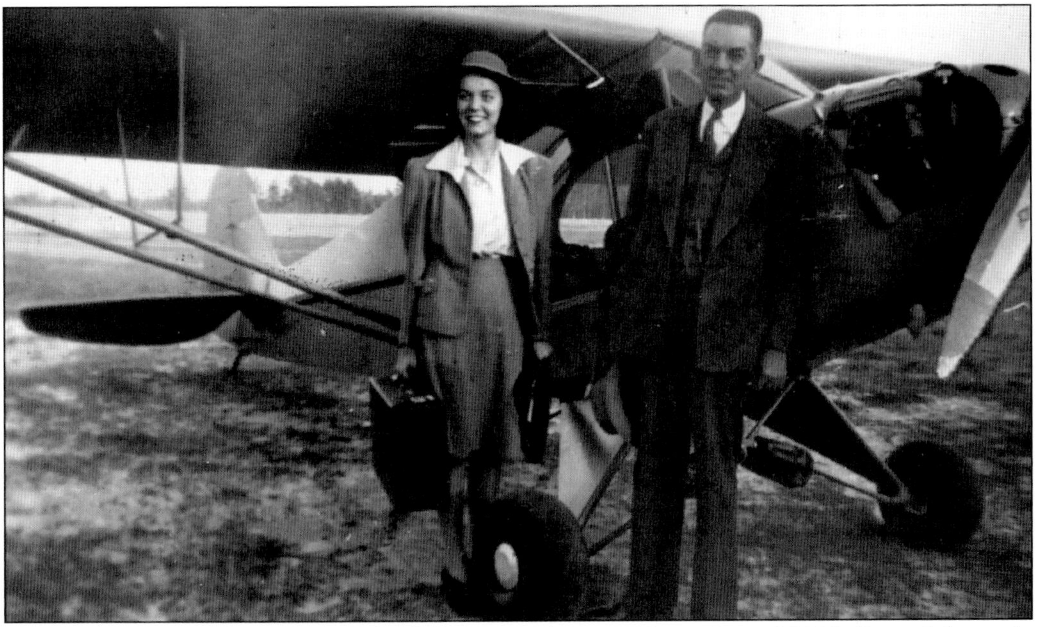

The first locally owned airplanes landed in Statesboro in November of 1936. One of the early pilots, Emmet Lee Barnes Jr., decided to fly his daughter, Esther Lee Barnes, to a state Beta Club convention in 1940. The yellow Piper Cub had no radio, and they landed at Atlanta's Harstsfield airport without instructions. Mr. Barnes founded the "Coffin Club," whose members included Charlie Olliff and Lannie Simmons. The name came from a make-shift airport telephone booth that Mr. Barnes, an undertaker, made from the shipping crate for a coffin.

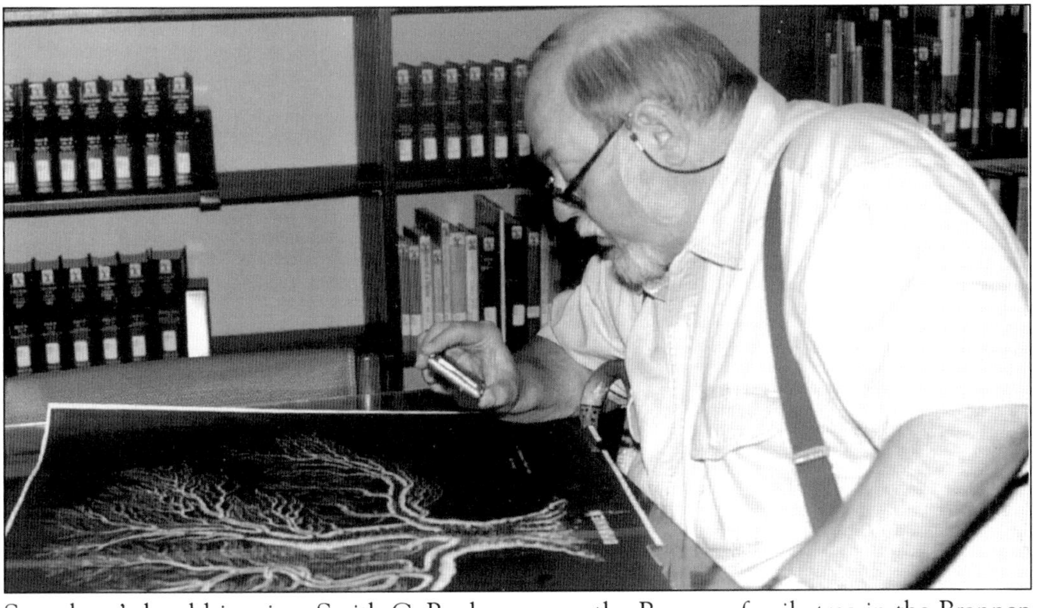

Statesboro's local historian, Smith C. Banks, peruses the Brannen family tree in the Brannen room of the Statesboro Regional Library. The room, built in the 1980s, honors the memory of the many Brannens who have lived and worked in Statesboro and Bulloch County. In 2003 the library's genealogy department has expanded into four rooms, two for books, one for microfilm, and a work room.

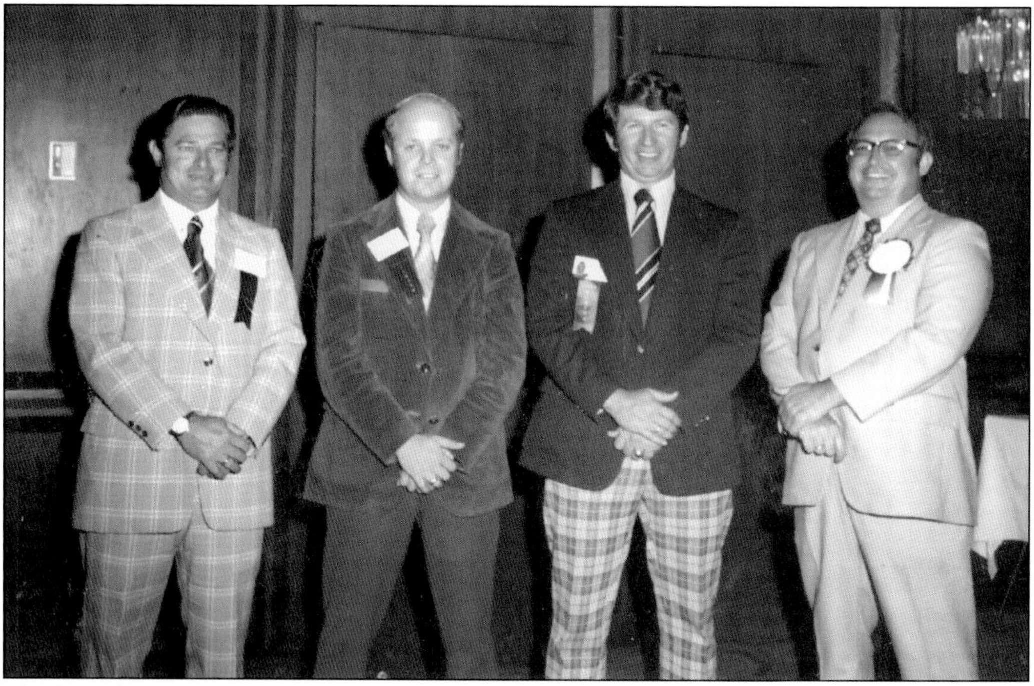

The Statesboro Recreation Center in the 1950s was recognized as the most successful recreation program for a town of its size in the United States. This photograph of the 1970s includes four early directors (from left to right), Tom Brown, Lonice Barrett, Ralph Turner, and founding director Max Lockwood. Mr. Barrett later became the director of Georgia's Department of Natural Resources. In 2003 Mr. Lockwood is mayor of Douglas, Georgia.

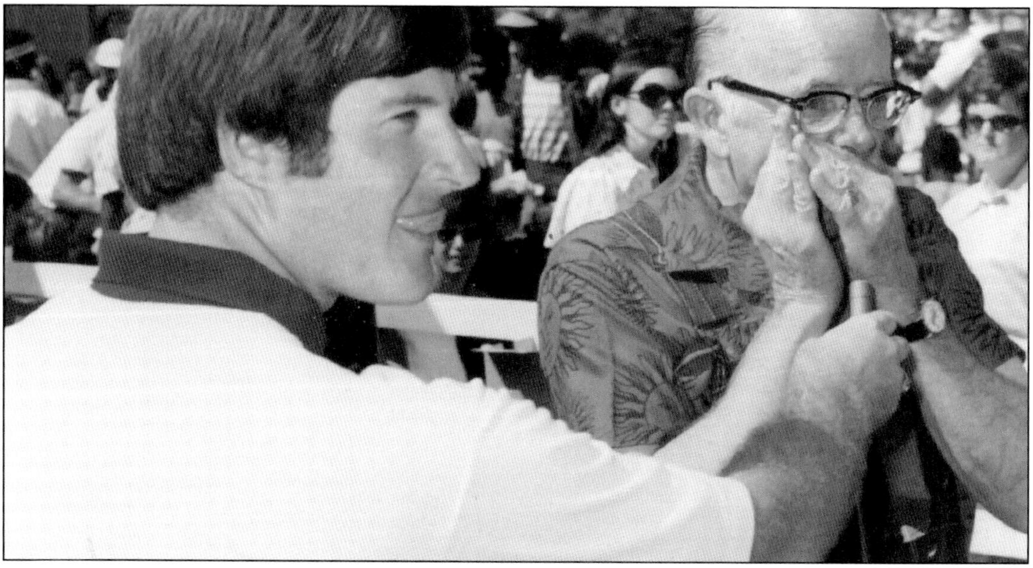

The director of the Statesboro Recreation Department in the 1970s, Frank Hook III, hosts Gov. Lester Maddox at the annual Robbins Fishing Rodeo, held each spring at Robbins Pond. Mr. Hook holds the microphone for the governor who entertains the crowd by playing the harmonica. The governor also enjoyed riding his bicycle backwards, to the delight of the audience.

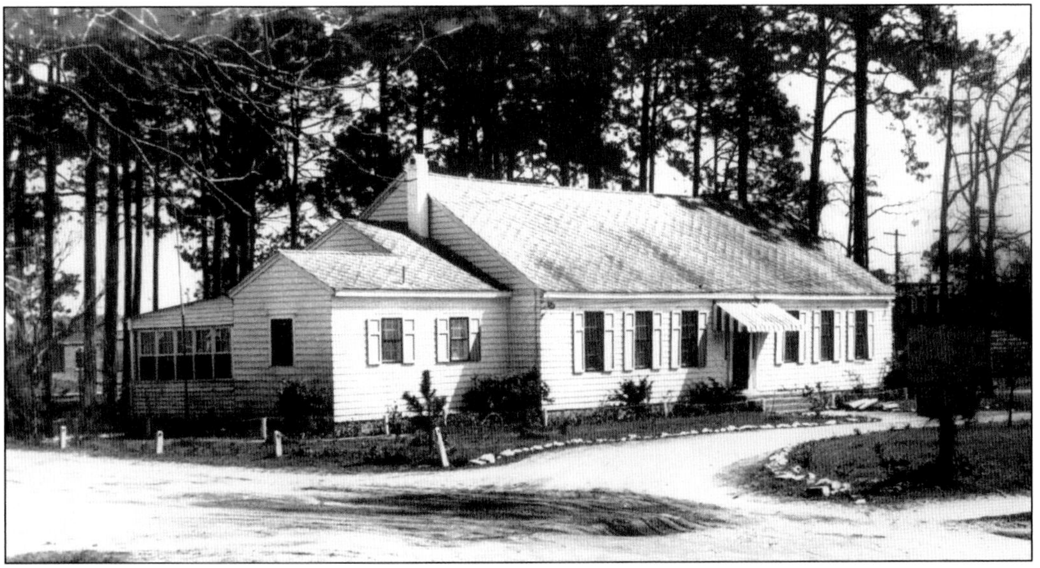

The Statesboro Woman's Club built their club building in 1937. Located on the east side of Fair Road, the building became a part of the Statesboro Recreation Center complex. In 1948, after Max Lockwood became the first director of the city's Department of Recreation, the football field on the grounds of the center was the site of all Statesboro High School home games. Many proms, dances, and bridge parties were held in this building. Today the Honey Bowen Building is located on this site.

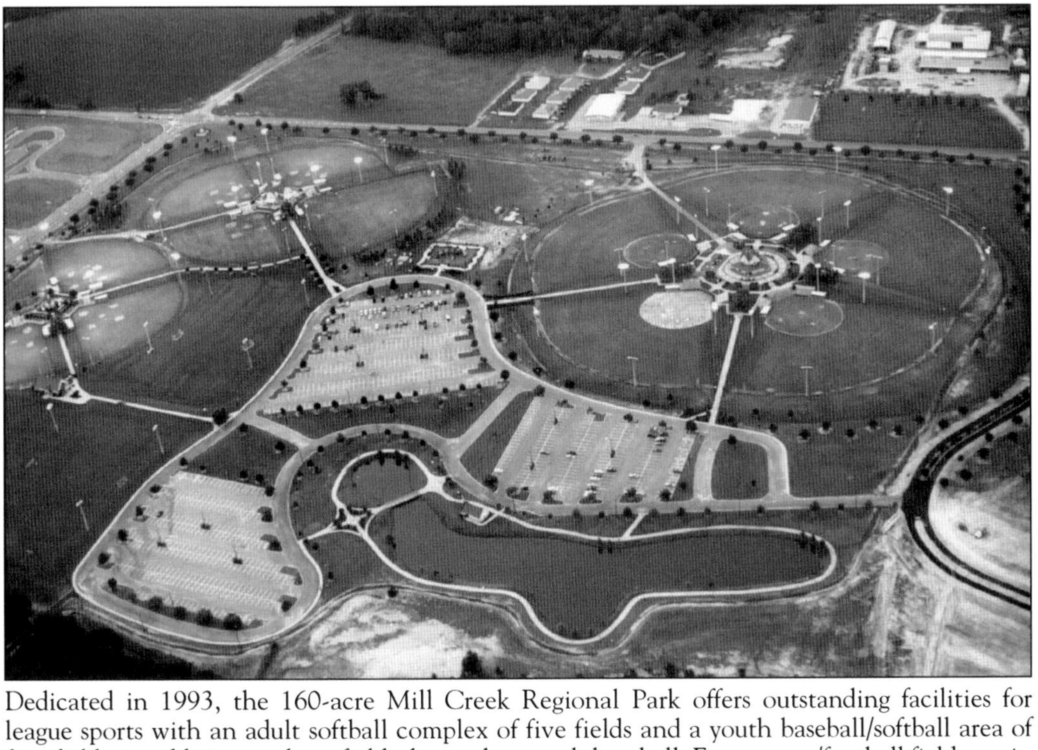

Dedicated in 1993, the 160-acre Mill Creek Regional Park offers outstanding facilities for league sports with an adult softball complex of five fields and a youth baseball/softball area of four fields, in addition to three fields devoted to youth baseball. Four soccer/football fields are in use almost year-round. Walkers especially enjoy the trails on the well landscaped grounds.

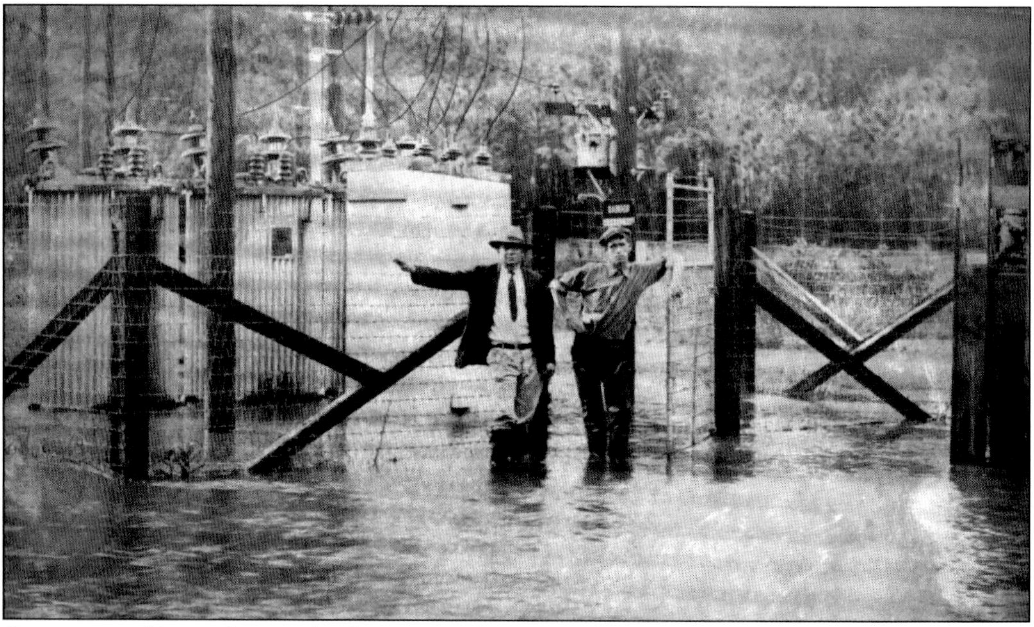

Citizens stand knee-deep in flood waters at the power plant off Hill Street in the 1920s. Located near the railroad, the power plant had provided electricity for the city's businesses and homes since the early part of the 20th century. Spring rains lifted the branches of Mill Creek well beyond their banks, flooding large areas of Statesboro.

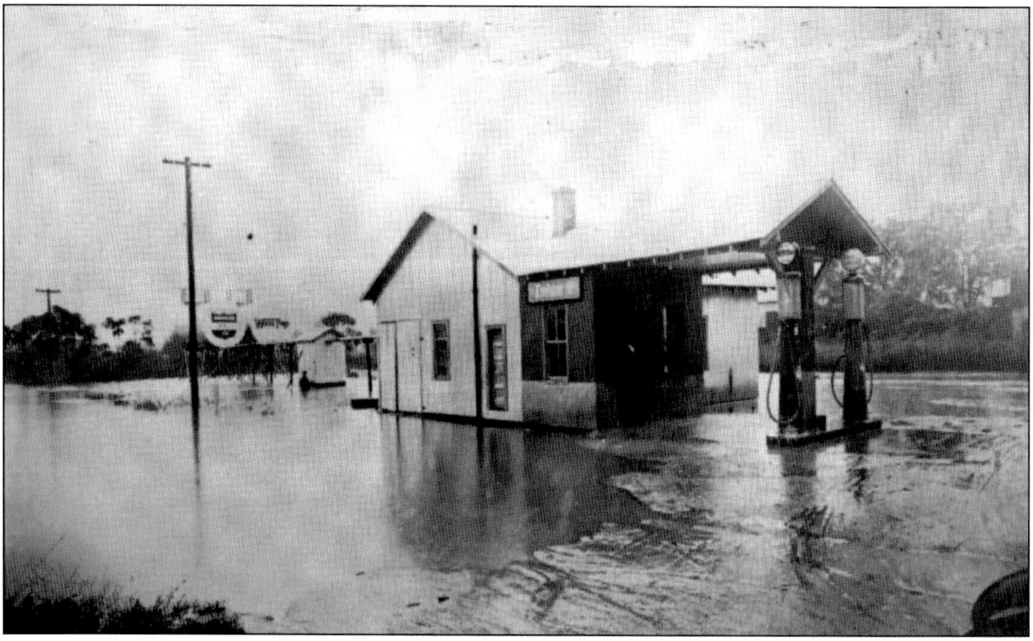

Another flood in 1929, caused by a downpour of over 10 inches, raised the level of the "Big Ditch" at the intersection of Johnson and West Main Streets. A Woco-Pep gasoline station is rendered unusable as a result. The ditch, a channel of Little Lotts Creek, historically overflows its banks during periods of heavy rains. In the background, Edwin Donehoo stands up to his waist in water near the little house in the background. The building still stands in 2003.

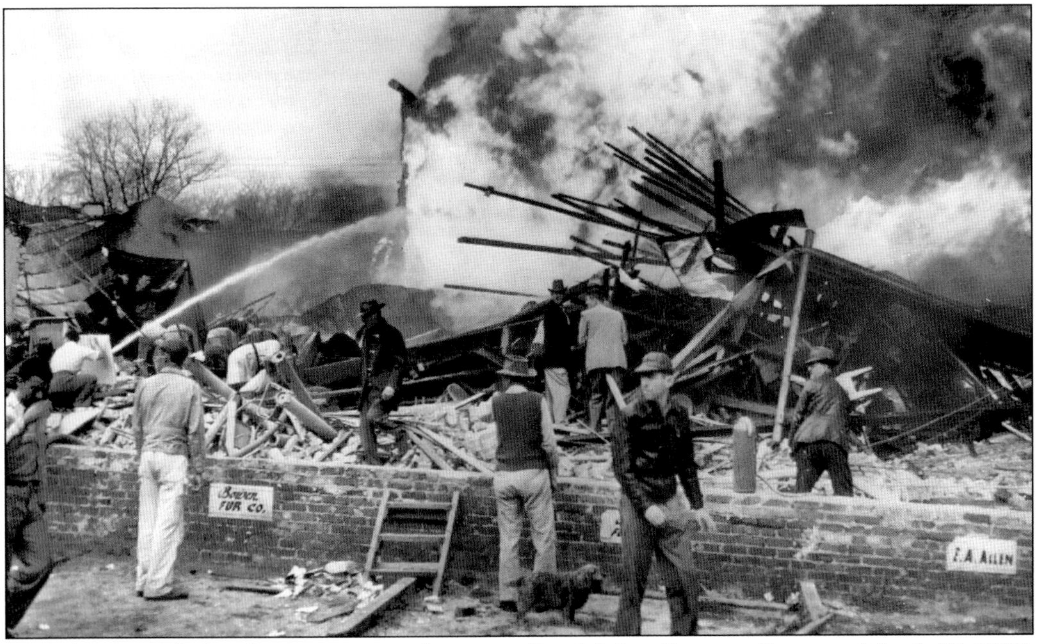

Statesboro was shaken by a massive explosion on South Main Street at 7 a.m. on March 18, 1950, when the gas heater in the Bowen Furniture Company exploded, trapping Emit Anderson and Kenneth Womack in the flaming debris. Olliff and Smith Feed Store and Warehouse, next door, was completely demolished, and 20 other stores nearby were severely damaged. Miraculously, no lives were lost. This photograph was taken in the alley behind the stores.

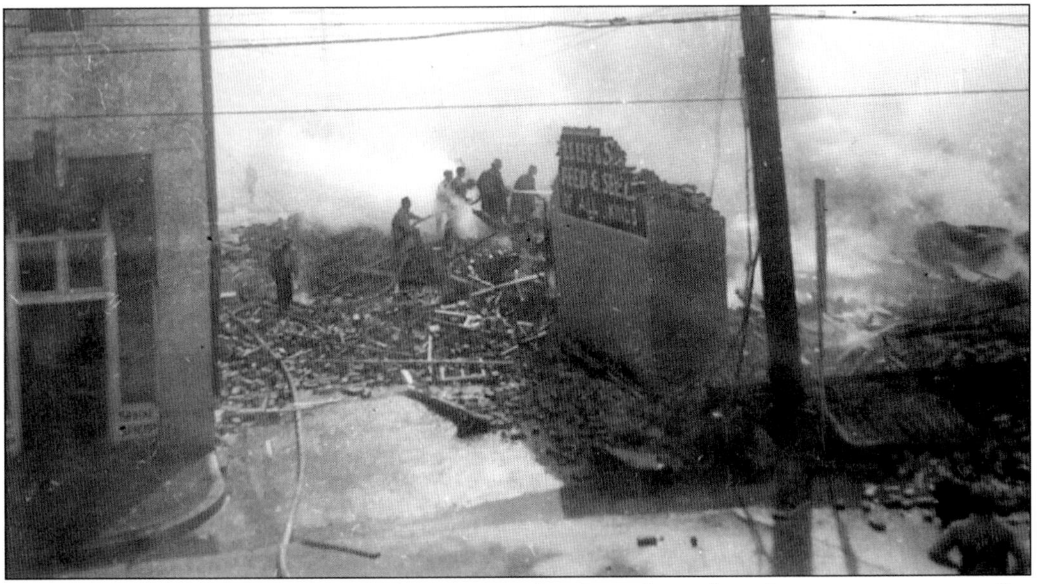

Fire trucks from Savannah rushed to assist the Statesboro fire department, joining fire fighters from neighboring towns of Millen, Metter, Swainsboro, and Sylvania. The diligent efforts of these men, combined with citizen volunteers, prevented the fire from sweeping downtown Statesboro. This photograph shows the scene from South Main Street. The Sea Island Bank building is on the left. The only standing wall is that of the Ollliff and Smith Feed Store and Warehouse.

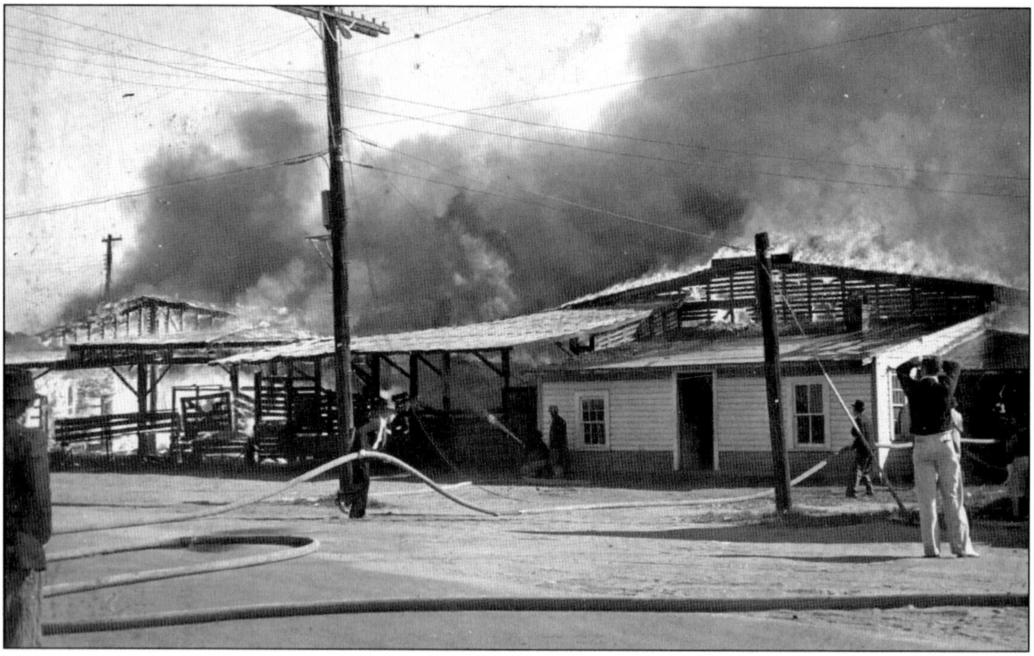

In October 1939, Statesboro's citizens heard alarming sirens and saw heavy clouds of dark smoke over the site of the Statesboro Livestock Exchange on West Main Street at Institute Street. The barns and stables housed great numbers of livestock, hogs, cattle, horses, and mules. Because the fire was so intense, very few animals could be saved. The smell of burnt animal flesh permeated the area for days afterwards.

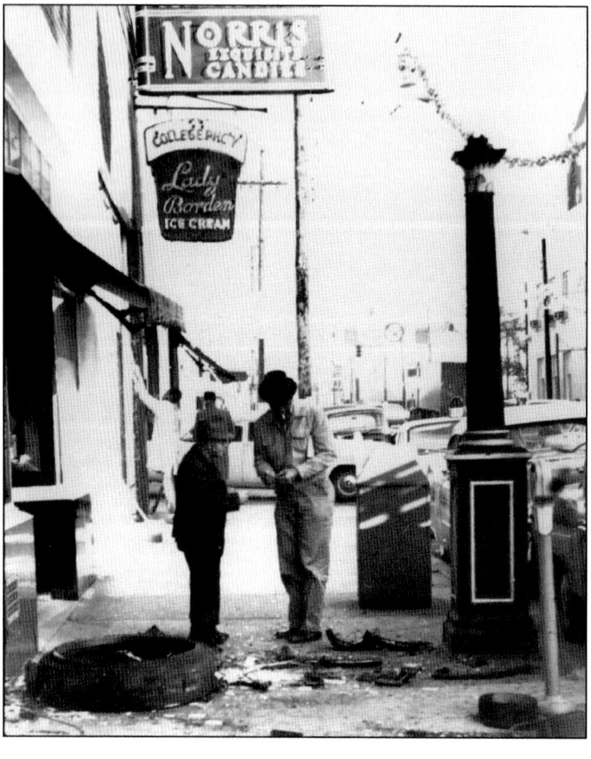

On Saturday morning, December 15, 1962, the sidewalk clock Maxie E. Grimes installed in front of his jewelry store in 1916 was destroyed when an unknown vehicle crashed into it. Burton Mitchell, left, was the watchmaker and jeweler at the Grimes Jewelry Store for many decades. He also was entrusted with winding up and maintaining the clock in the courthouse steeple. The store was located near the intersection of West Vine and South Main Streets.

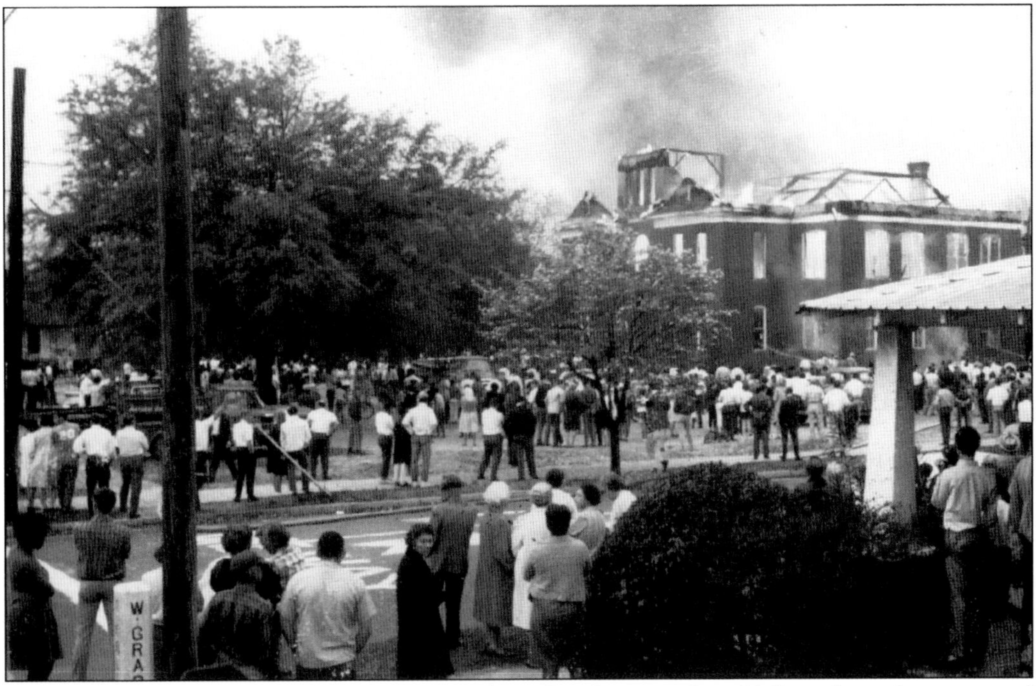

A crowd of several hundred spectators watch as fire destroys the old Statesboro Institute and Grammar School building at the corner of South College and Grady Streets in the early 1960s. The building, constructed in 1901, was designed to serve as both the grammar and the high school. In 1922 a new Statesboro High School was built behind this building on West Grady Street. In 2003 the Statesboro police department is on the site of the grammar school.

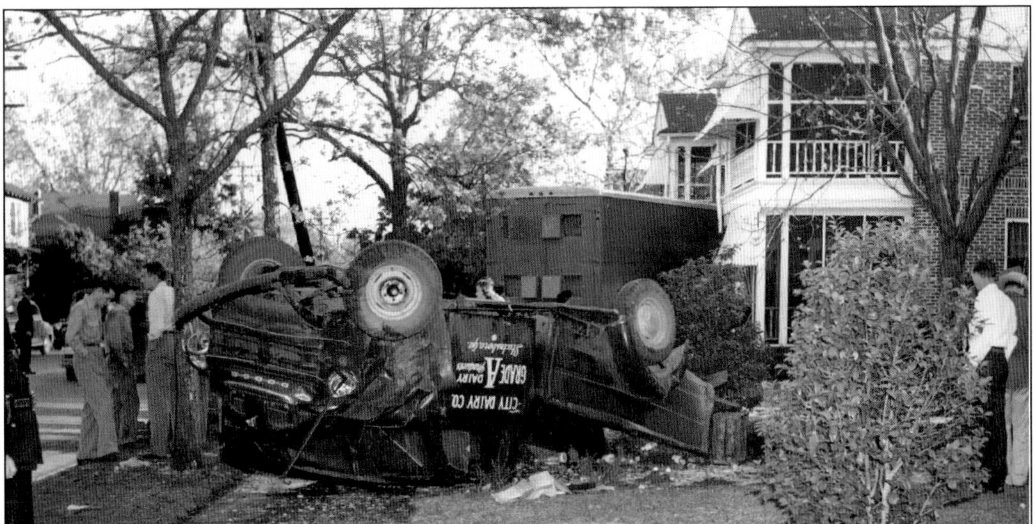

Early on an April morning in 1950, local residents were awakened by a loud crash, which resulted when a sleepy driver of a transfer truck hit a City Dairy truck and careened into the residence of F.C. Parker Jr. on South Main Street. The City Dairy truck was overturned and thrust into the front yard of F.C. Parker Sr. who lived next door. Every bottle of milk on the dairy truck was broken. The driver miraculously escaped injury.

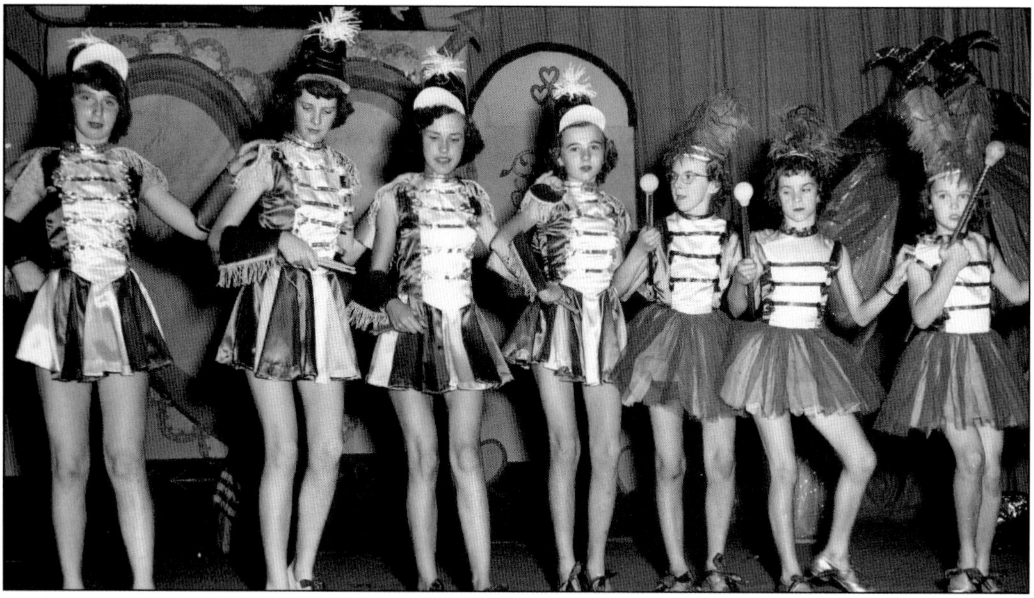

In the 1950s Marilyn Yeomans came from Savannah to teach dancing lessons to the young people of Statesboro and Bulloch County. On several afternoons each week she provided instruction in ballet, tap, baton, and ballroom dancing. Her spring recital was an important local ritual, as youngsters in colorful costumes performed a variety of routines. Shown here from left to right are Phoebe Kelly, unidentified, Faye Hagan, Linda Nessmith, unidentified, Jimmie Lou Lanier, and Judy Nesmith.

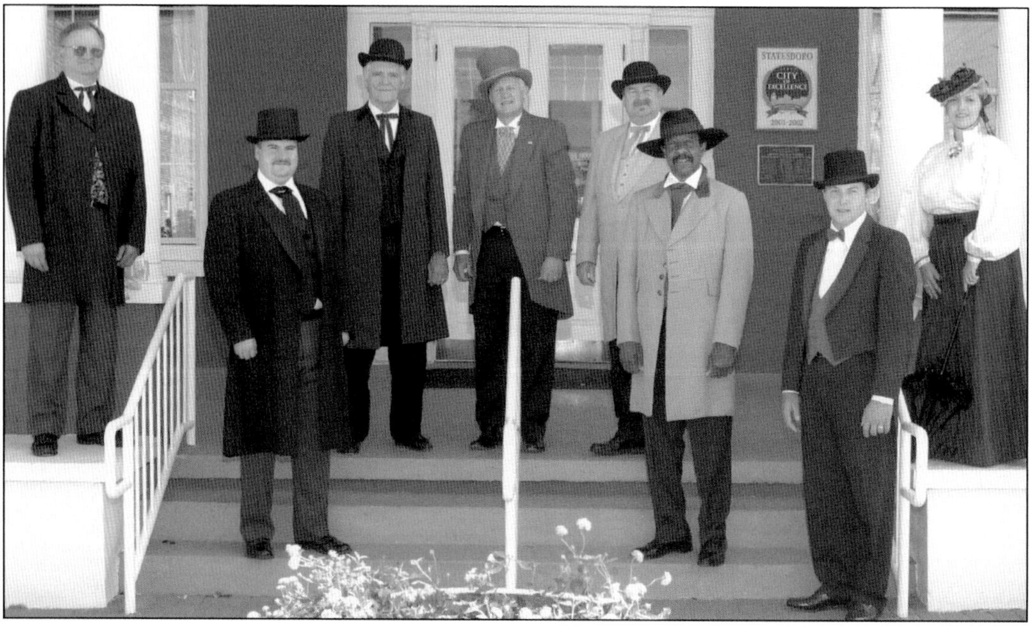

On April 24, 2003, Statesboro city officials pose on the steps of City Hall, wearing costumes appropriate for the first city council meeting held in 1889. The occasion was the mock city council meeting featuring students from local public schools. From left to right are George Wood, city manager; councilmen Merle Clark and Joe Brannen; mayor William S. Hatcher; councilmen Wendy Hagins, Gary Lewis, and John Morris; and city clerk Judy McCorkle.

Four

Reading, Writing, and . . .

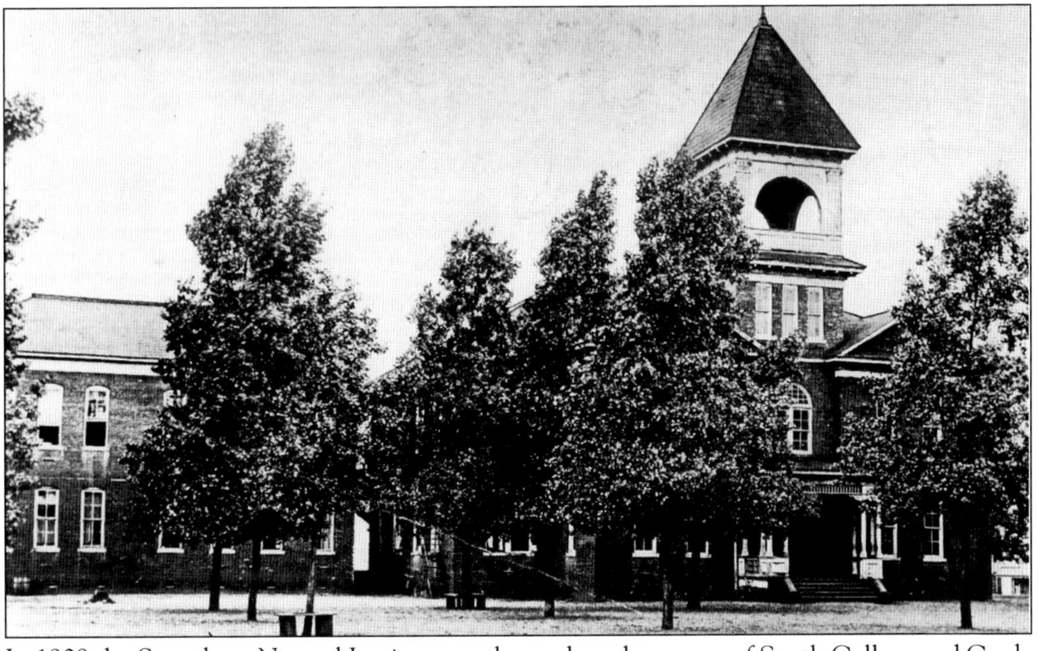

In 1908 the Statesboro Normal Institute was located on the corner of South College and Grady Streets at the 2003 site of the Statesboro police department. Trees planted in the schoolyard were named for members of the school board and other local citizens. Some of the trees survive today. The first building was completed in 1901. Additions in 1906 and 1913 (on left) provided more classrooms. The buildings burned in the 1960s.

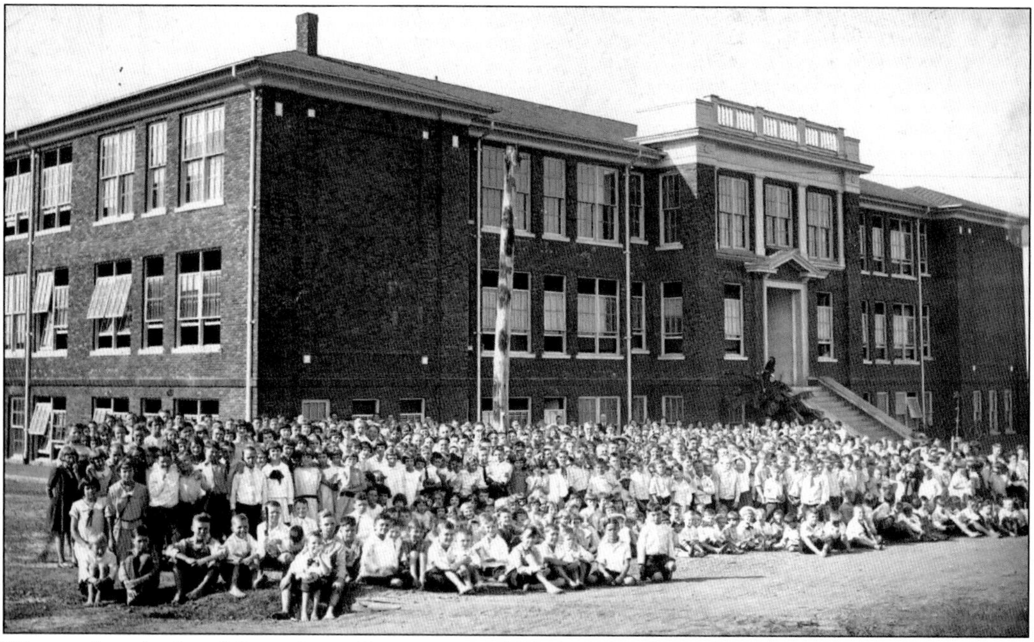

The student body of Statesboro Grammar and High Schools gathers for a photograph shortly after the building was completed in the 1920s at a cost of $46,265. It was located behind the Statesboro Grammar School on the south side of Grady Street between South College and Institute Streets, which in 2003 is the location of the Statesboro Fire Department.

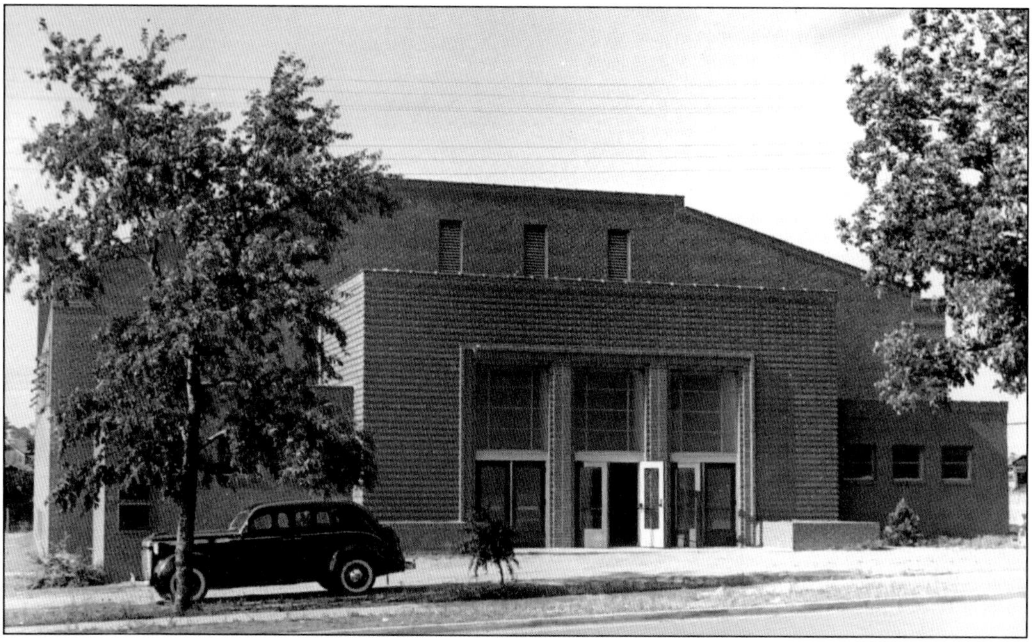

The Statesboro High School Gymnasium was completed in 1939 at a cost of $25,934. It was located directly across West Grady Street, opposite the Statesboro High School. It was the site of many memorable basketball games as well as many social occasions and dances. In the late 20th century it was the polling place for the 1209th G.M. district as well as a gymnasium for the Statesboro recreation department.

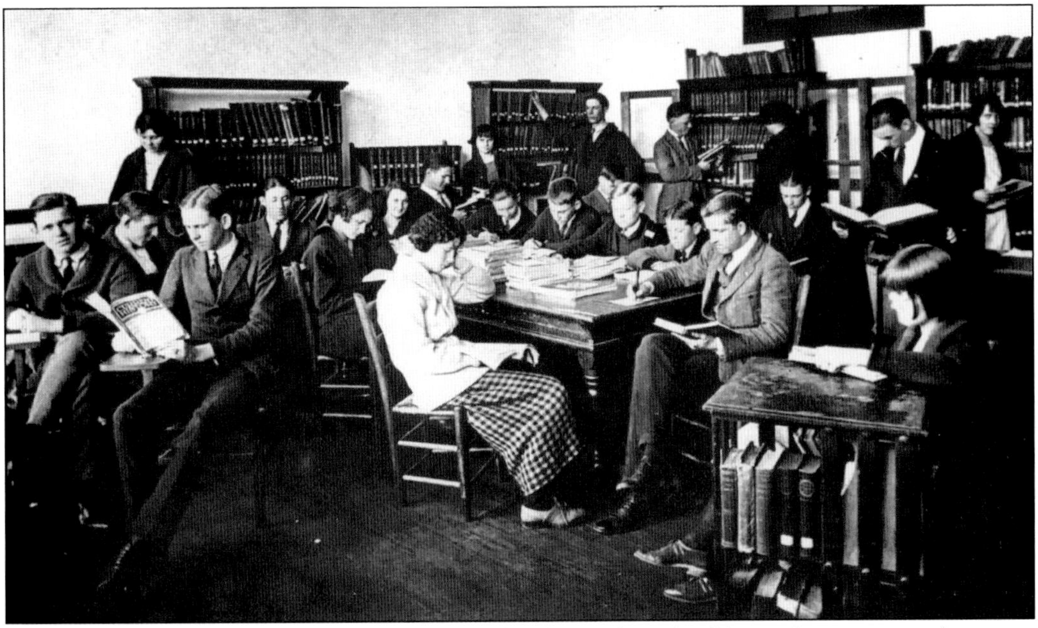

In the 1920s students at Statesboro High School posed in the library for a picture depicting an average study hall. Their serious demeanor indicates clearly that they were posing. In the left foreground, with magazine in hand, is George M. Johnston, who became a prominent local attorney.

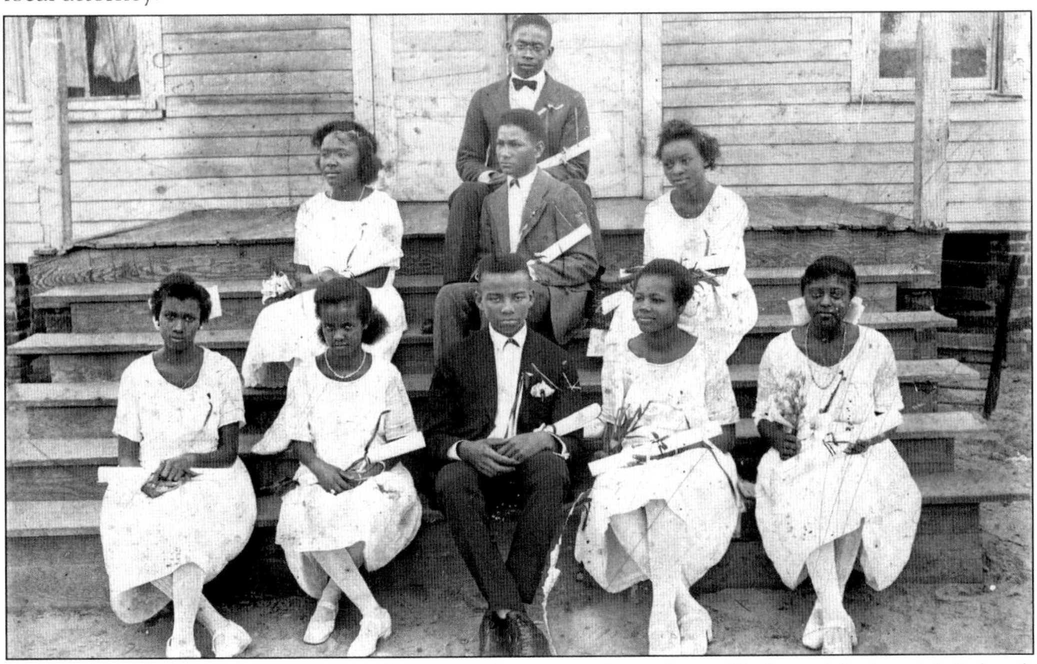

Middle School graduates were well prepared to enter Statesboro High and Industrial School, which was guided by the capable educator, Prof. William James. This photograph from the 1920s shows the steps of the original wooden building of two stories, which contained a steeple. Mr. James secured funding from the Rosenwald Foundation to support his highly regarded school, which he founded in 1906.

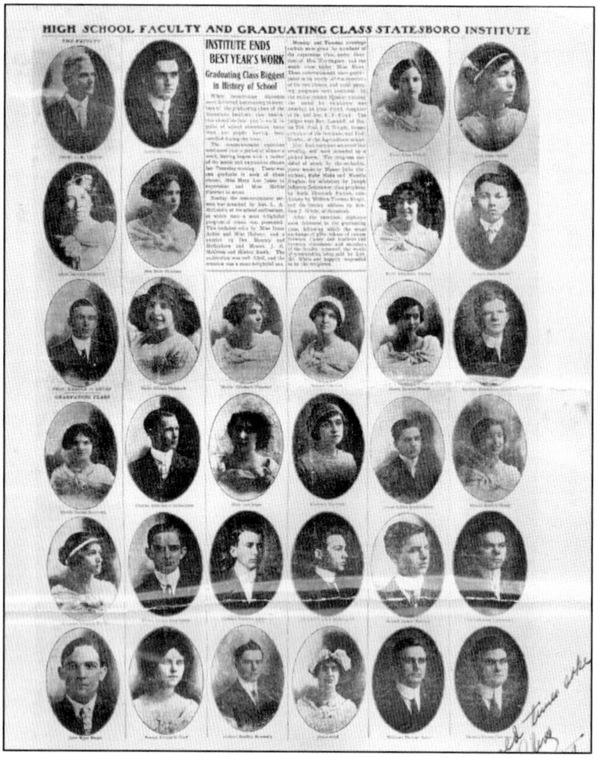

HIGH SCHOOL FACULTY AND GRADUATING CLASS STATESBORO INSTITUTE

INSTITUTE ENDS BEST YEAR'S WORK

Graduating Class Biggest in History of School

Faculty and students of the class of 1913 of the Statesboro Institute had a sheet of photographs rather than a high school yearbook. The school was located on the corner of South College and West Grady Streets. Fifty years later the class gathered again, as shown below.

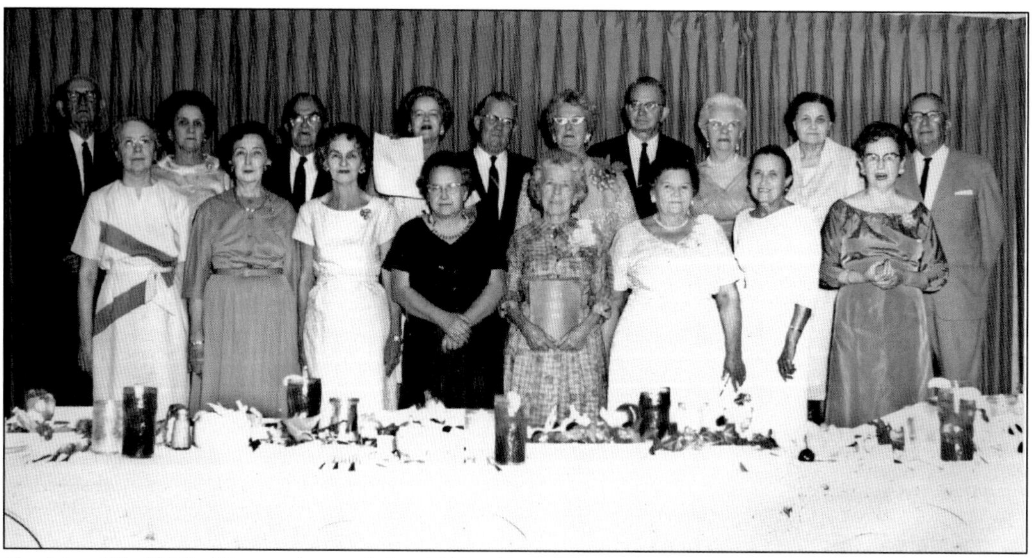

On May 25, 1963, 17 members of the 1913 class of Statesboro Institute gathered for the 50th class reunion. They are, from left to right, (front row) Mrs. Maybele (Brunson) McCormick, Mrs. Mary Lee (Jones) Cromartie, Mrs. Cleo (Lee) Hodges, Mrs. Sadie (Denmark) Waters, Miss Dreta Sharpe (teacher), Mrs. Myrtle (Anderson) Jones, Miss Hattie Powell, and Mrs. Ruth (Parrish) Donaldson; (back row) Lester E. Brannen, Miss Coramae (Blitch) Smith, Tom Zetterower, Mrs. Bonnie (Ford) Flemming, Dr. Julian Quattlebaum, Mrs. Jessie (Olliff) Averitt, Horace Z. Smith, Mrs. Kathleen (McCroan) Barron, Mrs. Mattie (Fletcher) Akins, and Durance Kennedy.

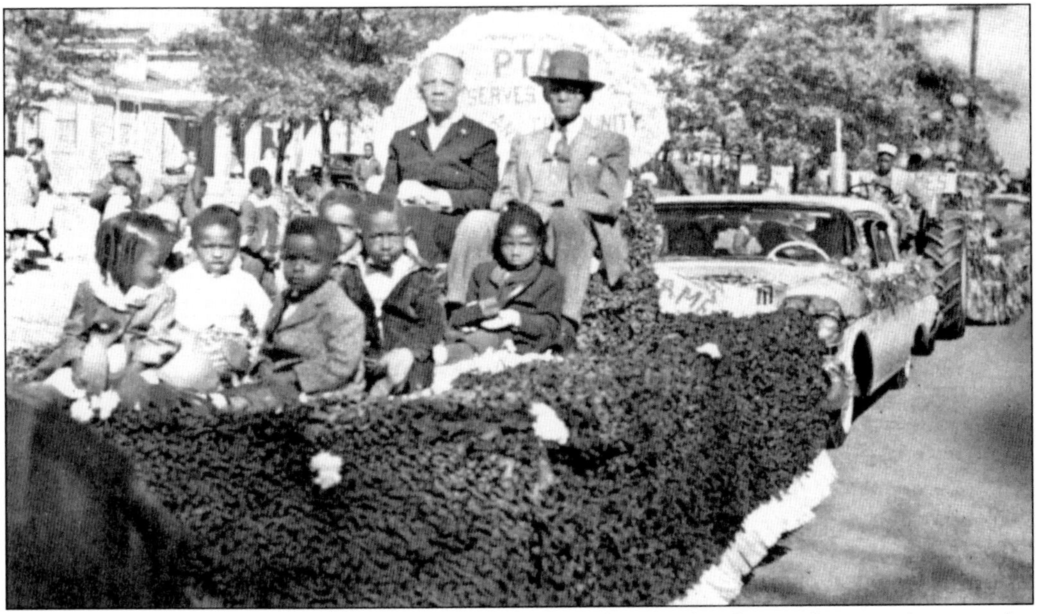

In the late 1950s, Mr. and Mrs. H.W.B. Smith Sr. were honored as featured personalities on the William James School PTA float. They were notable educators and leaders in the community. Mr. Smith taught school for more than 55 years. He lived to be 106 years old. His wife, Mrs. Amanda Love Smith, taught for over 40 years. After retirement, she established the first kindergarten for black children in the county.

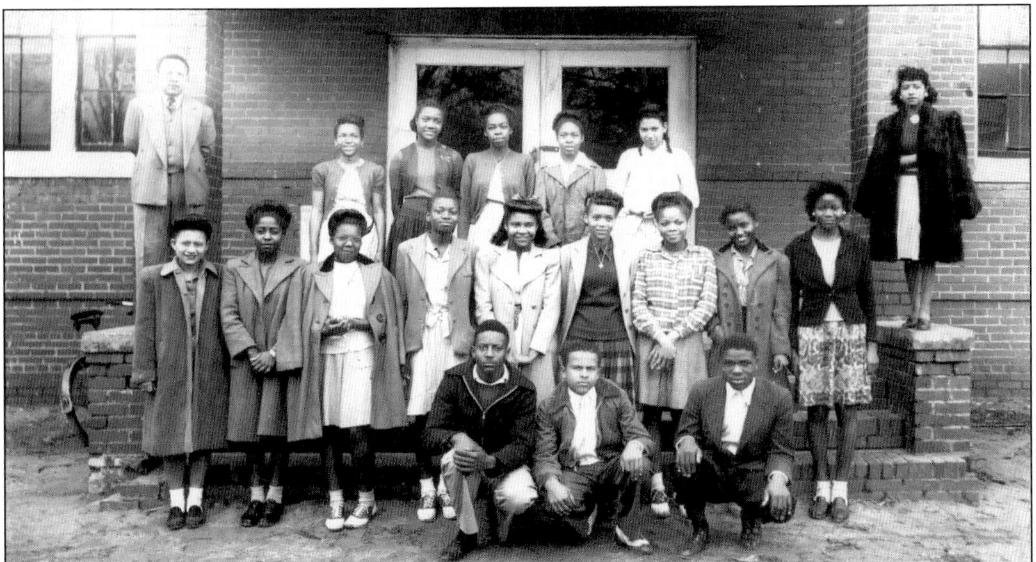

This is the class of 1949 of the Statesboro High and Industrial School, located at Cotton Avenue and Blitch Streets (now MLK Jr. Drive). Pictured from left to right are (kneeling) Hubert Lawton, Horace Jones, and ? Presley; (first row) Mary Lou Morgan, Della Swain, two unidentified, Betty Sue Williams, Dorothy Riggs, Lenora Rivers, and ? Mikell; (second row) Beatrice Brown, Ida Frank Robinson, Emma Lee Brockington, Johnnie Mae Mincey, and Loretta Ball. At far left is J. Griffin Green, principal, and at far right is Sarah Ayers Smith, science and math teacher.

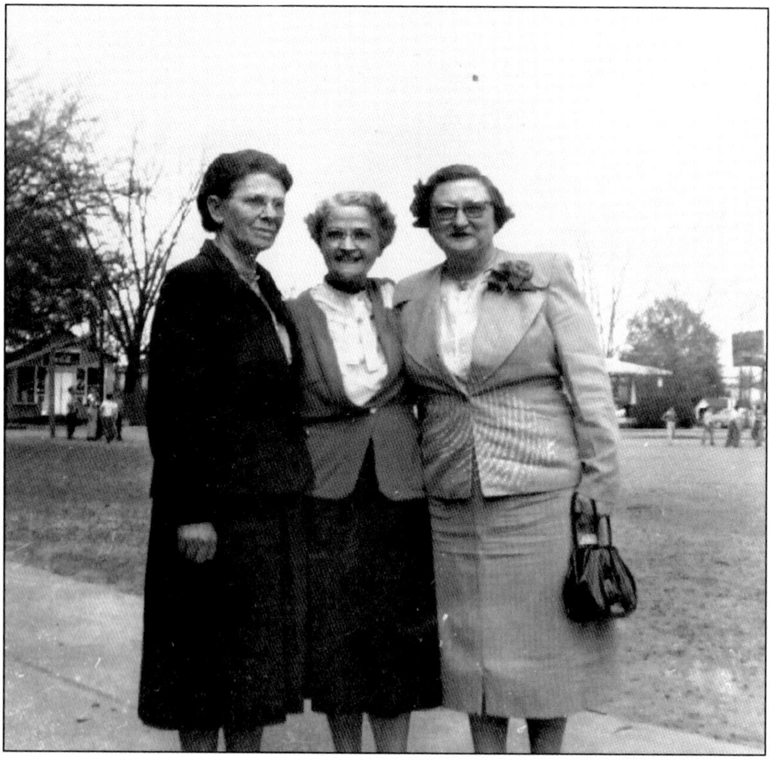

Three highly regarded sixth grade teachers at Statesboro Grammar School pose on the sidewalk on West Grady Street. On the left is Miss Sallie Zetterower, principal of the Grammar School and teacher of sixth grade students for over 50 years. Sallie Zetterower School was named in her honor. In this photograph from the 1950s, Miss Sallie Prine (middle) and Mrs. Tom (Nina) Kennedy (right) stand with their friend Miss Sallie.

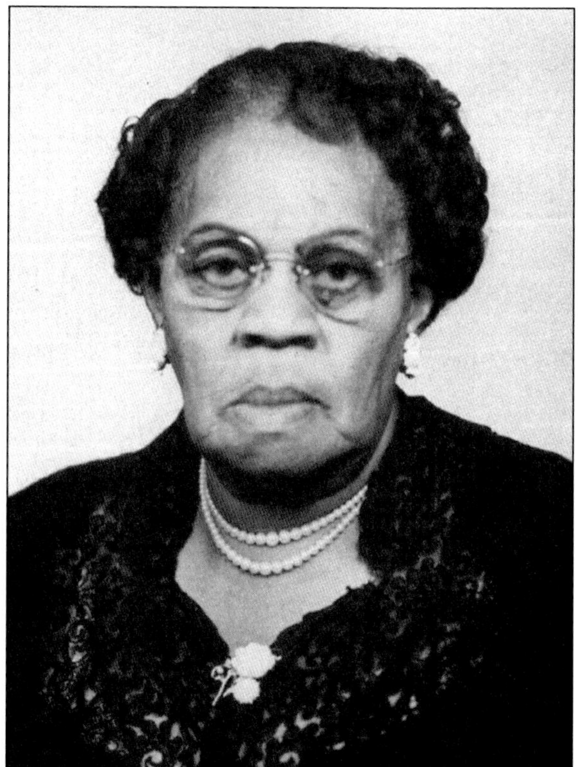

The namesake of Julia P. Bryant Elementary School was elected Teacher of the Year by the Bulloch County Teachers Association in 1956, and students at William James School dedicated the yearbook to her in that year. After receiving a certificate in art and design from Pratt Institute in Brooklyn, New York, she began a long career in education. Mrs. Bryant was a leader in several national organizations, including the Georgia Congress of the PTA. In Statesboro she was a Jeanes Supervisor and inspired both students and teachers in her classes in home crafts and industrial arts.

Dr. Billy Bice, former teacher, principal, and later superintendent of the Bulloch County public schools, poses as he presents a plaque recognizing the contributions of volunteers who built a new piece of playground equipment. The structure, made of rubber tires, not only is a recreational device but is also an imaginative sculpture.

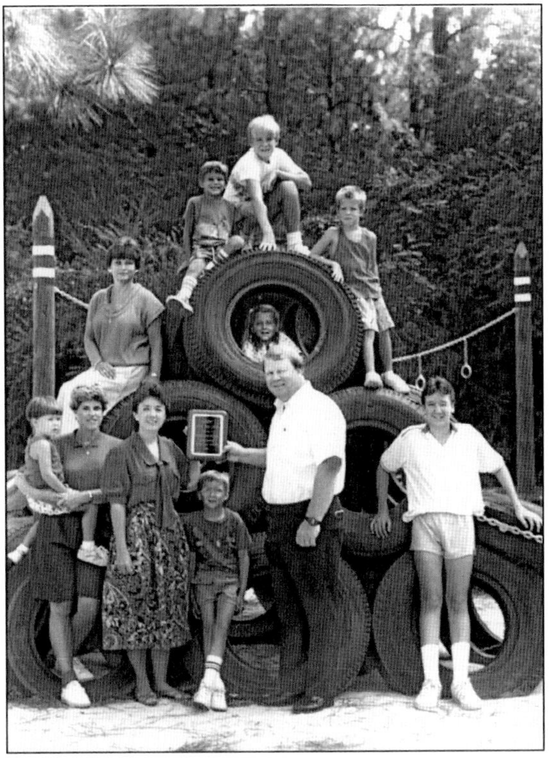

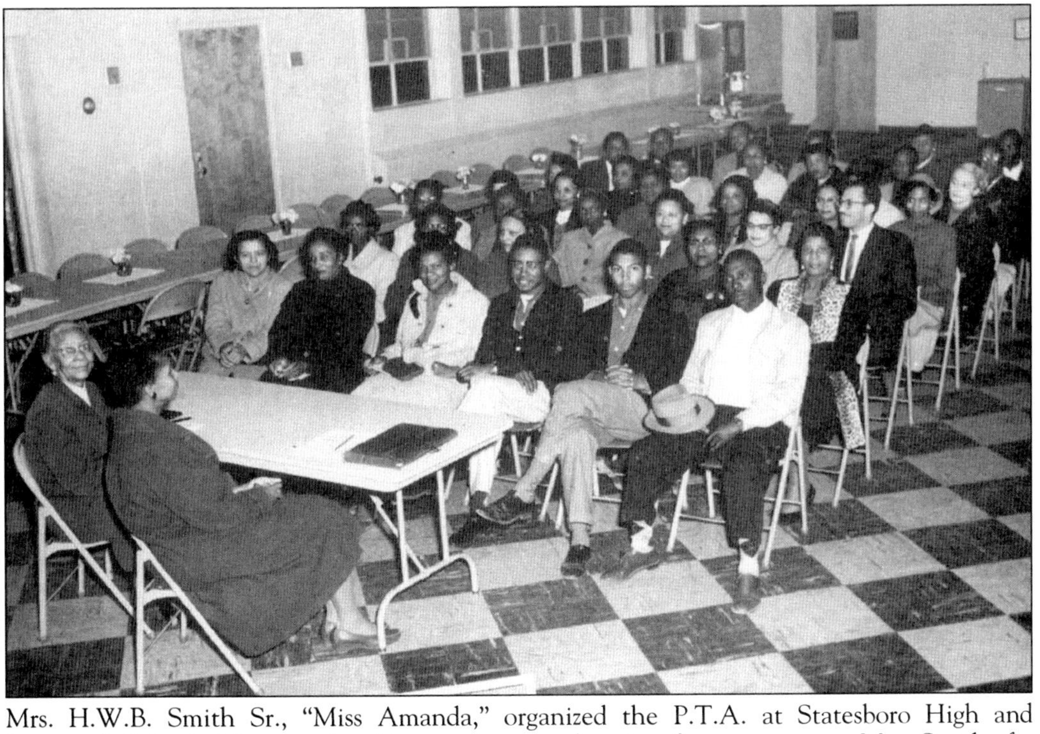

Mrs. H.W.B. Smith Sr., "Miss Amanda," organized the P.T.A. at Statesboro High and Industrial School. The membership was large and active for many years. Mrs. Smith, far left, presides over a well-attended meeting held in the school cafeteria around 1950.

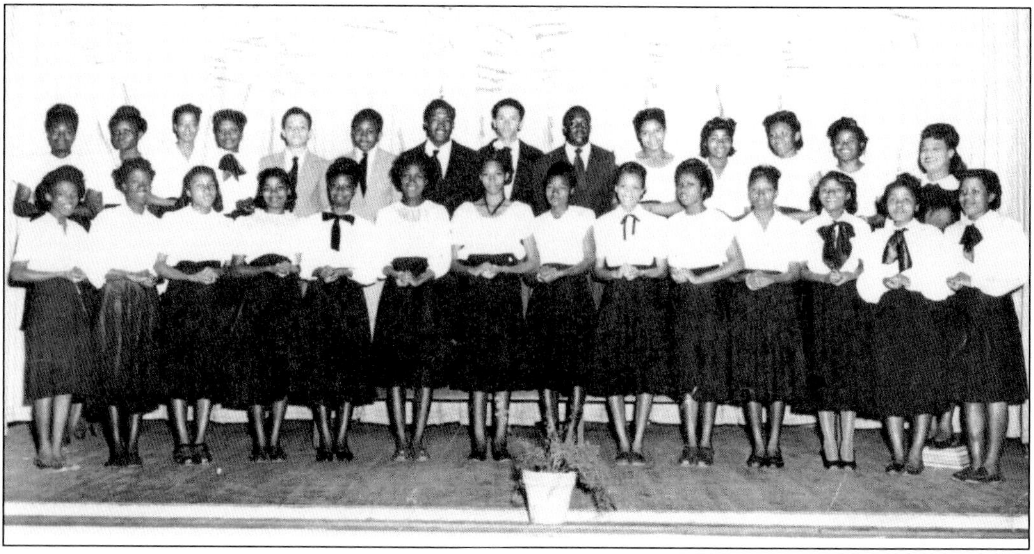

The Statesboro High and Industrial School Chorus in 1946 included the following, from left to right: (front row) unidentified, Jaunita Warren, Betty Douse, Verlie German, Alma Christian, Ida Robinson, Constance Millen, Willie B. Williams, Dorothy Riggs, Lovis Dickerson, unidentified, Almarita Shatteen, Julia P. Simmons, and Vena Simmons; (second row) Verlivian Lowery, Willie P. Mikell, Annie Jernigan, Iona Hendrix, Harvey Van Buren, J.H. Douse, Cleveland Hall, Patrick Jones, Collis Hall, Betty Williams, Mary Brown, Rebecca Linder, Betty Simmons, and LaBlanche Williams (director).

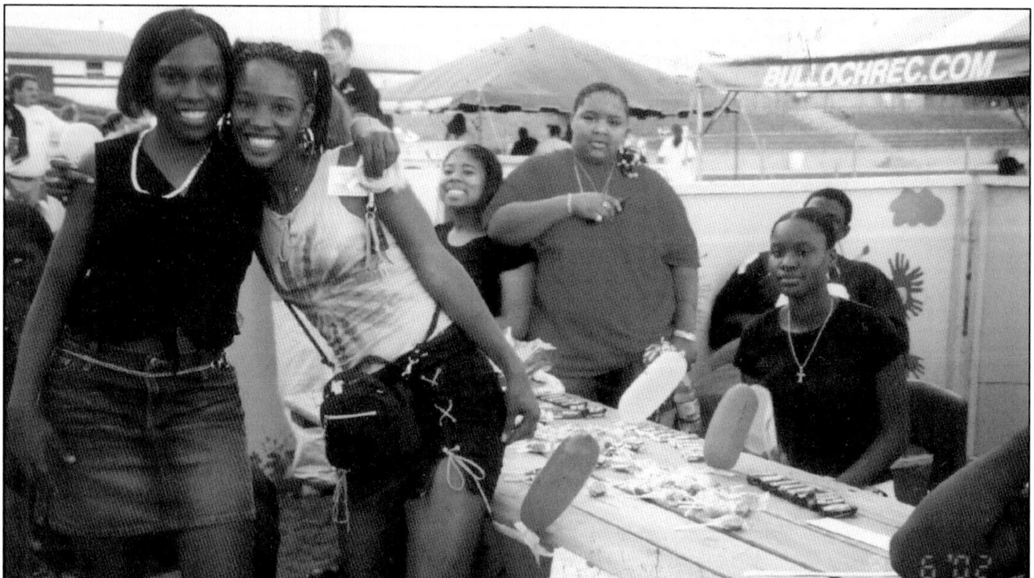

On September 6, 2002, students posed playfully for a picture at the booth of the American PRIDE Team at Womack Athletic Field at Statesboro High School. The official name of the event was the American PRIDE Cow Paddy Drop. PRIDE stands for Parents Resource Institution for Drug Education. The event raised funds to support drug awareness in Bulloch County. From left to right are Chiquita Fagans, Kim Natson, Sheddy Sikes, Christy Johnson, and Kim Rawls.

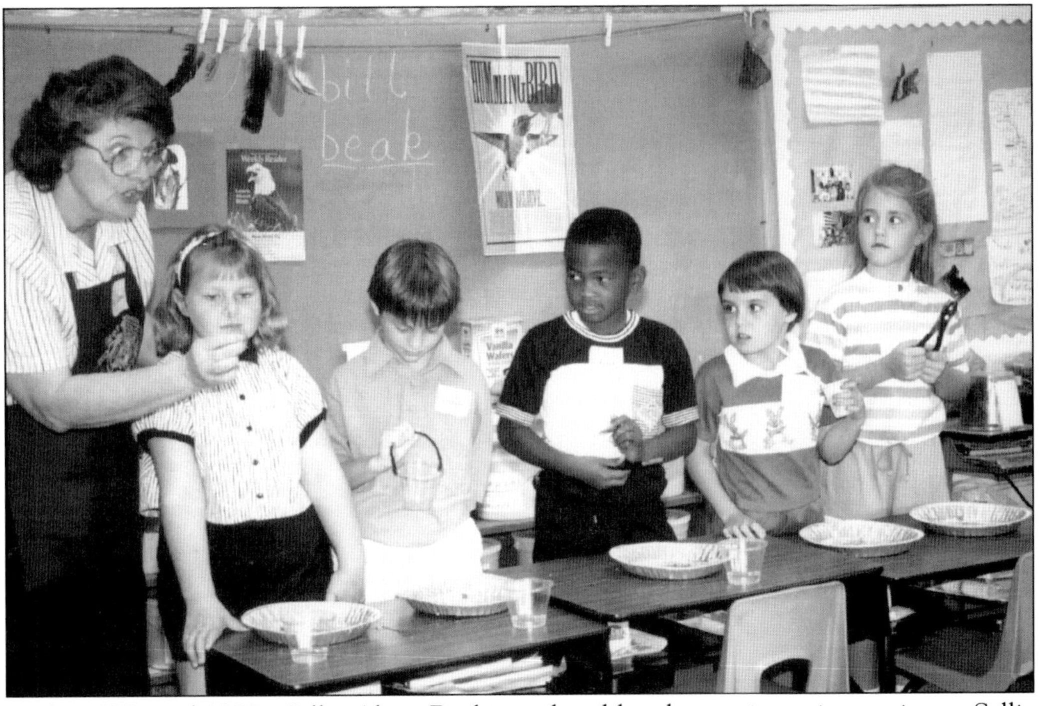

In the 1970s and 1980s, Sallie Akins Deal introduced hands-on science instruction at Sallie Zetterower Elementary School. Using ordinary objects from around the house, she helped students visualize scientific concepts. The school was built in 1953 on the south side of East Jones Avenue, near Gentilly Road.

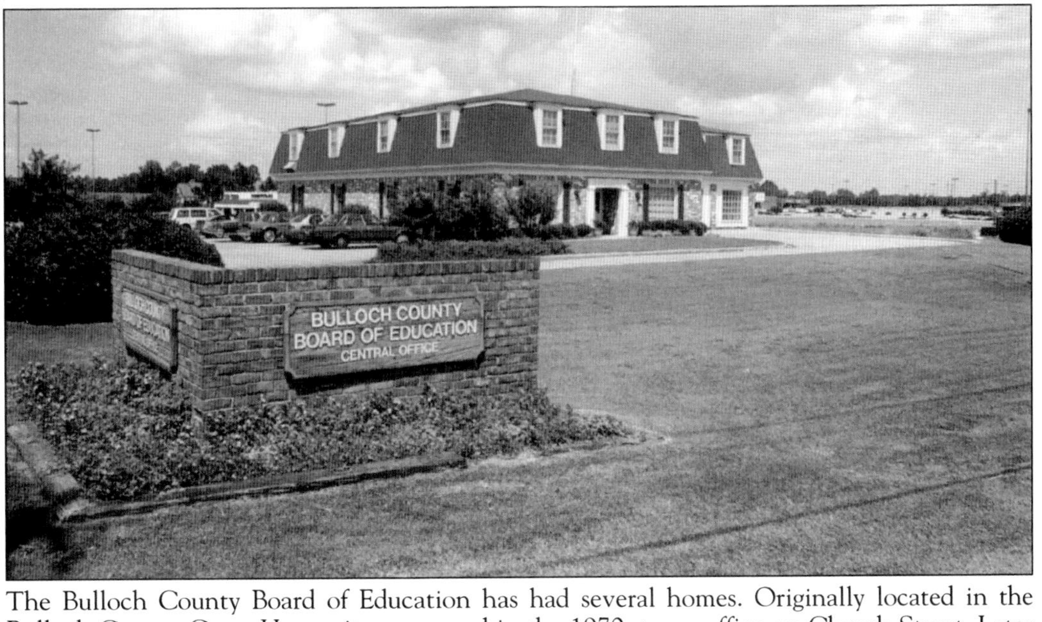

The Bulloch County Board of Education has had several homes. Originally located in the Bulloch County Court House, it was moved in the 1970s to an office on Church Street. Later the expanding department moved into a building on the corner of Northside Drive and Lester Road (above). In 2002 the building was demolished for a new drug store. In 2003 the Board of Education occupies the site of the former William James Middle School on Williams Road.

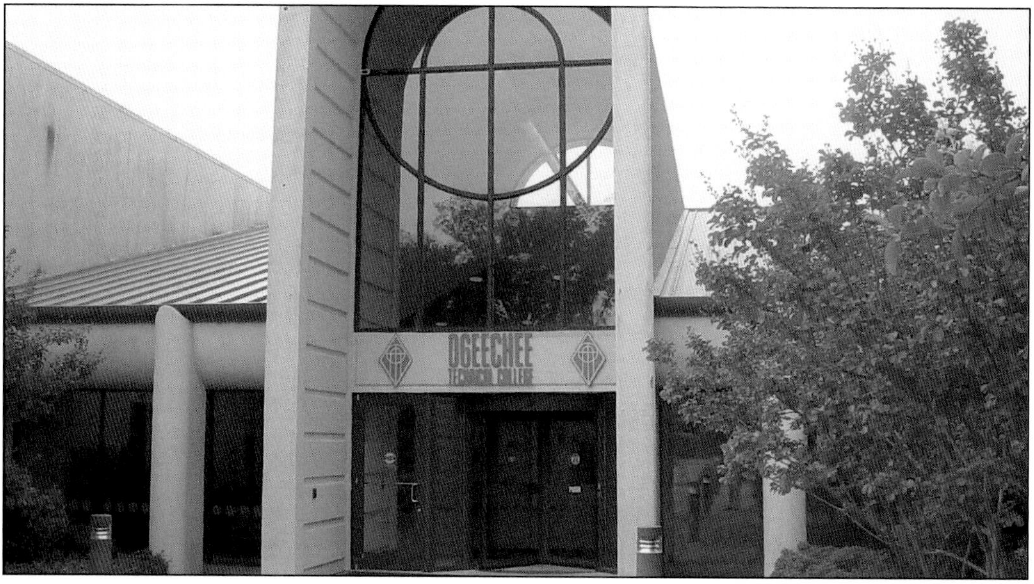

Since 1990 Ogeechee Technical College has been offering classes in a variety of fields. Originally called Ogeechee Technical School, the earliest students studied nursing. In July 2000 the state authorized a name change to Ogeechee Technical College, and students were enrolled in over 75 different programs of studies. Within a decade of its founding the student enrollment surpassed 2,000. This photograph shows the front entrance to a campus, which has numerous buildings and laboratories.

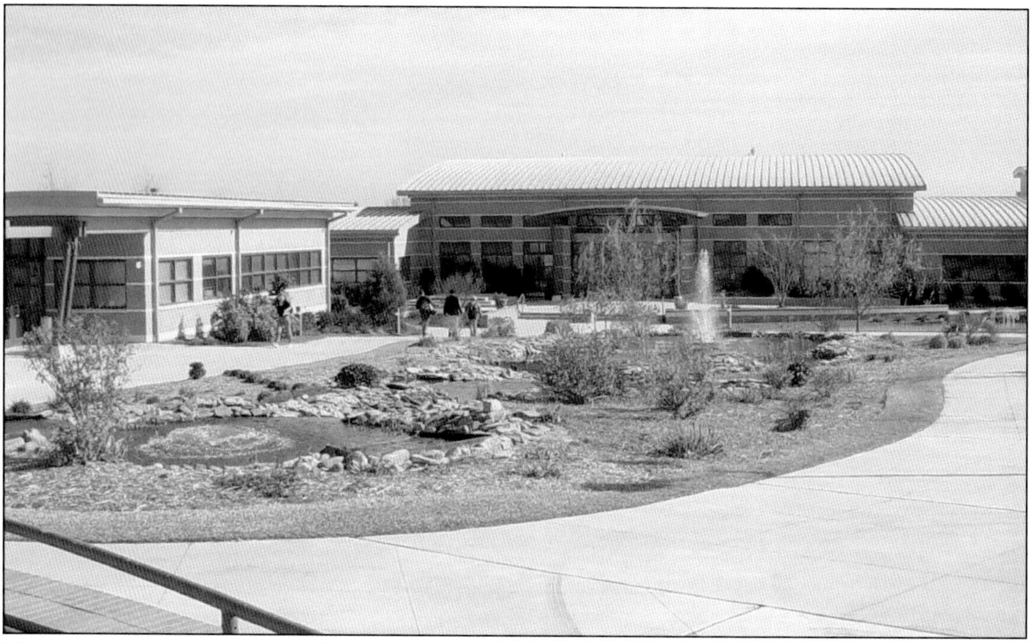

The central garden at Ogeechee Tech provides a quiet setting for students and faculty. This particular garden was developed by students of horticulture. Other majors include forensic science technology, welding, computer technology, electricity, cosmetology, funeral service education, and agriculture. The college offers a child enrichment center and a program in adult literacy and continuing education.

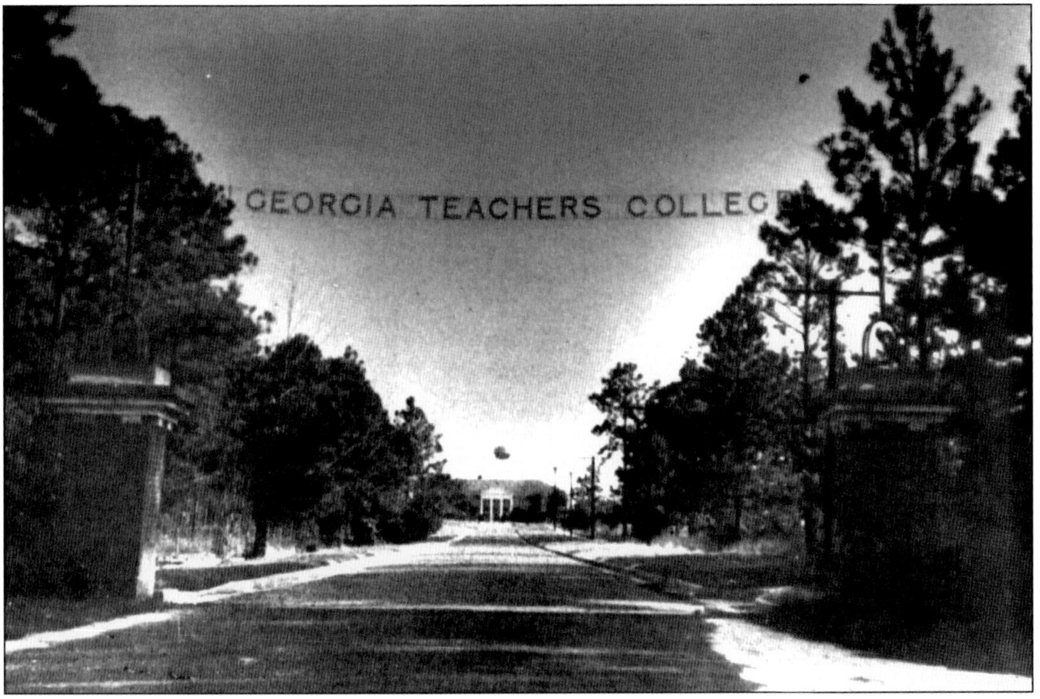

In 1939 the Board of Regents authorized the change in name from South Georgia Teachers College to Georgia Teacher's College, in response to persuasive arguments by Pres. Marvin S. Pittman. He visualized the college as a regional teacher training institution, and, indeed, Georgia Teachers College became a major center for advancing elementary and secondary education in the southeastern United States.

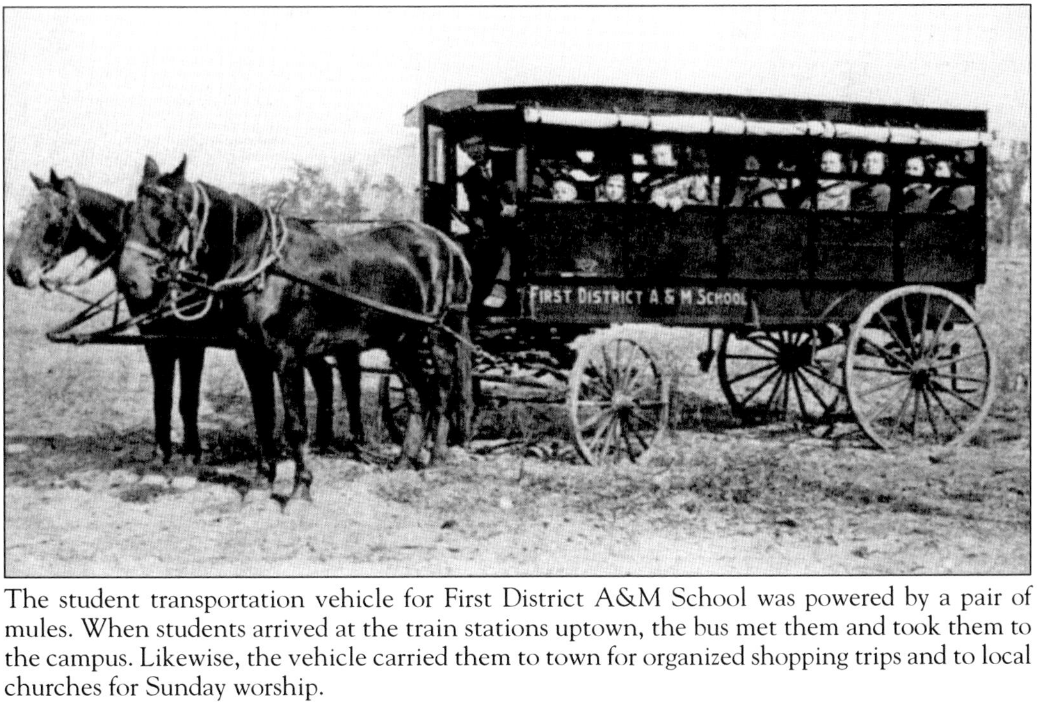

The student transportation vehicle for First District A&M School was powered by a pair of mules. When students arrived at the train stations uptown, the bus met them and took them to the campus. Likewise, the vehicle carried them to town for organized shopping trips and to local churches for Sunday worship.

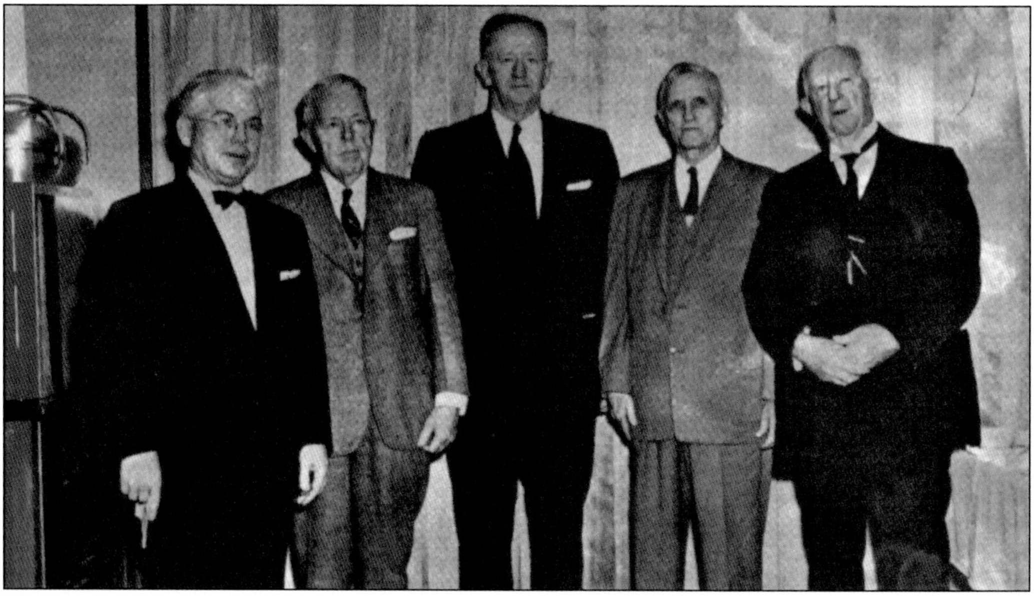

The 50th anniversary of the classes of the First District A&M School brought together the surviving early leaders of the institution that became Georgia Southern University. From left to right are Ernest V. Hollis, Guy Wells, Zach Henderson, E.C. Dickens, and J. Walter Hendricks.

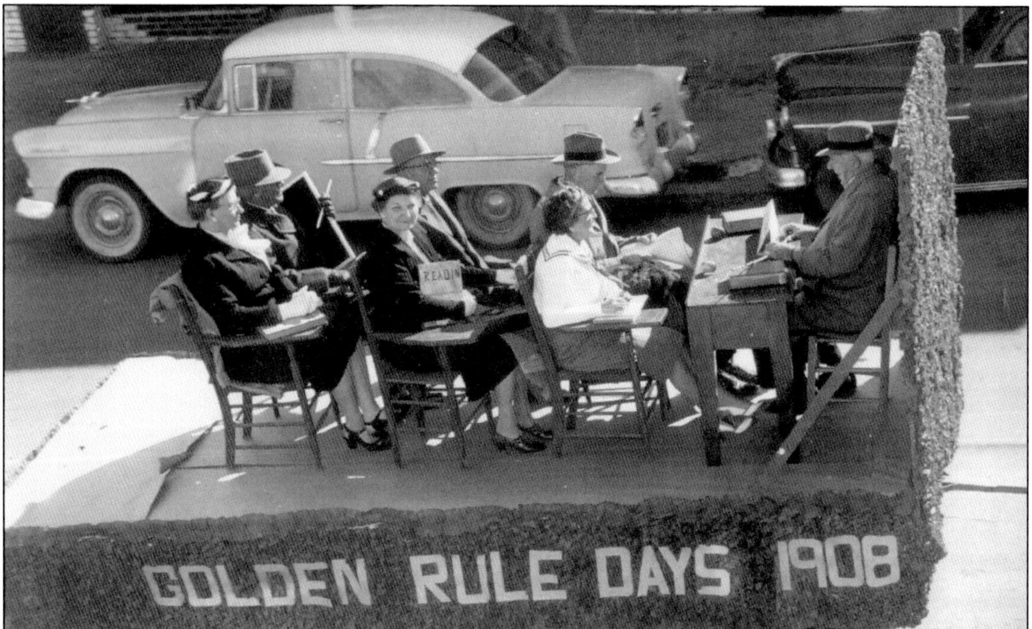

On February 1, 1958, the theme of the annual homecoming parade of Georgia Teachers College was the 50th anniversary of the beginning of classes at First District A&M School. A float included members the first class of 1908, and original teacher and president Elder J. Walter Hendricks at the front of a classroom. In the first row facing the teacher (from left to right) are Dan and Catherine Bland, in the second row are Juanita Strickland and Clayton Hollingsworth, and in the third row are Mr. and Mrs. James Arthur Bunce. Mr. Bunce, Mr. Bland, Mr. Hollingsworth, and Mrs. Strickland were in the first graduating class.

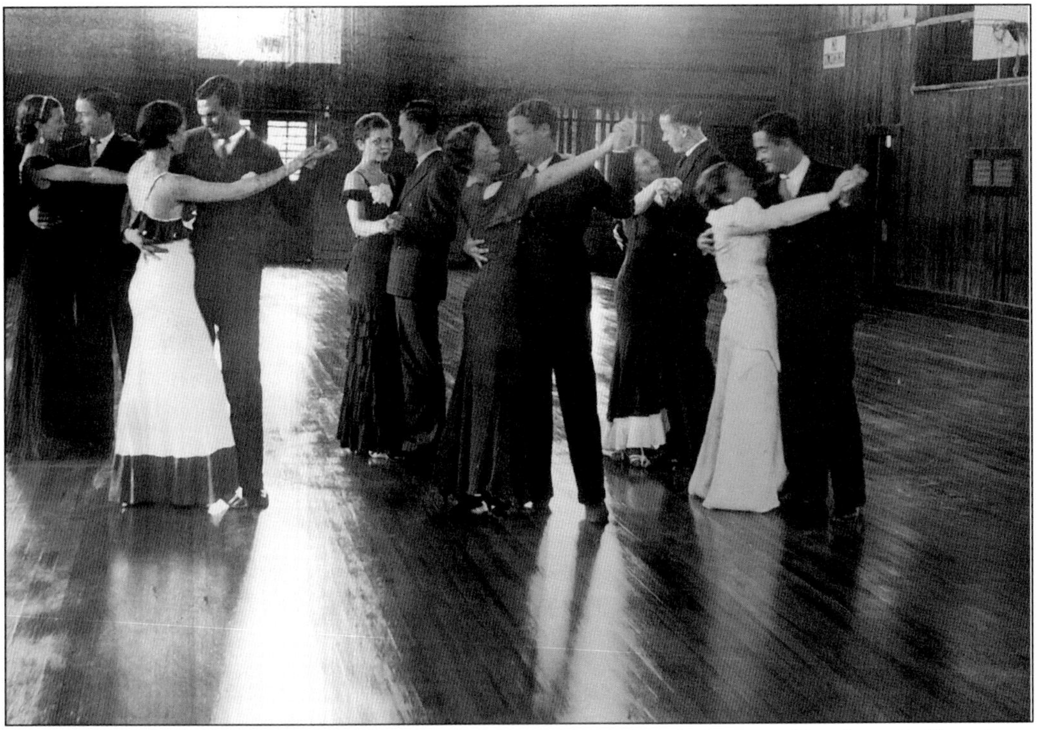

In 1935 the Great Depression did not prevent students at South Georgia Teachers College from enjoying the good life. Here a group participates in a formal dance at the college gymnasium. Often the faculty and students formed an orchestra which played songs made popular by the Dorsey brothers, Glenn Miller, and others.

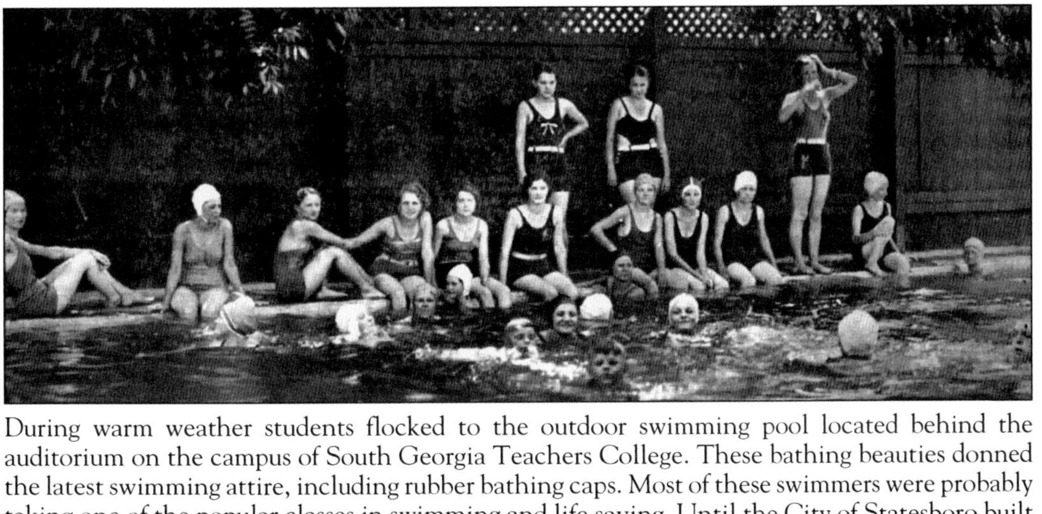

During warm weather students flocked to the outdoor swimming pool located behind the auditorium on the campus of South Georgia Teachers College. These bathing beauties donned the latest swimming attire, including rubber bathing caps. Most of these swimmers were probably taking one of the popular classes in swimming and life saving. Until the City of Statesboro built an outdoor pool at the recreation center in 1949, local children were permitted to swim there.

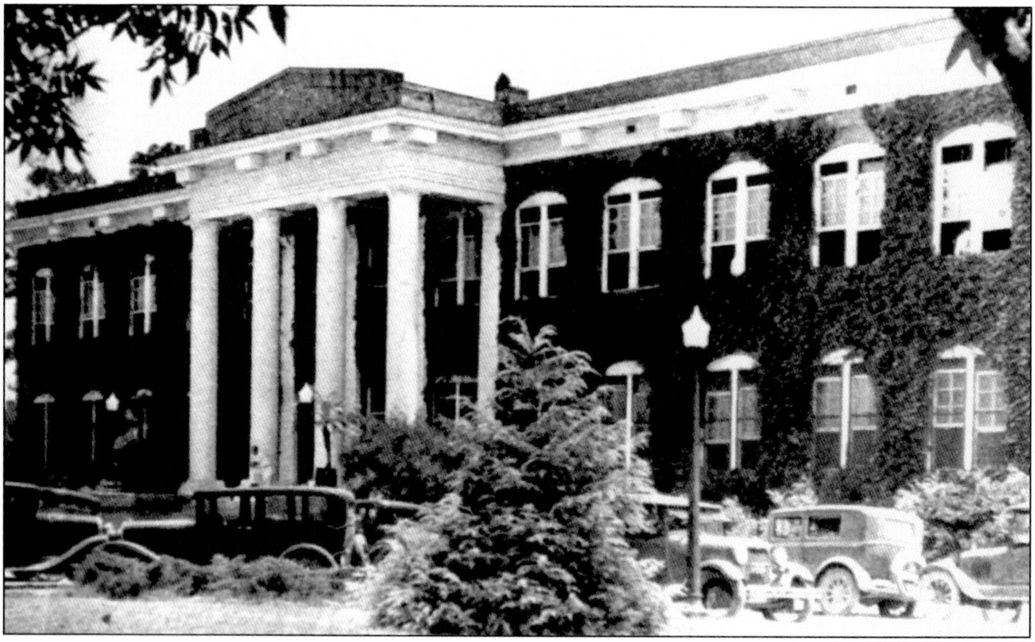

The Marvin Pittman Administration Building, erected in 1907 for the First District Agricultural and Mechanical School, has been a landmark on the campus for almost 100 years. This photograph was taken between 1924 and 1929 when the institution was known as Georgia Normal School. The multi-purpose structure provided classrooms, the library, an auditorium, and offices for faculty and staff. The roofline reflects the building's original design. The college expanded and renovated the structure *c.* 1930, and it has remained essentially unchanged to this day.

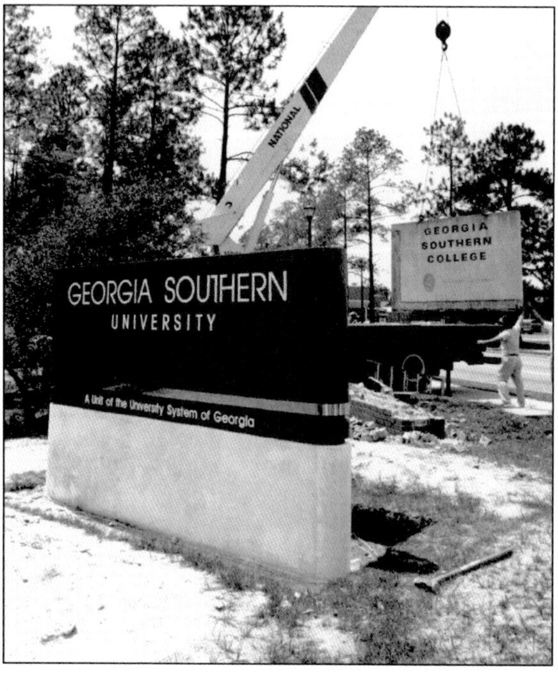

In June 1990 preparations were underway for the official transition of Georgia Southern College to Georgia Southern University on July 1. Workers readied new signage for the University Day Celebration, and just after midnight in the early hours of July 1, thousands of students, faculty, staff, and community members watched as the sign at the entrance to campus on U.S. Highway 301 was unveiled.

College president Dale W. Lick (left) and head football coach Erk Russell were featured on the cover of an early Eagles' game program. Lick led the drive to re-establish football as a varsity sport, which had been dormant since the United States entered World War II in 1941. He hired Russell, the University of Georgia's legendary defensive coordinator, as the Eagles' first modern coach. Russell coached his teams to three national titles between 1982 and 1989 and retired after a perfect 15-0 season.

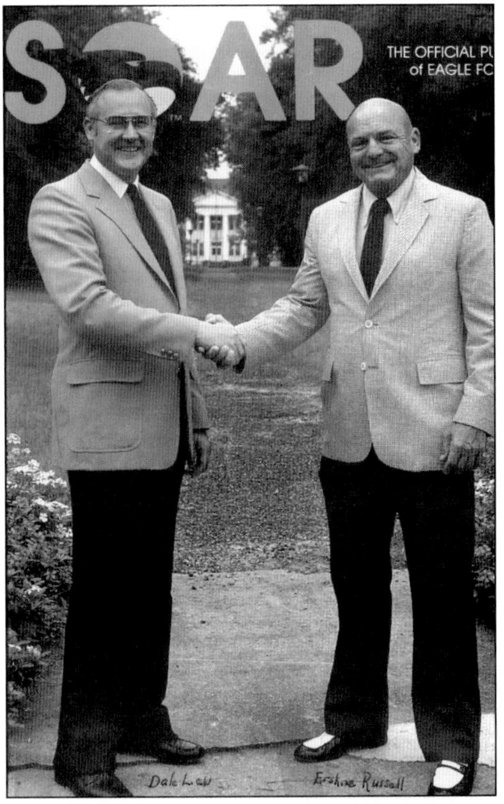

The introduction of a highly successful football program gave Georgia Southern national visibility and the college attracted students in record numbers, making it the fastest growing college or university in the U.S. from 1987 to 1992, when enrollment more than doubled. Fans have flocked to Allen E. Paulson Stadium since 1984 to see their Eagles capture NCAA Division I-AA national titles in 1985, 1986, 1989, 1990, 1999, and 2000. The enrollment boom that came with football contributed greatly to the college's successful bid for university status in 1990.

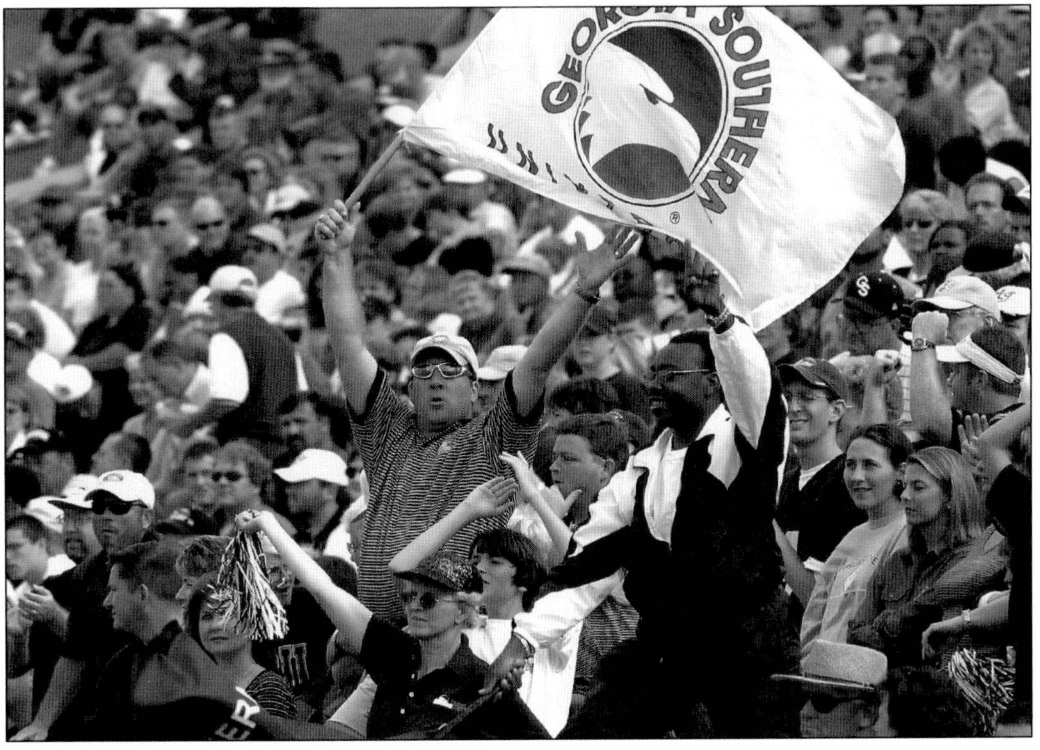

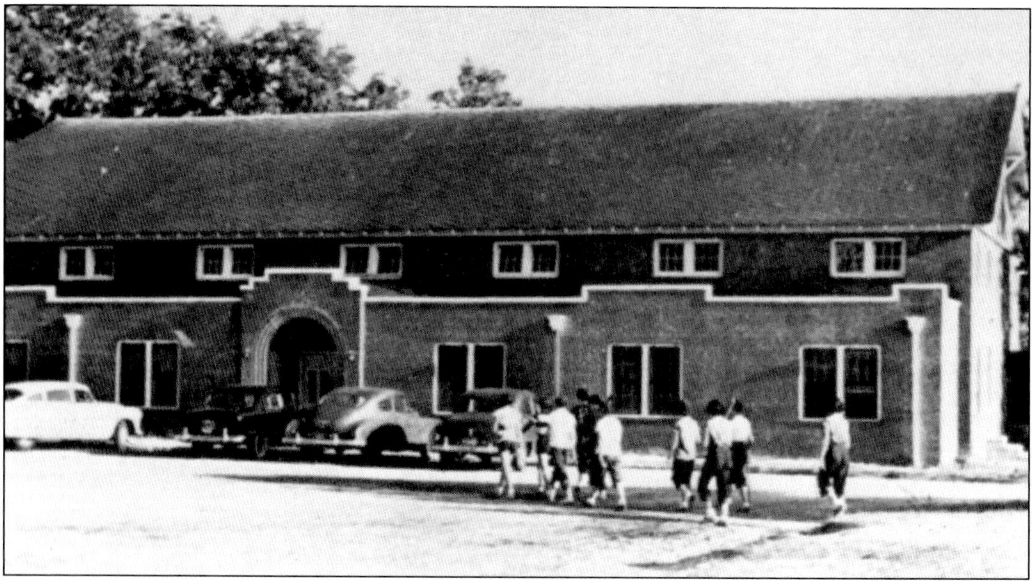

Prior to 1936, the college's basketball teams had to endure the indignity of hosting games in a local tobacco warehouse because they lacked an indoor campus facility. Contributions from alumni were largely responsible for funding the construction of what became known as Alumni Gym, the campus' first basketball arena. It served the college until the opening of the W.S. Hanner Gym in 1955, which was home to the basketball Eagles until 1970 when 5,400-seat Hanner Fieldhouse was constructed as part of an expansion to the Hanner complex.

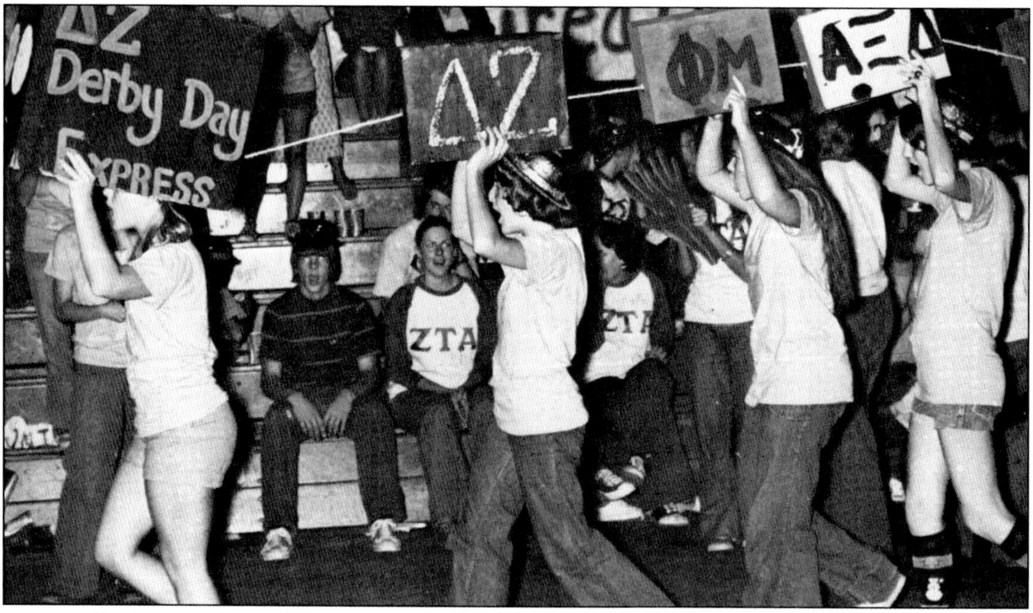

Nationally chartered social fraternities and sororities were established on campus in the 1930s, and Greek Life programs have grown to 21 organizations for men and women. Greeks are highly involved in campus events and community-based charitable projects. While some Greeks leased off-campus housing for decades, the university made arrangements beginning in the early 1990s for groups to finance the construction of their own houses along Olympic Boulevard. Seven fraternities and six sororities have established homes to date.

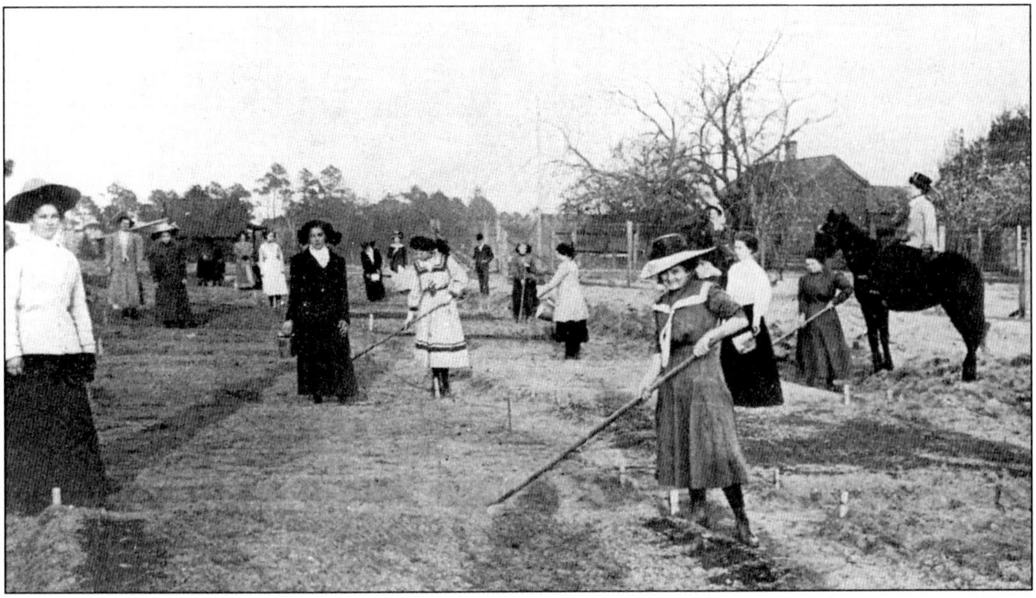

Female students in 1909 planted and maintained flower gardens as part of their tuition at First District A&M School. Male students learned how to grow basic crops such as peanuts, cotton, corn, and garden vegetables as well as animal husbandry. Female students took courses in domestic sciences, in addition to the required general curriculum. For many years the gardens and dairy provided food for the entire student body.

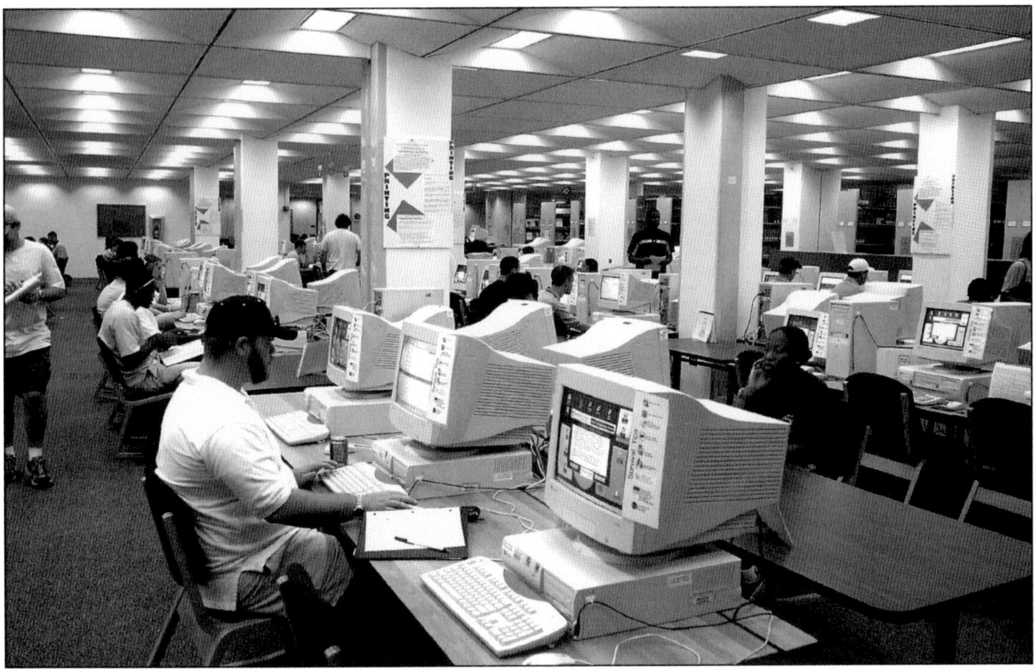

As the Information Age unfolded, the late 1980s saw the advent of computer-based word processing and research in Henderson Library and other facilities across campus. At present, more than 1,400 personal computers are available for student use in the library, classrooms, and labs, enabling students to write assigned papers and conduct internet research.

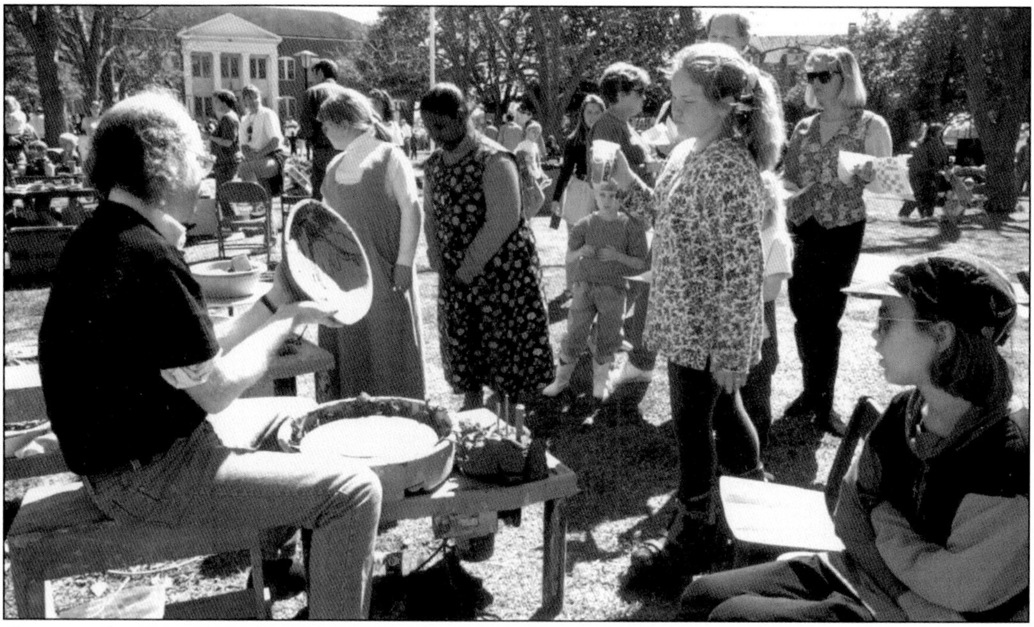

Georgia Southern has always welcomed community participation in university events like the annual Youth Arts Festival, which brings thousands of area children to Sweetheart Circle each spring. Sponsored by the Betty Foy Sanders Department of Art, the festival hosts painters, woodcarvers, potters, weavers, singers, and dancers from across the Southeast to teach and entertain school-aged kids and their parents.

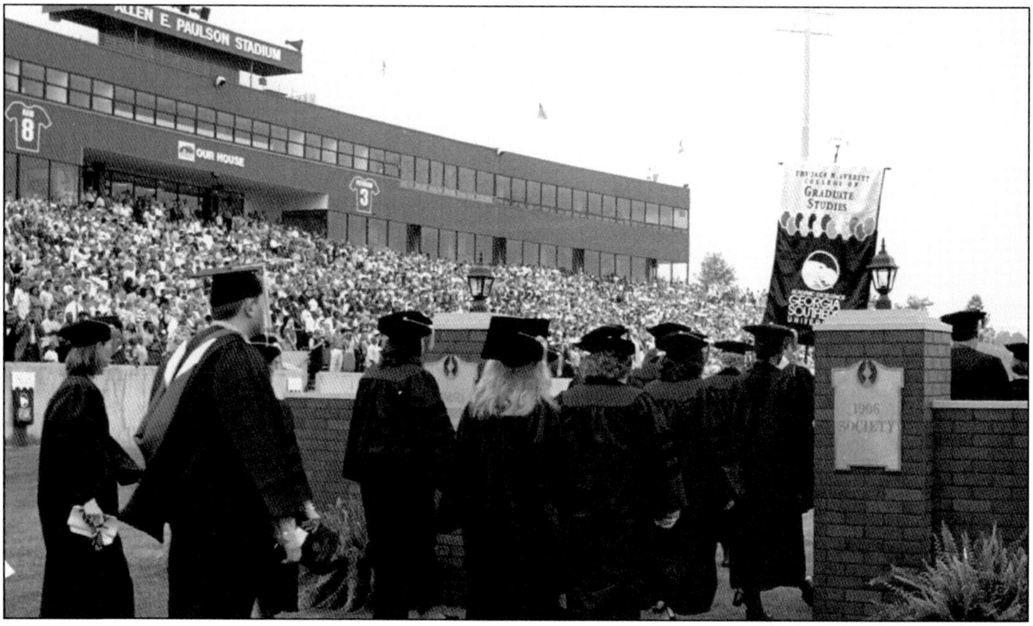

Spring Commencement has evolved from multi-session exercises in a gymnasium to a single ceremony in spacious Paulson Stadium. Each May, a crowd of more than 15,000 family and friends gathers to watch graduates process into the stadium before being called to the stage to receive their degrees. Last year, Georgia Southern awarded nearly 2,300 bachelor's and advanced degrees.

Five

From Then to Now

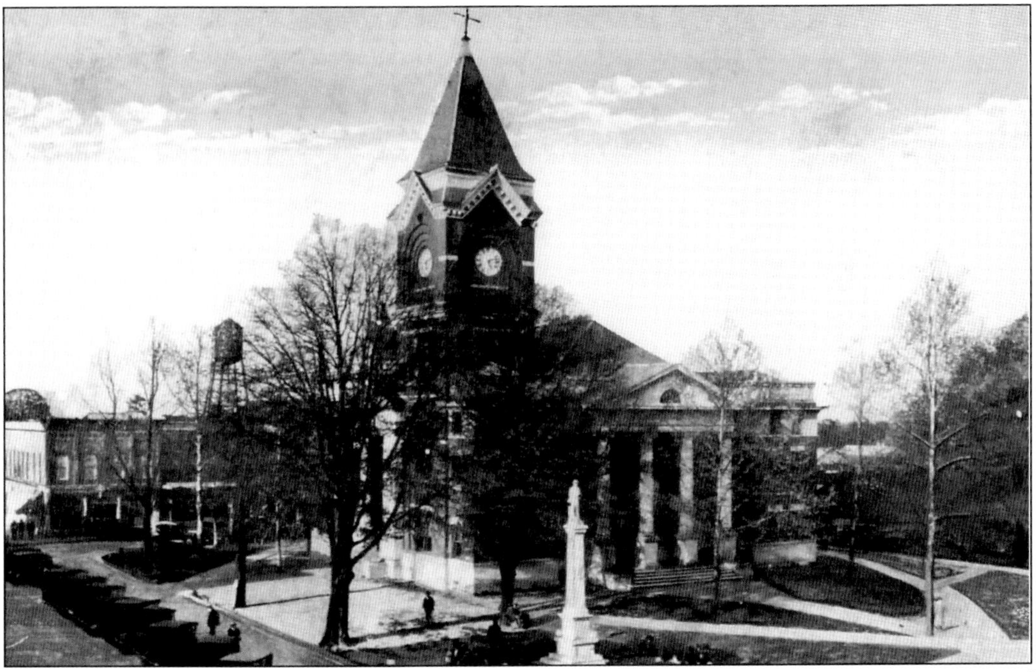

The town of "Statesborough" was born on December 19, 1803, and it served as the seat of Bulloch County. Until 1894 judges and lawyers held court in wooden buildings, the first of which was made of logs. A larger structure fell to the torch of Union soldiers in December of 1864. The replacement, a two-story structure, was inadequate for a growing county in the 1890s. This building, which stands today, was completed in 1894 and has been renovated on several occasions. This view of 1920 shows an expanded building, featuring porticos with Ionic columns that were added in 1914.

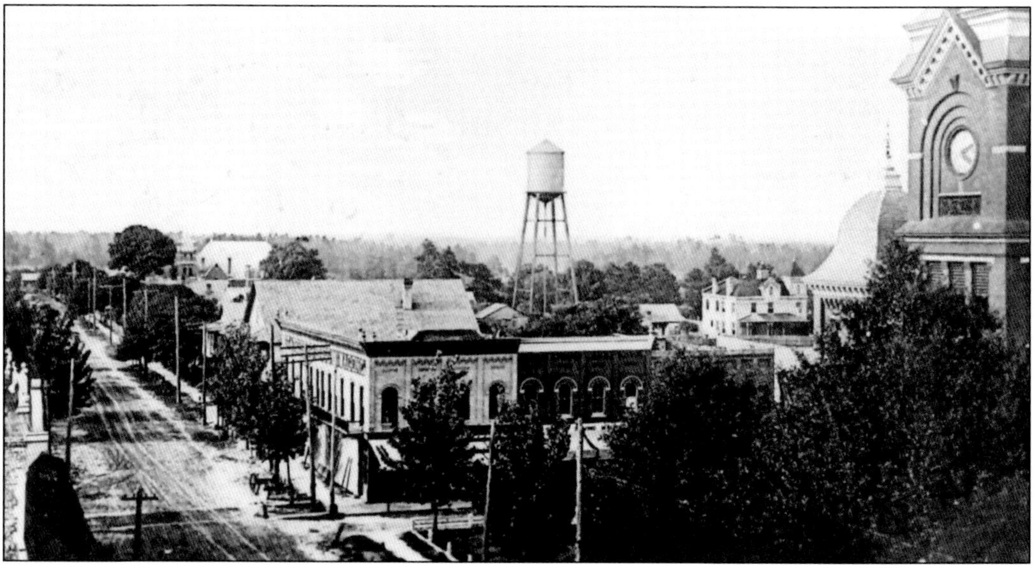

The photographer stood atop R. Simmons Company's three-story building to take this dramatic view of the northern part of town in 1908. The city's water tank is to the left of the Bulloch County jail. On the left is the tower of the Statesboro Missionary Baptist Church (now First Baptist). In 1896 the Statesboro City Council passed an ordinance specifying that the town's main streets would be planted with water oaks. Some of these trees remain in 2003.

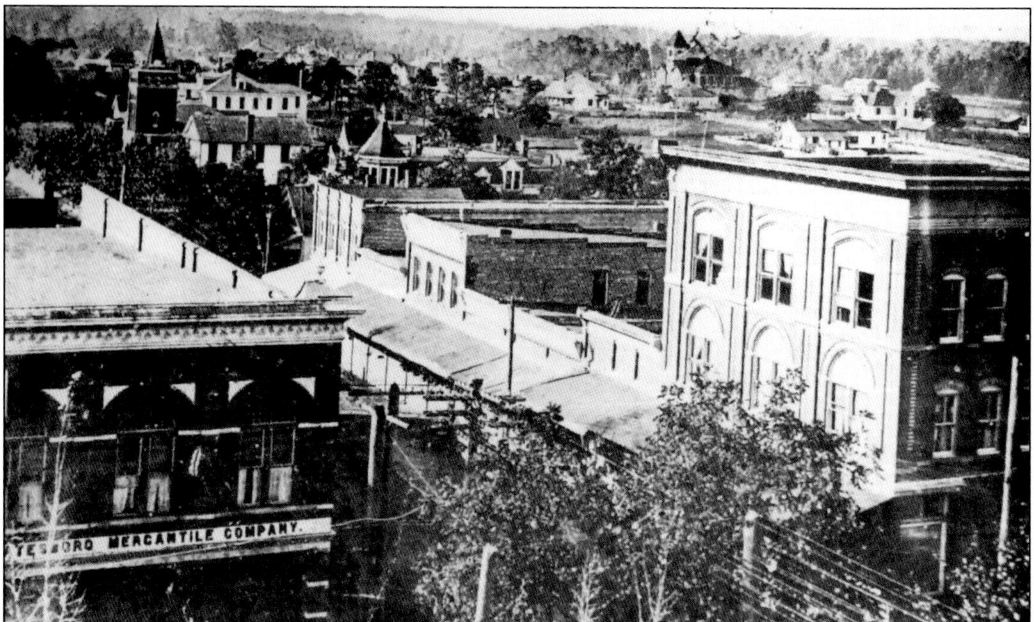

This photograph shows South Main Street and the city as viewed from the courthouse steeple in 1908. In the left foreground is the Statesboro Mercantile Company (site of the Sea Island Bank in 2003). In the left background is the tower of the Methodist church. The R. Simmons Company (later Minkovitz) is located on the right. In the background is the bell tower of the Statesboro Normal Institute (later Statesboro Grammar School), located on the corner of South College and Grady Streets.

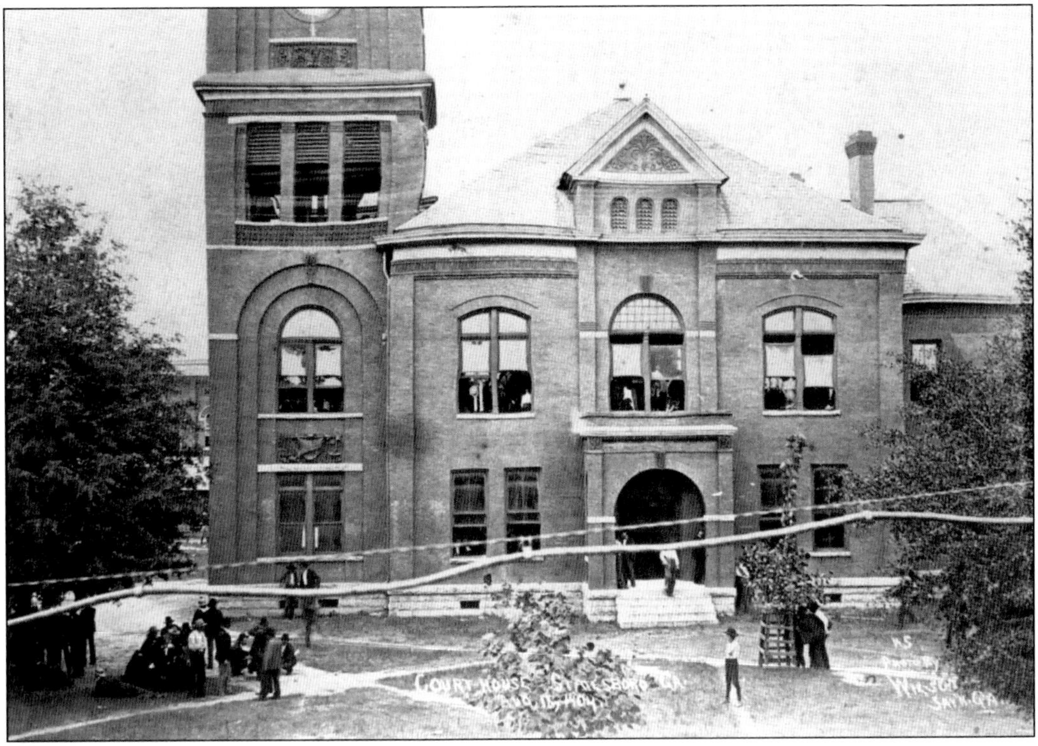

This photograph was taken in August 1904. Shown is the south entrance of the courthouse facing East Main Street. Note that the windows are open, showing crowds of people inside. The activity inside and outside the building indicates this could have been a court day. Of special interest are the electric power lines shown in the foreground. The lines had just been installed by the city to provide electricity throughout the downtown area.

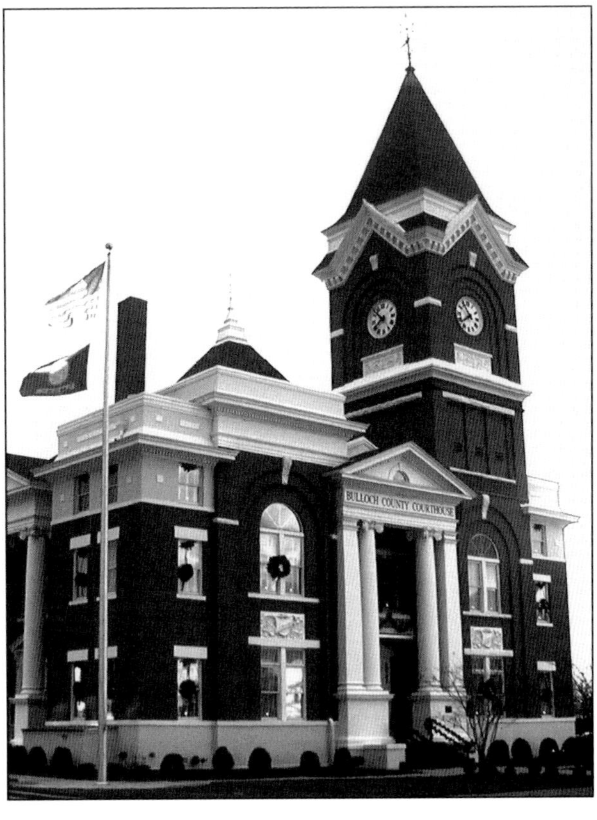

The Bulloch County Courthouse on Christmas morning of 2002 shows its most recent renovation completed in the year 2000. In 1970 the building had been modernized, providing space for offices, and the red brick exterior was painted white. The most recent renovation restored the appearance of 1914, and additions of 1970 were removed. It was rededicated on August 20, 2000, to serve the needs of the courts, including the judge of probate.

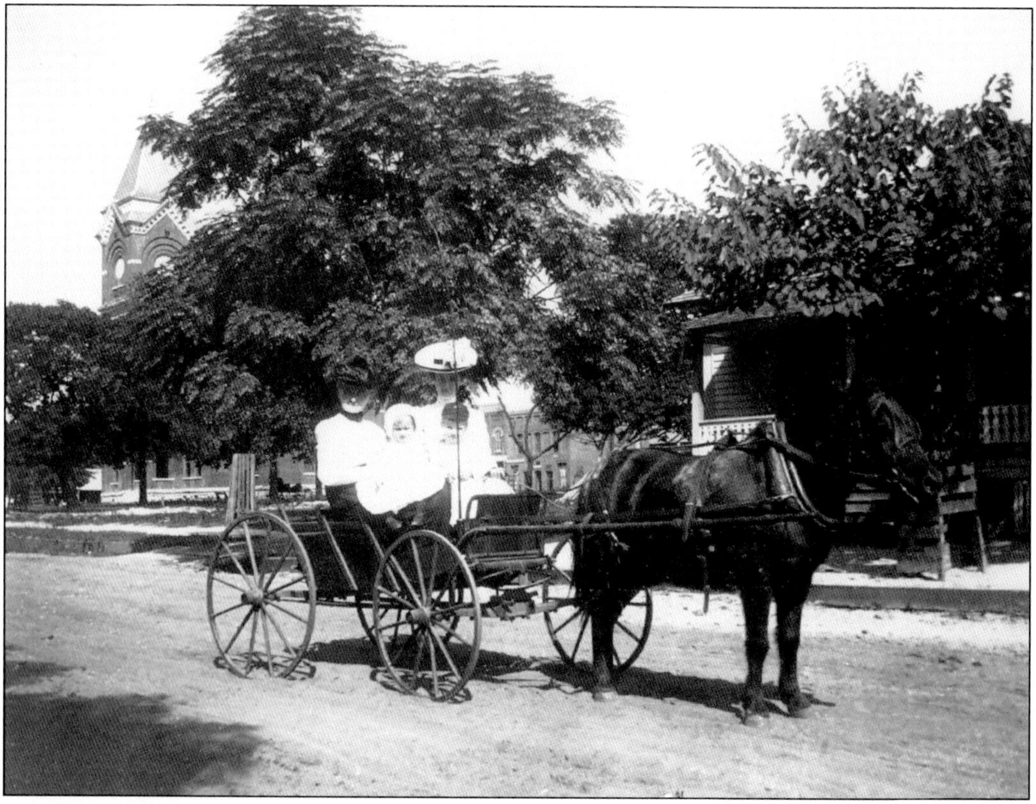

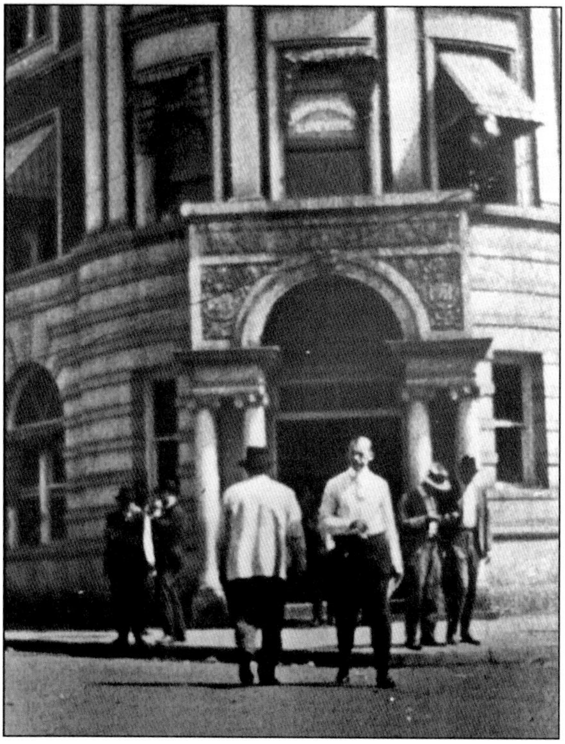

Members of Mrs. Greene S. Johnston's family are pictured in a buggy on East Main Street in 1894 as they sit in front of the boarding house of Capt. W.N. Hall near the corner of Siebald Street, the present site of the Bank of Statesboro building. In the background note the courthouse is under construction, as windows have not yet been installed.

Paul G. Franklin Sr. leaves the Bank of Statesboro for his drug store directly across the street in 1932. The attractive building was constructed in 1911 on the corner of Siebald and East Main Streets. Established in 1894 it was the first bank in Statesboro. It survived the financial crisis of 1929 until 1932, the last bank in town to close its doors. The bank did not survive the Depression. Note that directly above the entrance of the bank is the law office of Johnston and Son (Greene S. and George M. Johnston).

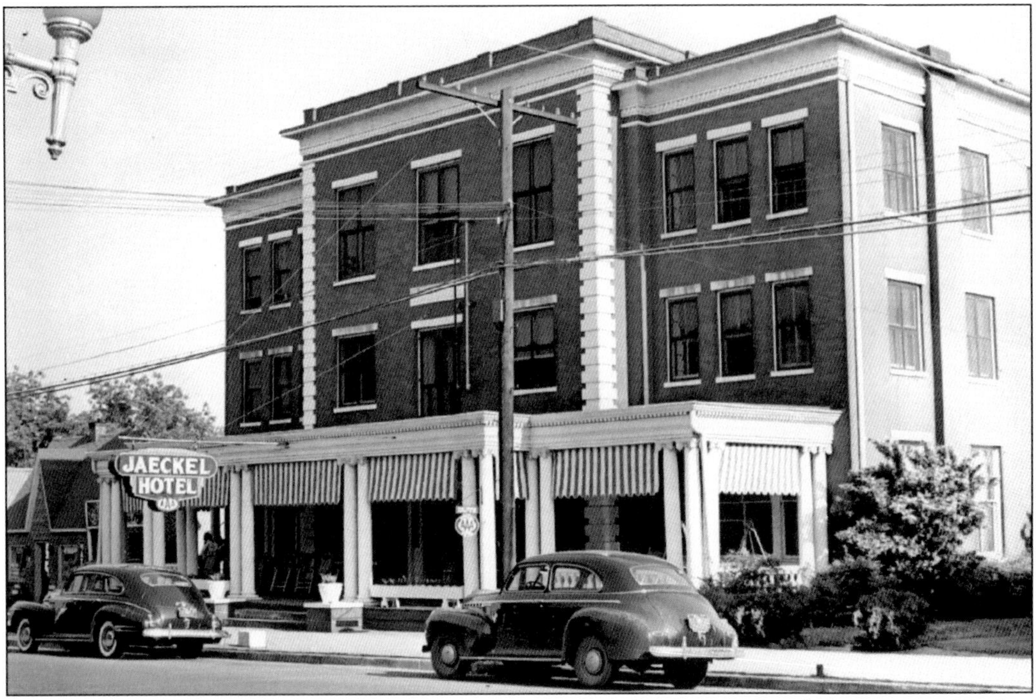

The Jaeckel Hotel was opened in 1905 on East Main Street by Gustave Jaeckel, a native of Berlin, Germany. For over 40 years the hotel had the reputation of offering the best accommodations in Bulloch County. Many dignitaries lodged here, including William Jennings Bryan (see cover), Henry Ford, Cornelius Vanderbilt, and several governors of Georgia. This photograph from 1940 reveals in the top left foreground a decorative bracket for a street light.

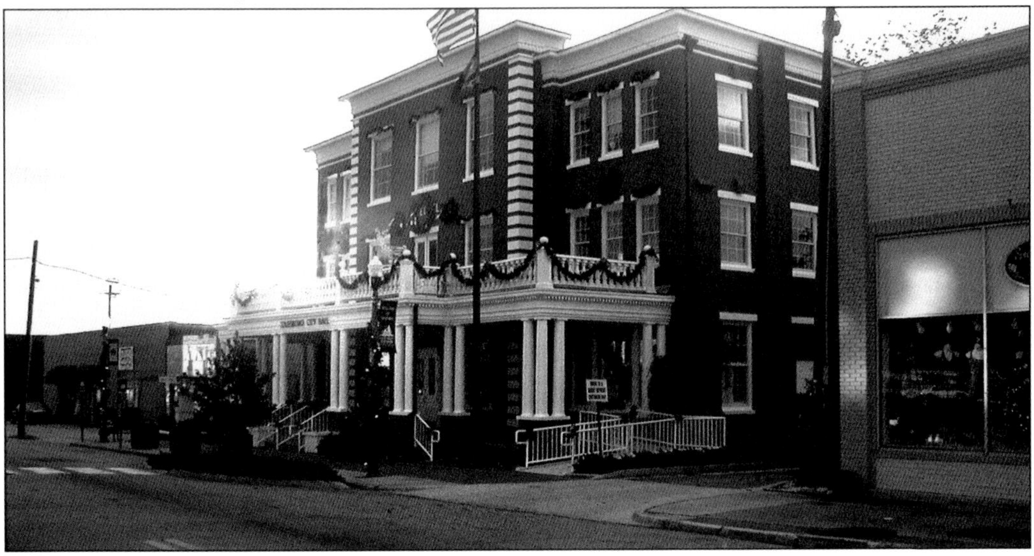

On Christmas morning of 2002 the Jaeckel retains much of is original charm, even though it is now the Statesboro City Hall. In the 1990s the city acquired the Jaeckel Hotel property and extensively renovated the structure inside and out. The new City Hall was dedicated on February 13, 1996. The structure's brick facade, previously painted white, was restored to its original color.

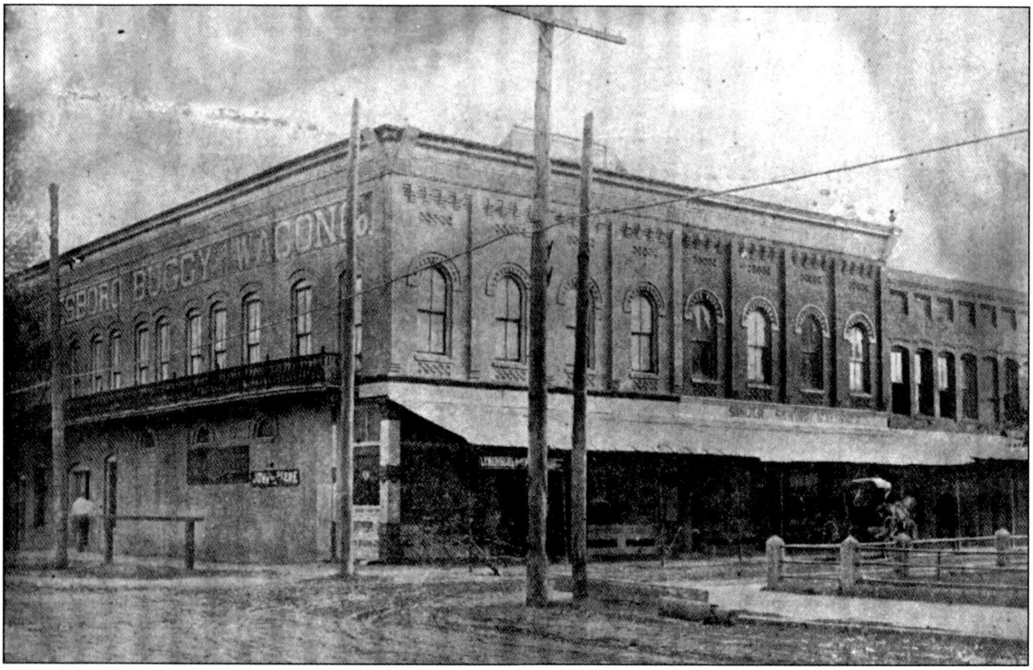

In 1905 the Statesboro Buggy and Wagon Company stood on the corner of Courtland and North Main Streets opposite the courthouse. The streets were unpaved and muddy in rainy seasons. However, a canopy covered the wooden sidewalks. Next door was the Singer Sewing Machine Company office. B.T. Outland built the structure in 1902 and sold it in 1905 to the Statesboro Buggy and Wagon Company, which was a familiar business name for almost 80 years.

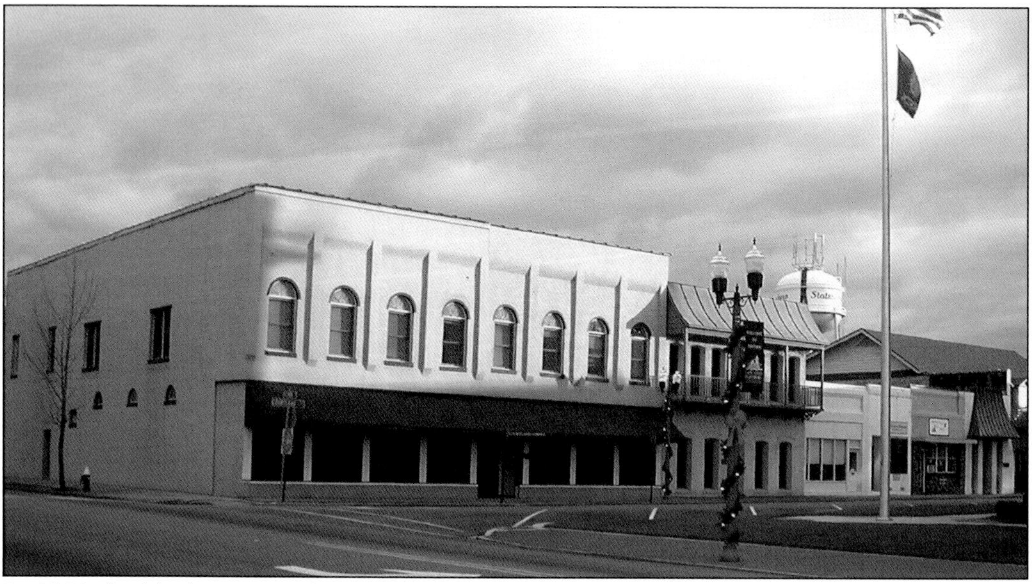

In 2003 the block running from the corner of North Main and Courtland Streets to Siebald Street has been renovated and modernized, providing office space upstairs and downstairs for attorneys and other business operations. The old Buggy and Wagon building has a stucco facade, but the basic structure remains intact.

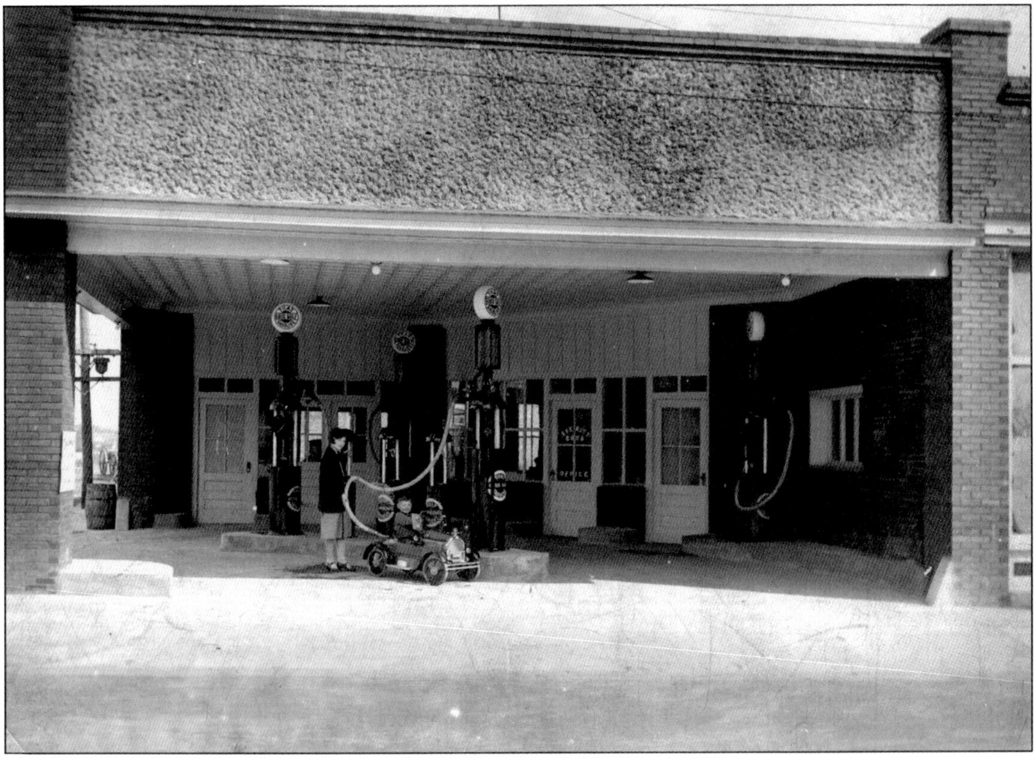

In the 1920s Averitt Brothers Motors, GM Dealer, occupied half of the block east of the courthouse, excluding the Bank of Statesboro. The In & Out Filling Station stood on the corner of Siebald and Courtland Streets. In February of 1926, young Jack Averitt, age four, asks company secretary Lilla Mae Oglesby (Mrs. Ernest C. Carter) to provide a pretend "fill up" of a promotional toy roadster.

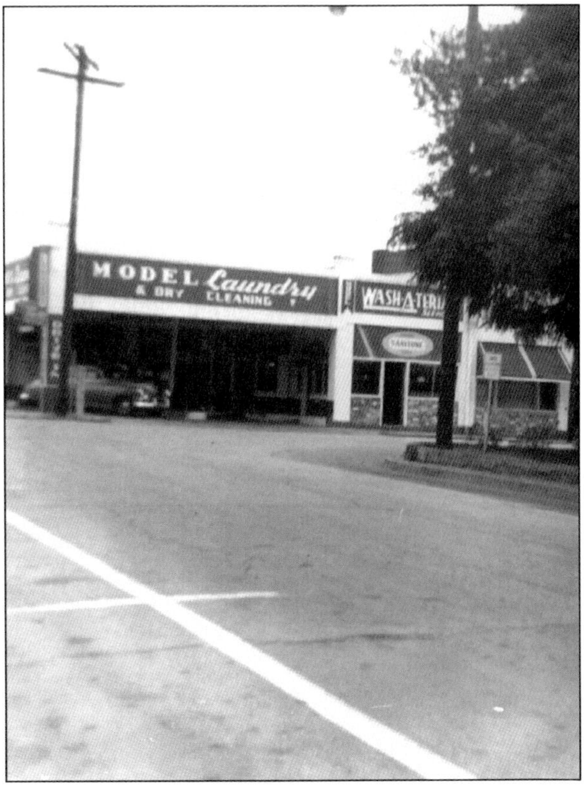

In the 1940s J.E. "Buster" Bowen operated his Model Laundry and Dry Cleaners in the buildings formerly occupied by Averitt Brothers Motors. For almost 20 years local citizens used what had been the driveway for the In and Out Filling Station as a drive-through to drop off laundry. In later years Bowen moved his business to a new facility at the corner of West Main and North College Streets, renaming it "Klean Korner," known as "Andrews Klean Korner" in 2003.

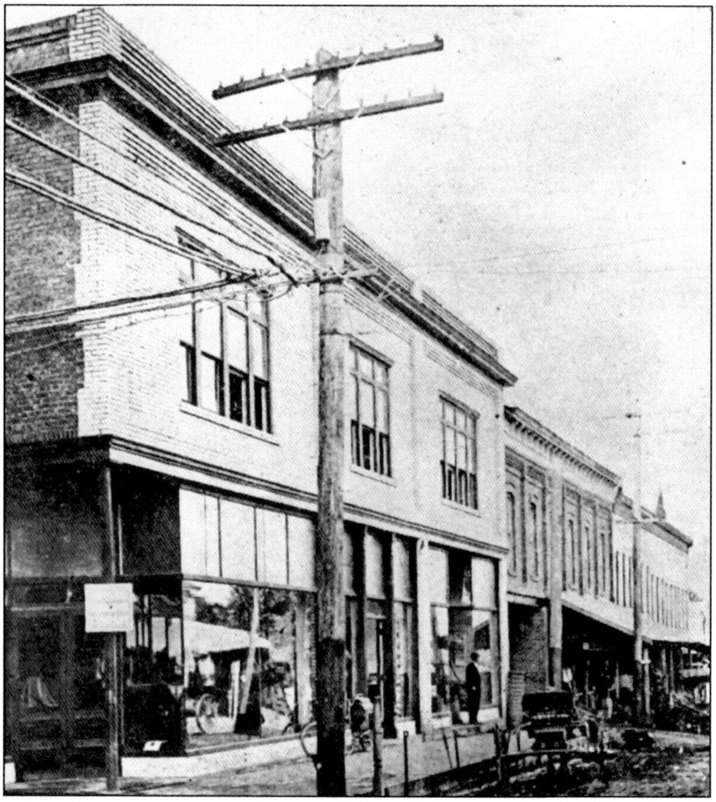

In 1914 the south side of West Main Street shows in the foreground the Brooks Simmons Company, a leading department store. The First National Bank was located in the central part of the building. A United States Postal Service mailbox appears on a post near the telephone pole. The sidewalk, with hitching posts, is much higher than the street. In the 1940s and 1950s this was the location of Griner's Hardware Store and the State Theater. In the 1960s Loy Waters acquired the property and opened a furniture store.

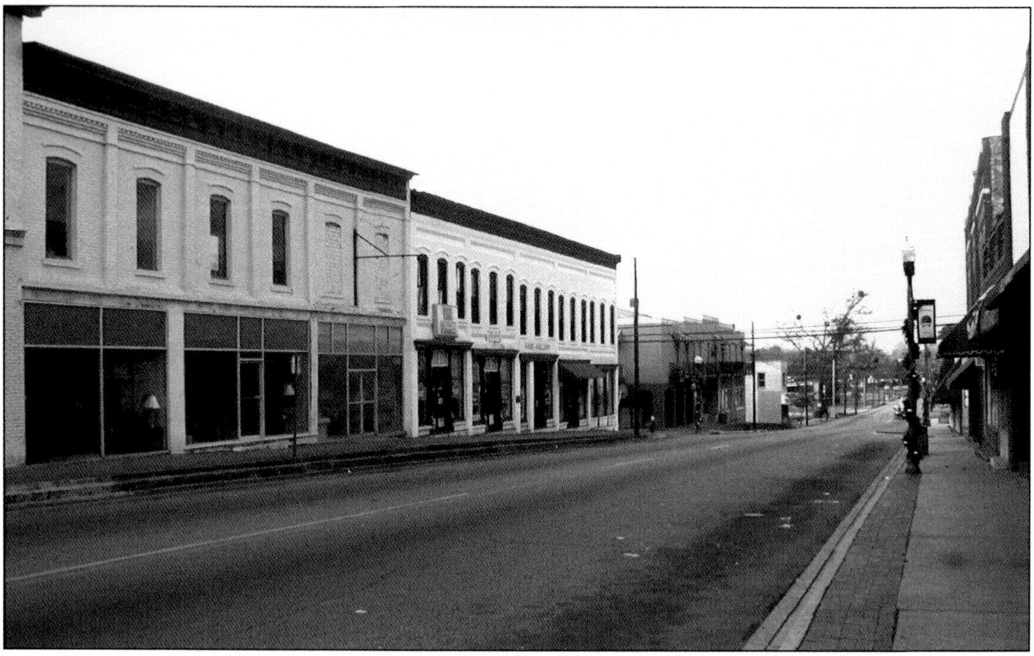

The south side of West Main Street in 2002 shows on the left a furniture store owned by the Waters family and other nearby shops. The sidewalks are still elevated well above the street level. Absent are the hitching posts and mail box, which were familiar sights for so many years.

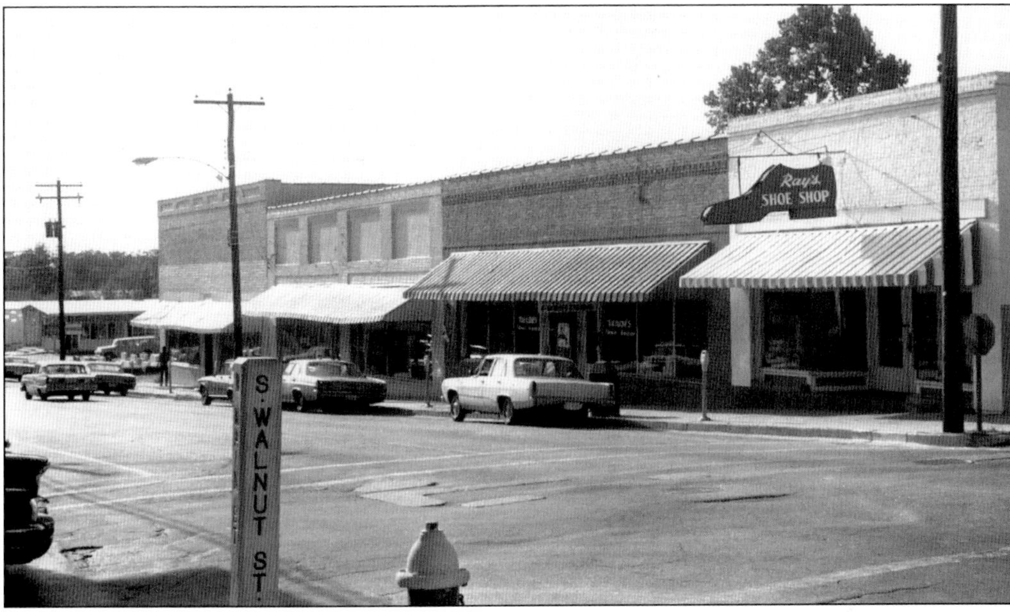

This is a 1960s view of the north side of West Main Street between North College and North Walnut Streets. The shoe shop on the corner is the oldest building, operated by the Grady Smith family and later by Frank Ray. The next building served two businesses, which sold television sets and furniture. The third building from the right was the original location of the USO during World War II, serving the soldiers stationed at the Statesboro Airport. In later years it was a furniture and carpet and tile store. On the end was the original site of a dealership for Ford tractors. The lot on the corner of West Main and College Streets was owned by the Thayer Monument Company.

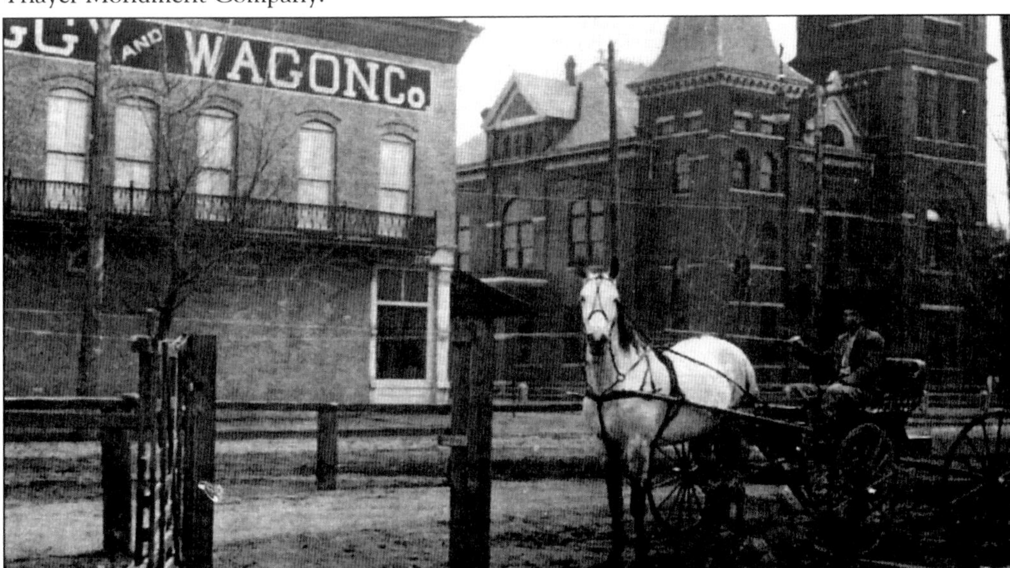

This is a view of North Main Street c. 1910 near the entrance to what is in 2003 the Simmons Shopping Center. Note the Statesboro Buggy and Wagon on the corner of Courtland Street and the "new" courthouse as it looked before it was remodeled in 1914. Driving the buggy is O.L. McLemore at the entrance to the Buggy and Wagon stable yard.

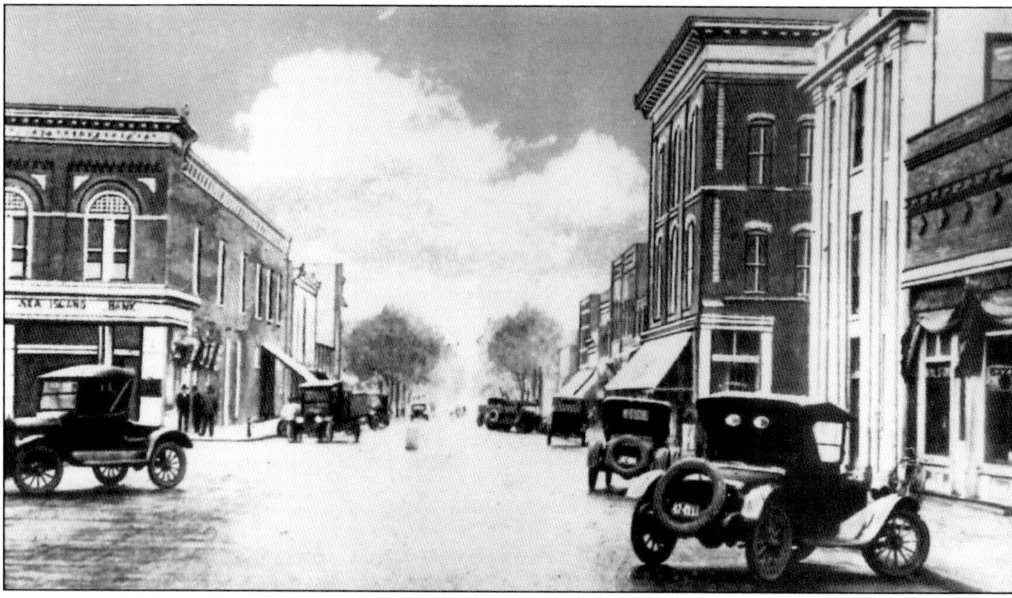

Around 1925 Statesboro had all the appearances of a prosperous town. Recent model cars lined the streets, which had been paved in 1919. Note the marble block at the intersection of the Main Streets. A policeman sometimes stood on the block and directed traffic. On the left is the Sea Island Bank, and on the far right is the three-story home of the First National Bank, built in 1917. On the southwest corner stood the R. Simmons Company, built in 1900.

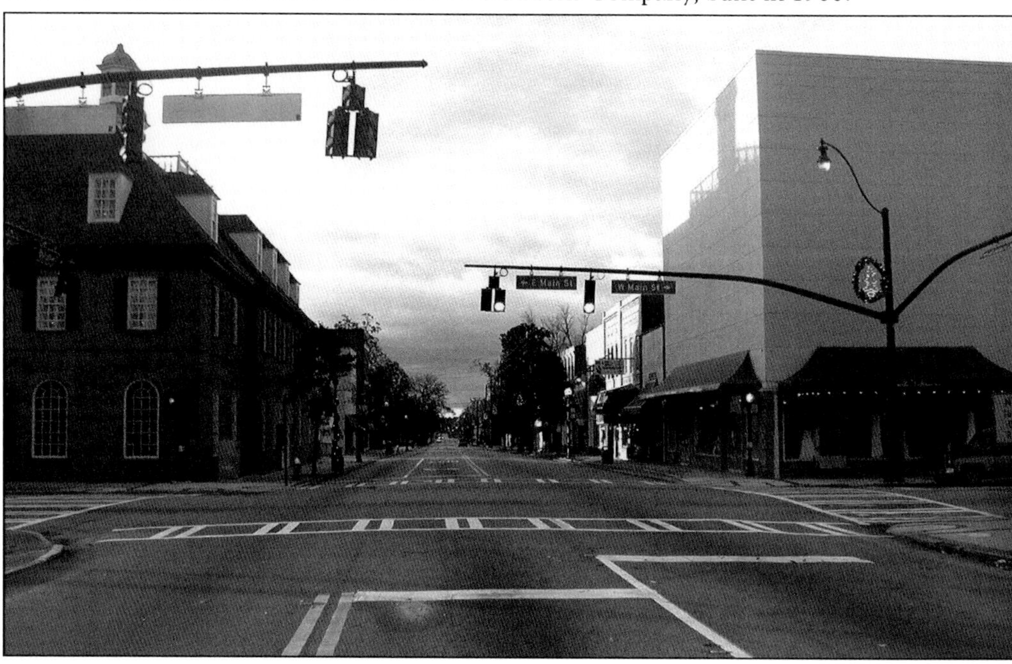

Early on Christmas morning 2002, few cars or trucks appeared, and the photograph is an excellent contrast with the scene above. On the left is the Sea Island Bank building, which has operated in this location since 1912. The new building was completed in 1970. The R. Simmons Company building still stands, although renovated, and is now a formal clothing store for women. Note the Christmas decorations and recently installed traffic light fixtures.

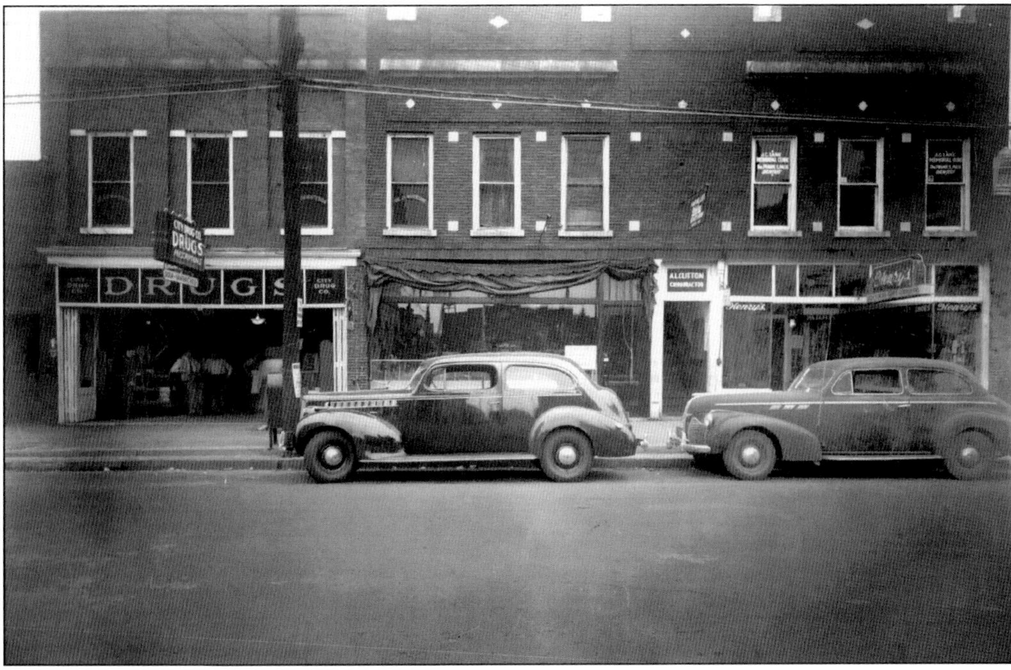

The first block of East Main Street, across from the courthouse, contained several popular businesses and offices. The following can be seen from left to right: the City Drug Company; the Men and Boys Clothing Store; and a staircase entrance to second-floor professional offices, including Dr. Clifton, a chiropractor, Dr. J.C. Lane, dentist, and W.G. Neville, attorney. On the far right is Henry's Department Store, operated by Henry Moses.

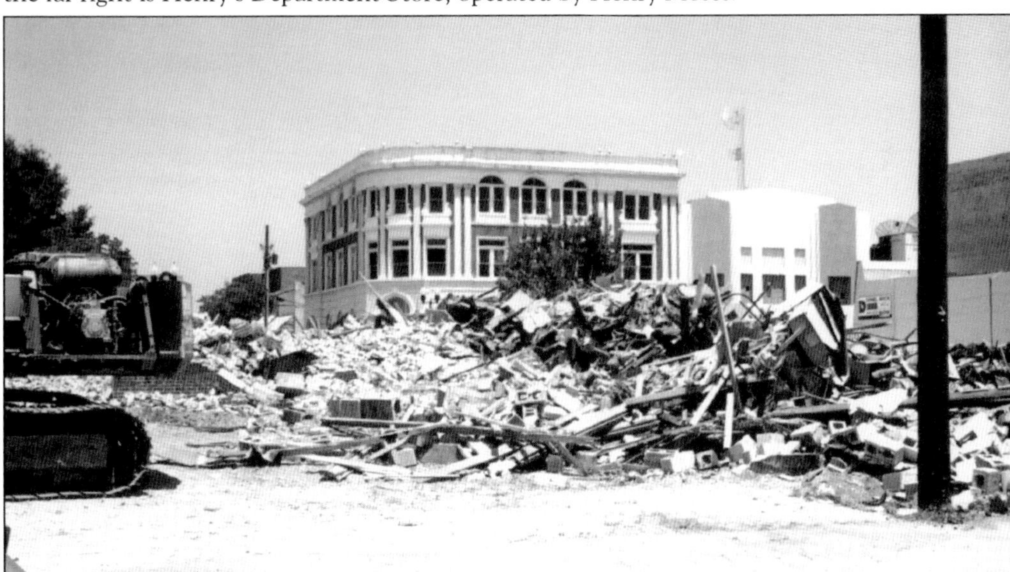

In 2001 the Sea Island Bank acquired all the property pictured above and razed it in order to expand the present business and provide a spacious parking lot for its customers. In the distance is the old Bank of Statesboro building and the Georgia Theater, which will become the Hal Averitt Community Arts Center. Both facilities will be remodeled by 2004 to retain the original appearance of these historic structures.

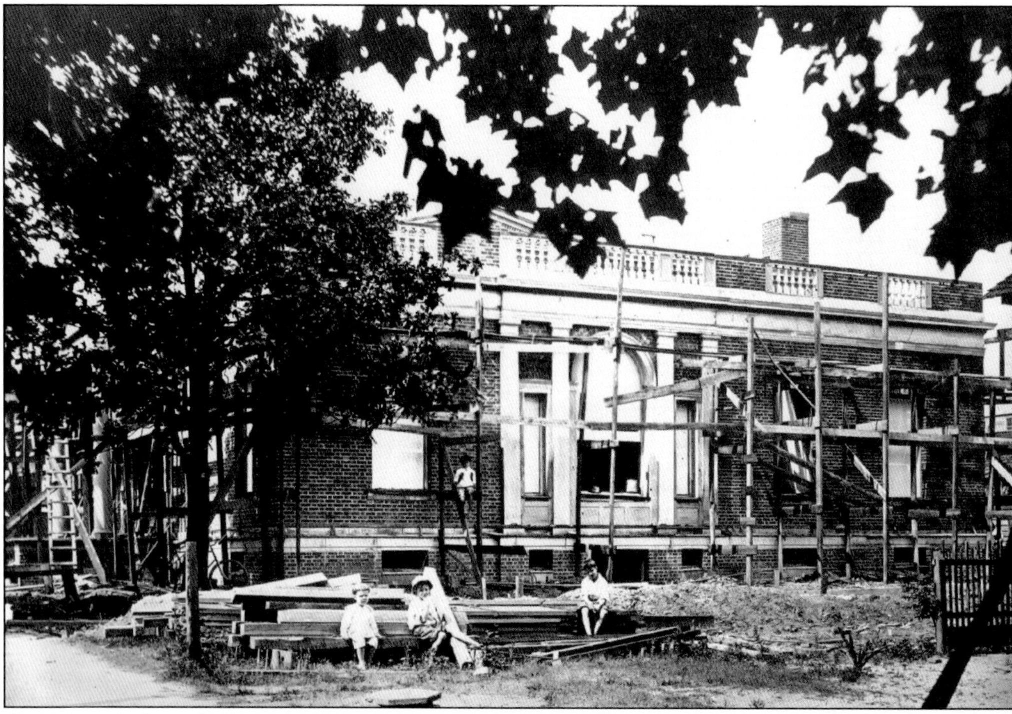

Statesboro's Post Office was an impressive structure when it was built on the corner of East Vine and South Main Streets in 1918. This image shows the south side of the building. After the post office moved to the Prince Preston Federal Building in the 1950s, the building was sold to the City of Statesboro. It was used as the city hall until the late 1990s. It is interesting to note that the boys in the picture are the four sons of P.H. Preston Sr., who lived next door—Benton, Prince H., Montgomery, and Tom. Prince Preston Jr. later became the first district congressman.

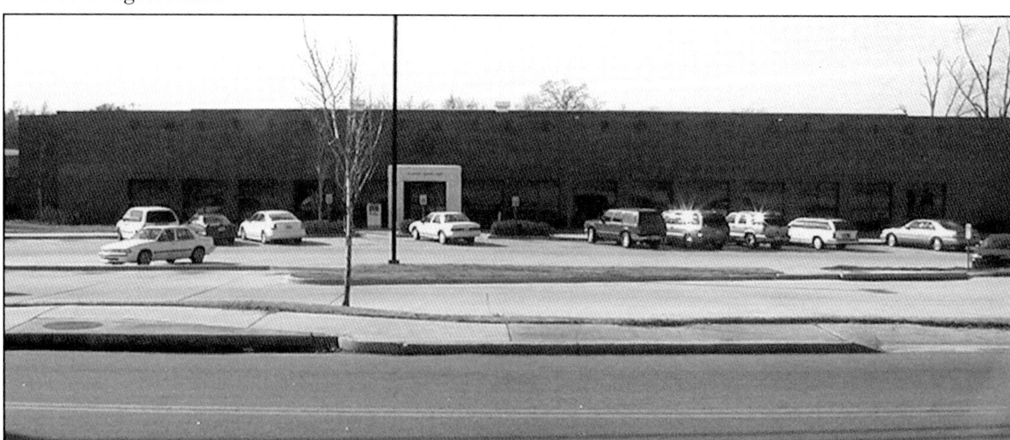

The new Statesboro Post Office is located in the first block of South College Street at West Main Street. The site covers several acres and extends to what is now MLK Jr. Drive. Originally the property housed the Olliff Hotel and other residences. It also included the site of the Georgia and Florida Railroad depot. This new facility was opened to the public in October 1992. The Prince Preston Federal Building on North Main Street is now a federal courthouse building.

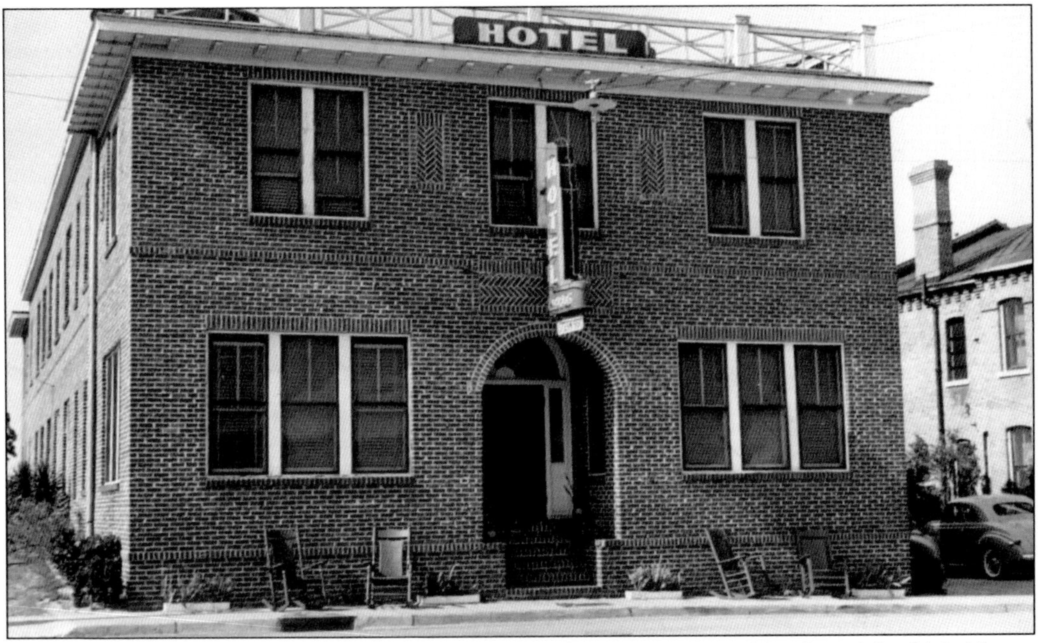

In 2003 the Norris Hotel building reflects few changes since 1938 when Mr. J.M. Norris remodeled and bricked the building for a hotel. However its original use was quite different from its ultimate destiny. The building was Statesboro's first hospital. Dr. R.L. Samples built the Statesboro Sanitarium in 1908. It was designed to serve 40 patients. One of the first "outside" doctors to move to town because of the new facility was Dr. F.F. Floyd. In 1912 he and Dr. L.W. Williams purchased the hospital which served the town until the Bulloch County Hospital was built on East Grady Street in 1936.

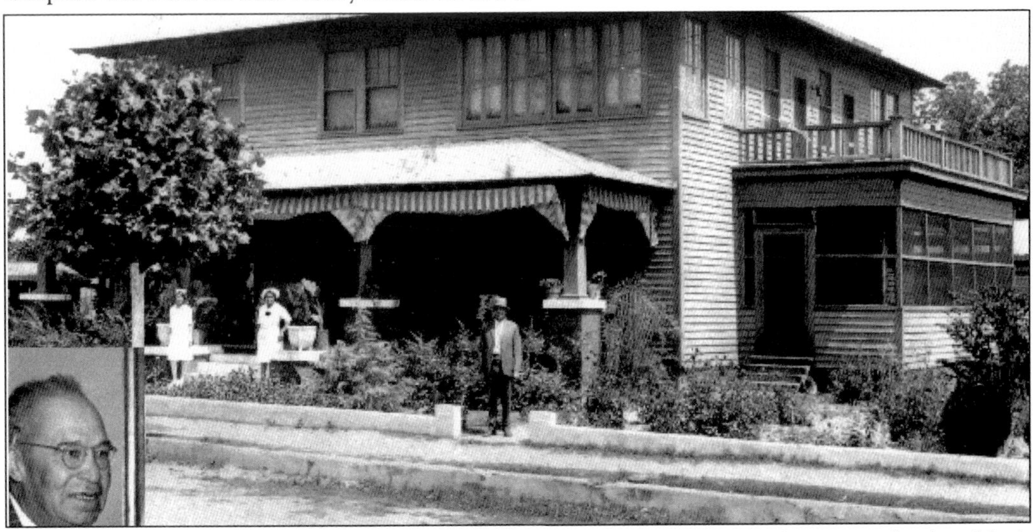

Dr. Harvey VanBuren (insert on left), a native of Sumter, South Carolina, was the first black physician in Statesboro. After receiving his M.D. degree from Howard University in 1915, he moved to town. Three years later he opened a 12-room hospital on Elm Street. Known as the VanBuren Sanitarium, the facility grew into a major health service. Dr. VanBuren received much acclaim for his service to the community during the great flu epidemic of World War I. He was a civic leader and lifelong member of the Republican Party.

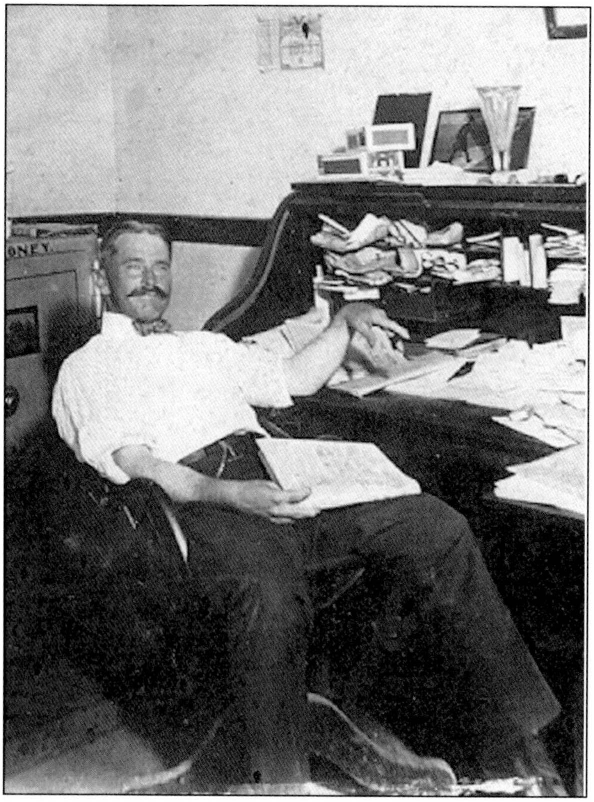

In the year 1900 Dr. A.J. Mooney moved to Statesboro from Millray (near the Ogeechee River) and began the practice of medicine. He was a contemporary of Dr. R.L. Samples and Dr. A.W. Quattlebaum. He was active in his profession and a community leader until his death in 1946. For many years his office was located on Siebald Street near the site of the Statesboro Sanitarium. His son, Dr. John Mooney, occupied the same office and opened Willingway Hospital in 1970. The third generation of the Mooney family still practices medicine in Statesboro through Willingway.

The Bulloch County Hospital was built in 1936 on the corner of East Grady and Donehoo Streets at a cost of $84,000, using property donated by local attorney Hinton Booth. Walter Aldred was the architect. This photograph from the late 1960s shows several popular vehicles of the day.

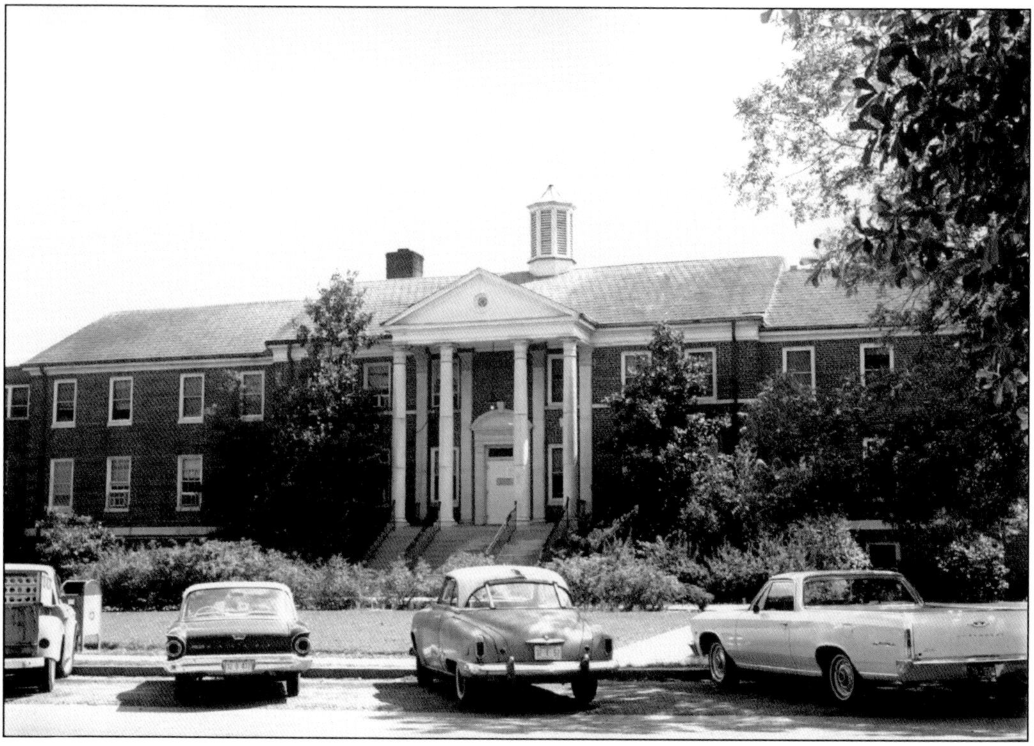

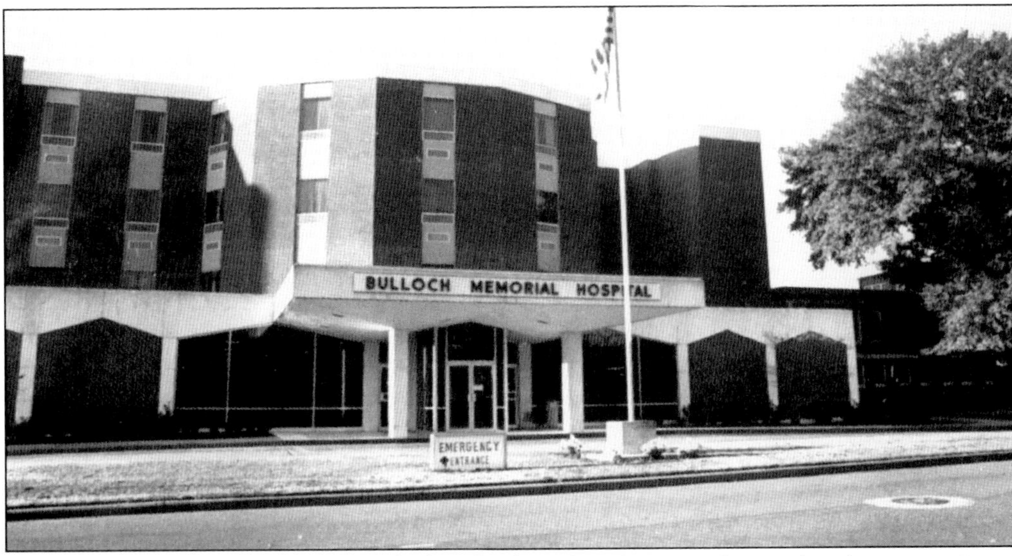

In 1966 Bulloch Countians approved a bond referendum for a new hospital and a renovation of the old Bulloch County Hospital. Designed by Ed Eckles, AIA, a local architect, the facilities were joined, offering expanded care and modern technology. The new name was Bulloch Memorial Hospital which continued to serve local citizens until the late 1990s.

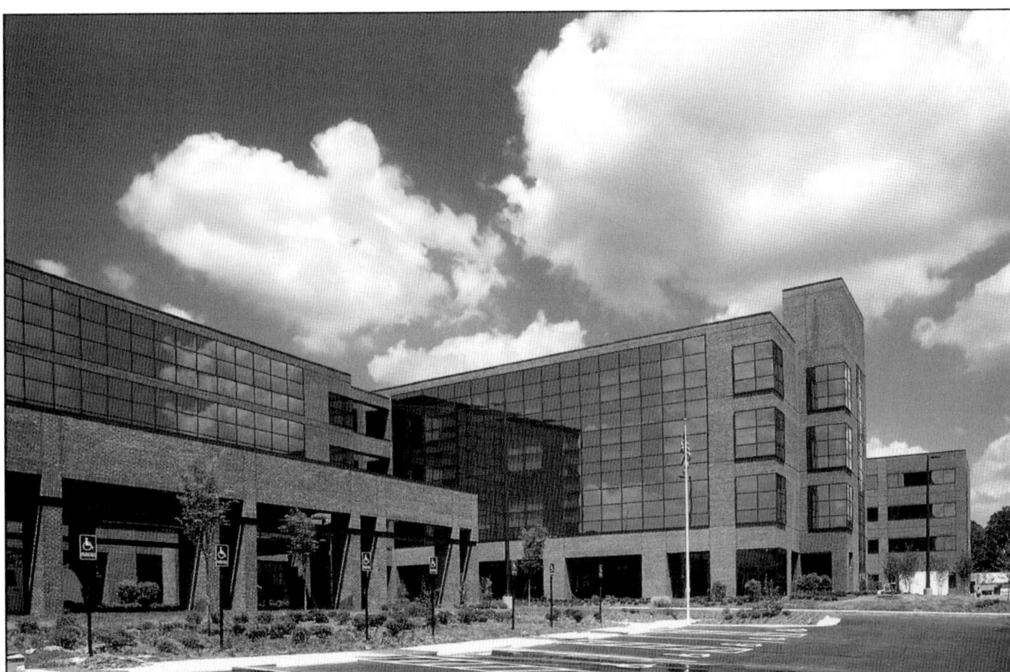

In 1995 Health Management Association, Inc. (HMA) purchased the Bulloch Memorial Hospital and operated it until their new and ultra-modern facility could be completed at 1499 Fair Road under the name of East Georgia Regional Medical Center. With 150 beds, the hospital serves a nine-county area and has an employee base of more than 700. It provides state-of-the-art health care, using the most modern techniques and equipment. The women's pavilion delivers more than 1,200 babies each year.

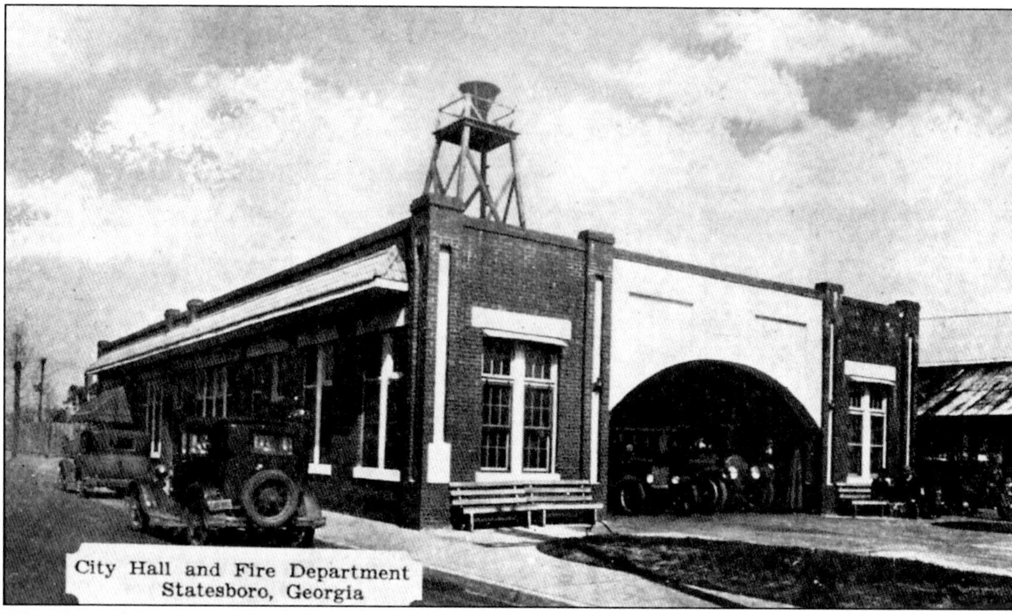

The Statesboro Fire Department and City Hall occupied the same building on the corner of Siebald and Courtland Streets in 1933; it was built during the hard days of the Great Depression. Some labor for the new structure was provided by unemployed citizens who worked to pay off their taxes and water bills. Two firetrucks are parked in the arched bays, and the city hall entrance is at the left rear. On the right side of the building is the jail, commonly known as the "Calaboose."

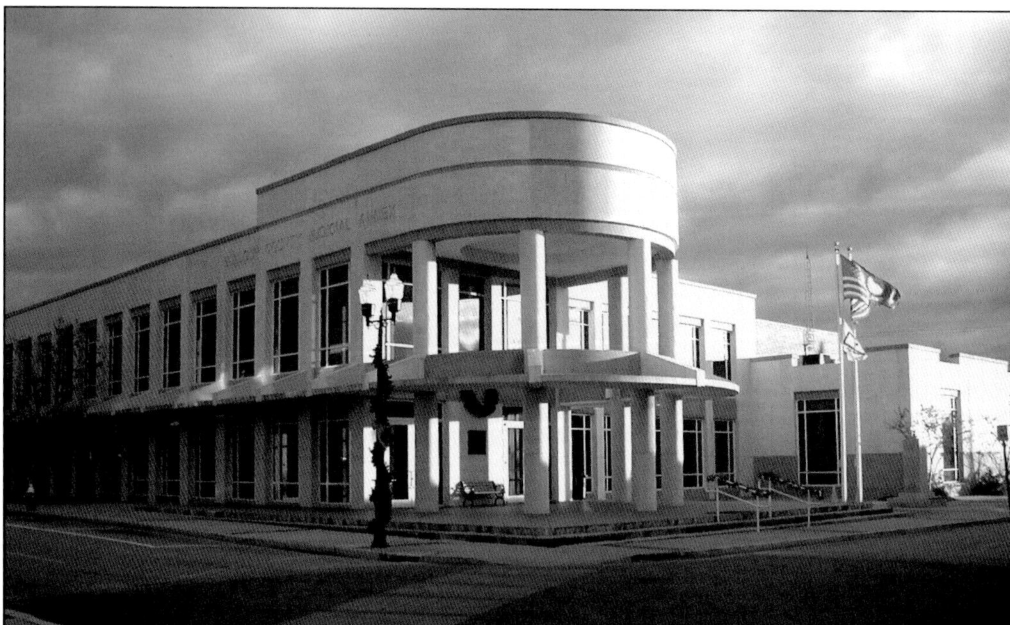

The Judicial Annex of the Bulloch County courthouse was built on the site of the old City Hall and fire department in the late 1990s. The building houses a large courtroom and vault of the clerk of court, in addition to various judicial offices. On the far right on the edge of the terrace is an eternal flame dedicated to the memory of veterans of Bulloch County.

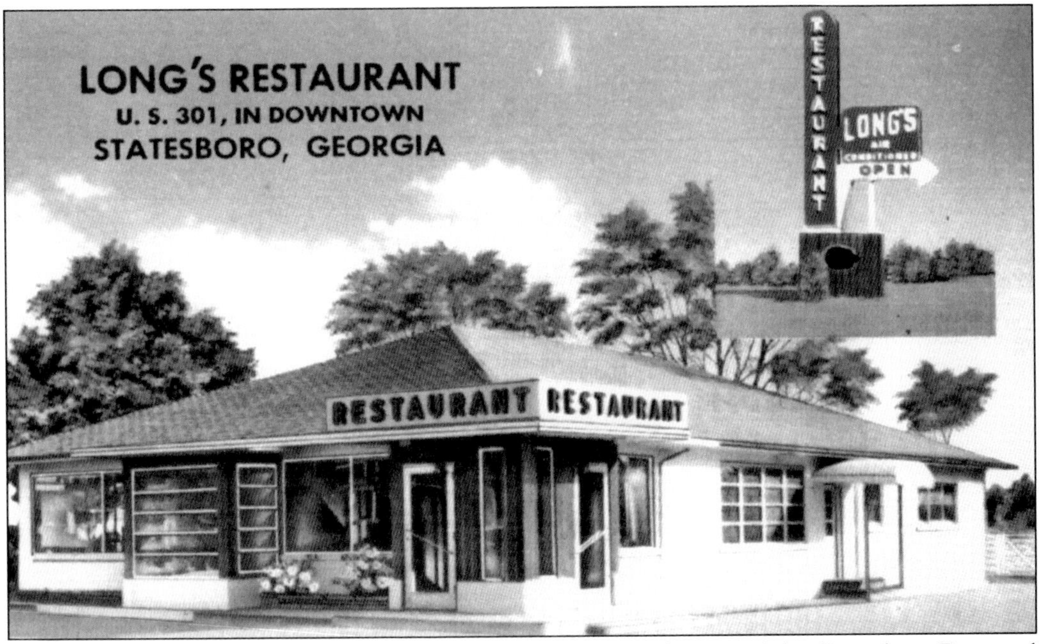

Long's Restaurant was located on South Main Street near the site of the Statesboro Regional Library in 2003. It was known as the Lafayette Grill until Mr. Long bought the business. Later the building was used as a beauty shop, accounting firm, and real estate office. The first building on the property was the home of the Rushing family, who operated the Rushing Hotel next door.

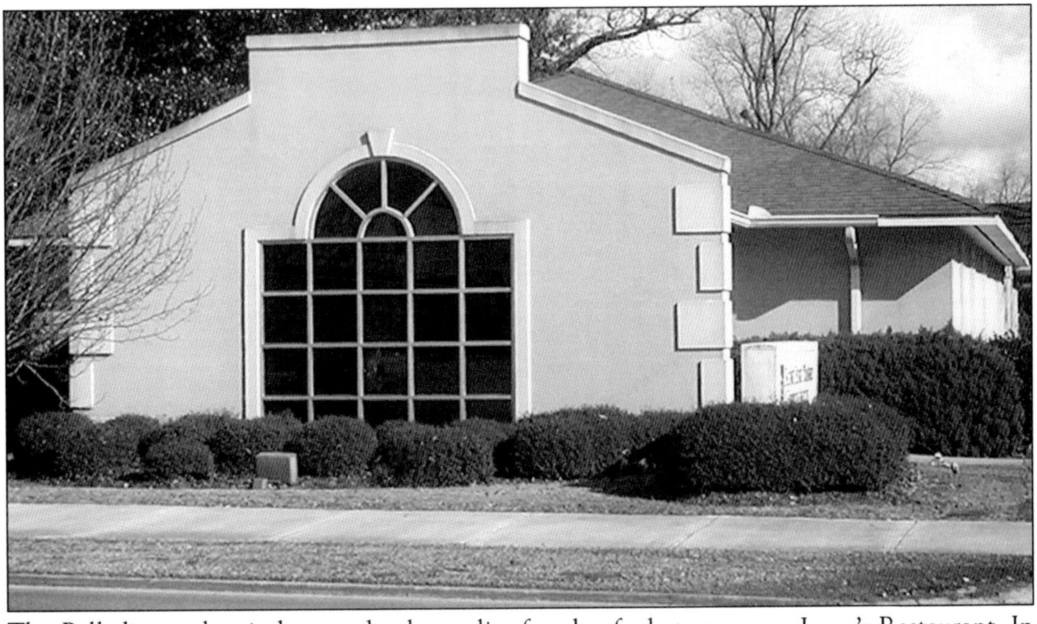

The Palladian-style window masks the earlier facade of what once was Long's Restaurant. In 2003 the structure is the home office of Blount, Burke, Wimberly, and Hendricks Insurers. The company continues a historic Statesboro business begun by C.A. Sorrier who moved here from Arcola, Georgia, in 1888. The family maintained an interest in the business until late in the 20th century.

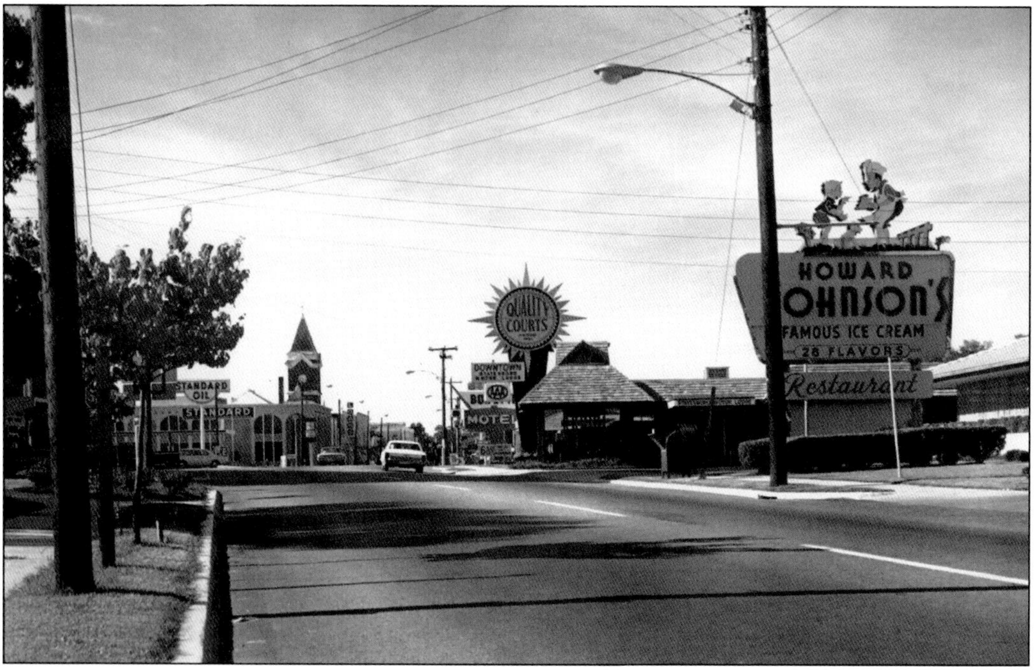

This view of North Main Street, looking south, reveals how tourists saw Statesboro when U.S. Highway 301 was the major route from Maine to Florida. Pictured here are a restaurant and two motels. Howard Johnson's offered counter and table service, specializing in 28 flavors of ice cream. Adjacent was the Downtown Statesboro Motor Lodge, next door to the Bonette Motel. Travelers could fill up their gas tanks across the street at the Standard Oil Service Station.

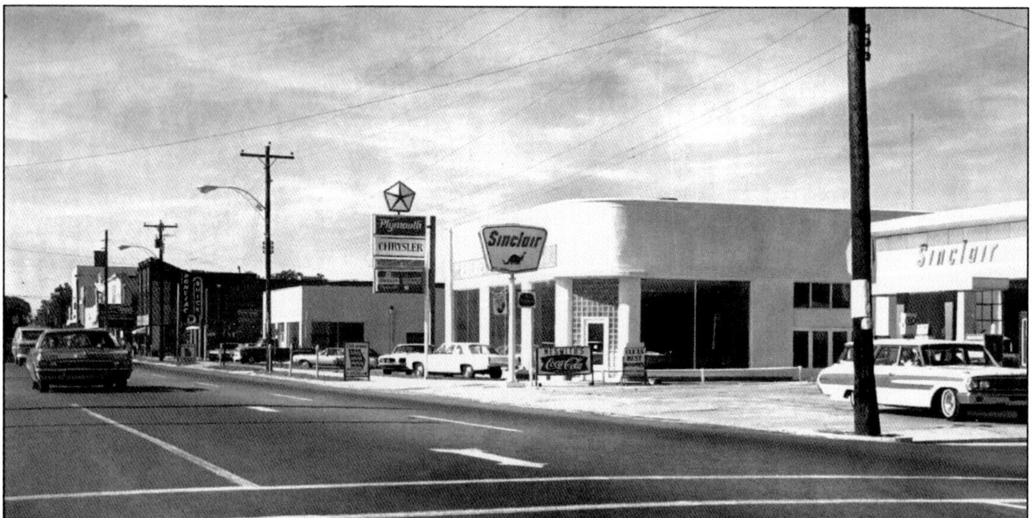

Farther down North Main Street at the corner of Elm Street the traveler views Nesmith's Sinclair Station. Next door, a classic Art Deco building houses Everett Motor Company, the authorized dealer for Plymouth and Chrysler. Altman Pontiac Company was located in an adjacent building. In the 1990s the Statesboro Telephone Company razed the Sinclair station and Everett Motors for their new facility. In 2003 the Core Credit Union building occupies that space.

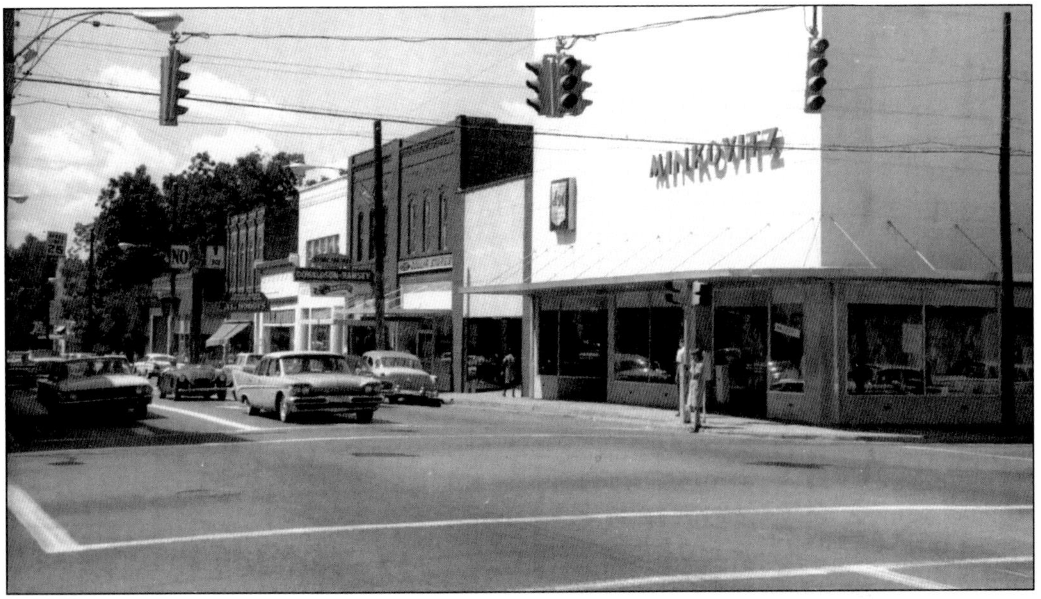

In the late 1960s Minkovitz Department Store was the anchor of the retail business community in uptown Statesboro. It occupied the space built by R. Simmons and Company in 1900. The Minkovitz family came to Statesboro in 1936 and operated the store as H. Minkovitz and Son. Later it was called, simply, Minkovitz. Note that the store offered the incentive of S&H Green Stamps that could be collected and traded in for merchandise. Down the street are H.W. Smith Jewelers, the Dollar Store, Donaldson and Ramsey Men's Store, Statesboro Telephone Company, J.L. Hodges, and Rosenbergs. Across West Vine Street is College Pharmacy.

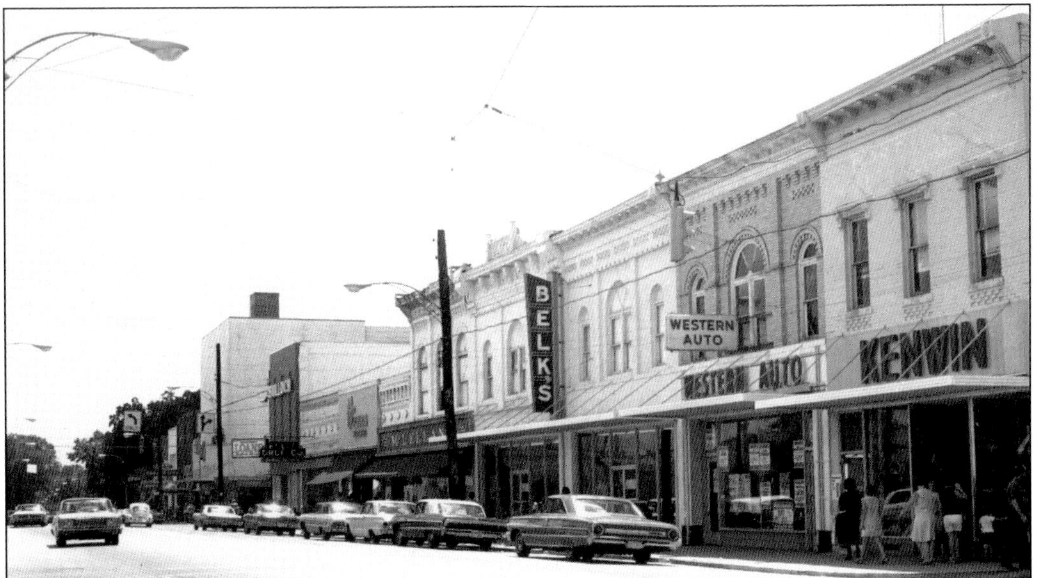

In the 1960s the first block of North Main Street across from the courthouse was part of the central shopping district in Statesboro. The following can be seen from right to left: Kenwin Ladies Shop, Western Auto, Belk's Department Store, McClellans 5&10 Cent Store, Diana Dress Shop, Ellis Drug Company, and the Bulloch County Bank. During this period, as well as decades earlier, businesses uptown all closed their doors on Wednesday at noon.

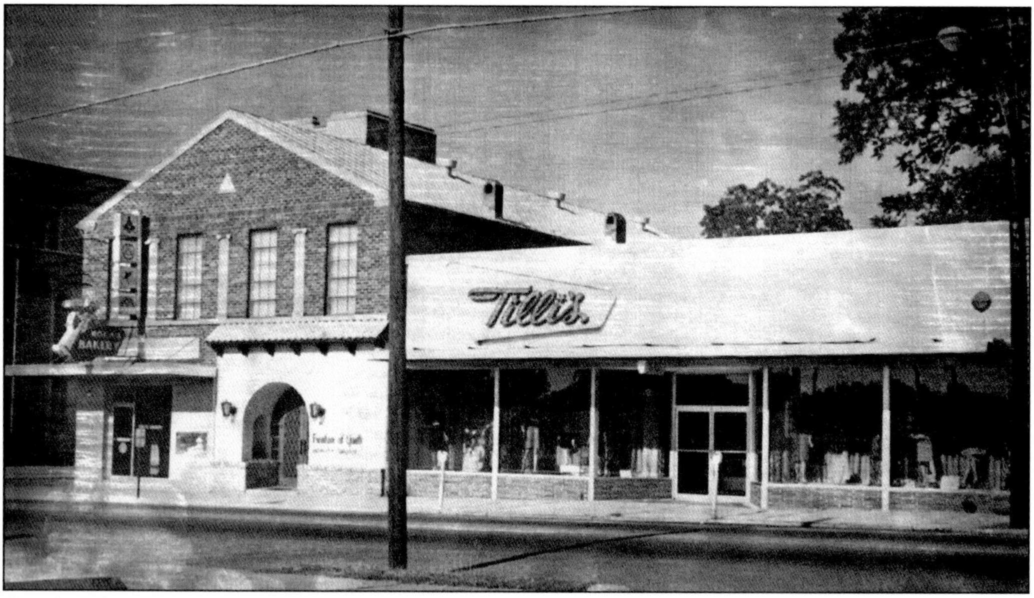

On South Main Street at Cherry Street in the 1960s, three stalwart shops were Tilli's, the Fountain of Youth Beauty Salon, and Mock's Bakery. Tilli's specialized in women's fashions. It was operated by A.M. Seligman, a member of a family active in Statesboro's retail community since the early 1900s. He named the store to honor his wife, Tilli. For many years the Seligmans operated the Fair Store, a clothing store for ladies. John Mock, formerly a Navy cook, opened his bakery in the late 1940s. Both the bakery and beauty parlor rented space from the Masonic Lodge, which has owned this corner property since 1874.

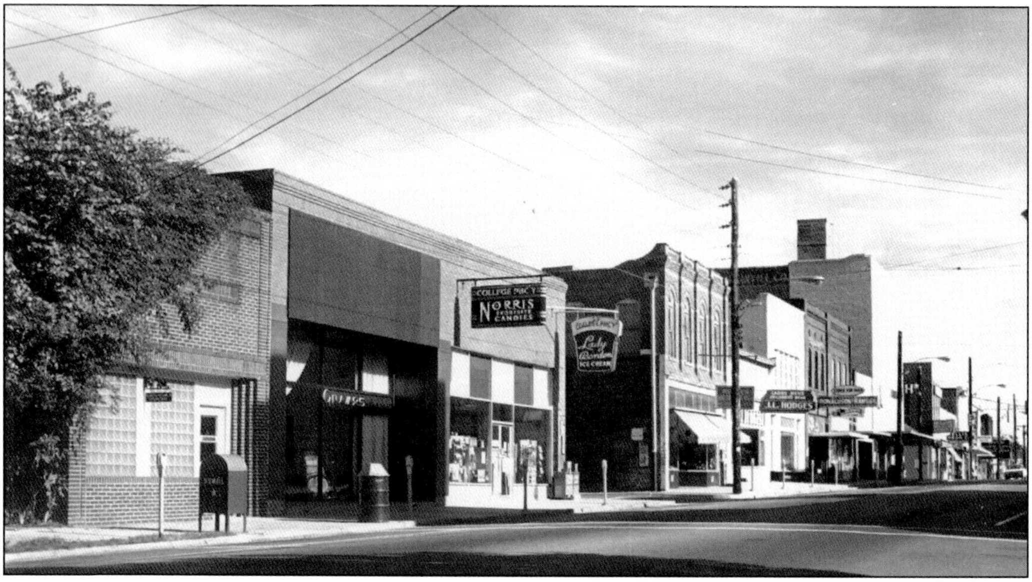

This is an unusual view of the businesses on the west side of South Main Street in the late 1960s. The tree on the far right is the Magnolia on the lawn of the M.M. Holland House. Because of the noise of birds roosting in the Magnolia, the large Victorian house was known as the "Chatter Tree." At the left are the offices of Roger Holland, optometrist; Grimes Jewelry; and the College Pharmacy.

A familiar landmark since 1909, the Confederate monument on the southwest corner of the Courthouse Square was erected through donations by members of the United Daughters of the Confederacy. This view of businesses in the first block of East Main shows Ben Franklin's 5&10 Cent Store and Burton's Shoe Store, the authorized dealer of Red Goose shoes. For many decades the beautiful cedar tree on the left became a colorful Christmas tree each December.

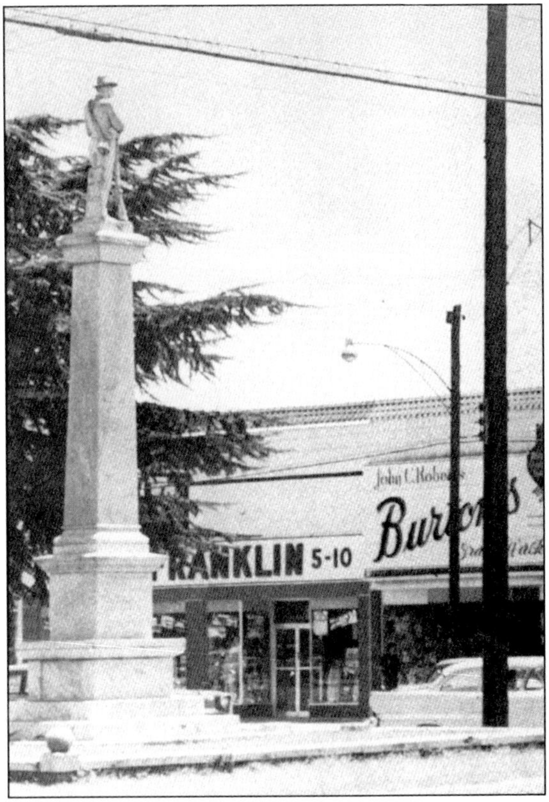

The south side of East Main Street in 2003 shows the modern facades of renovated buildings. At the far left is a portion of the new city hall, and other shops include Craig's Deli and Lori Grice Photographic Studios. Frank Parker has an office in a building he renovated, which for several decades housed the W.C. Akins and Son Hardware Company. The building's upper floors now contain several unique and modern apartments. Daniel Brick Company is on the corner of East Main and the alley.

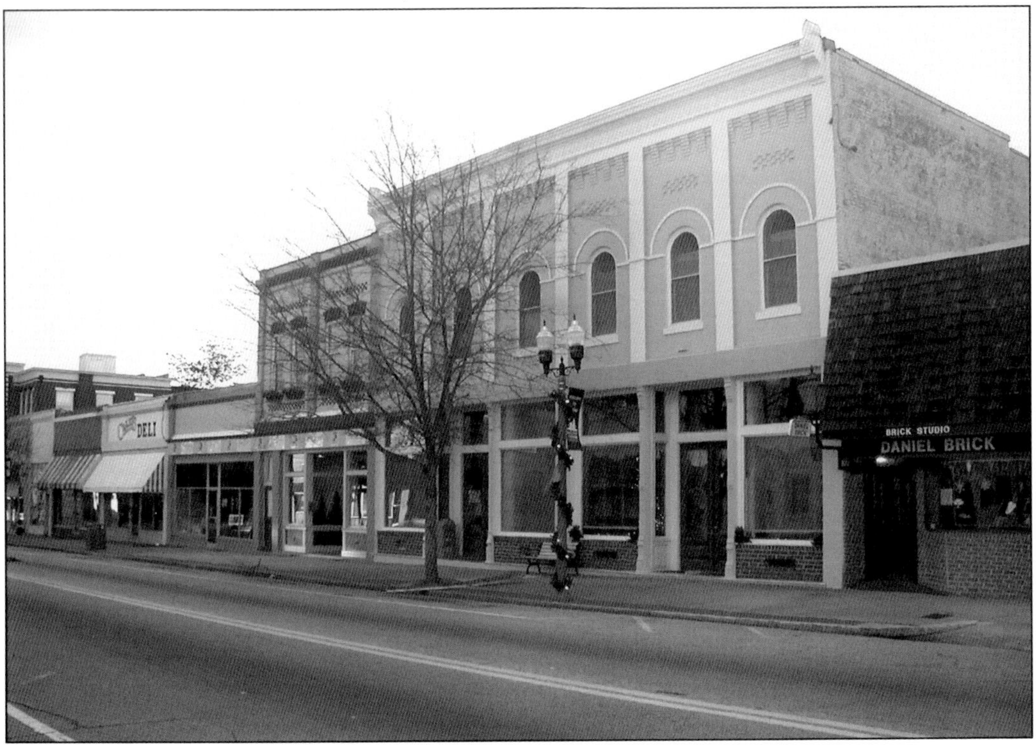

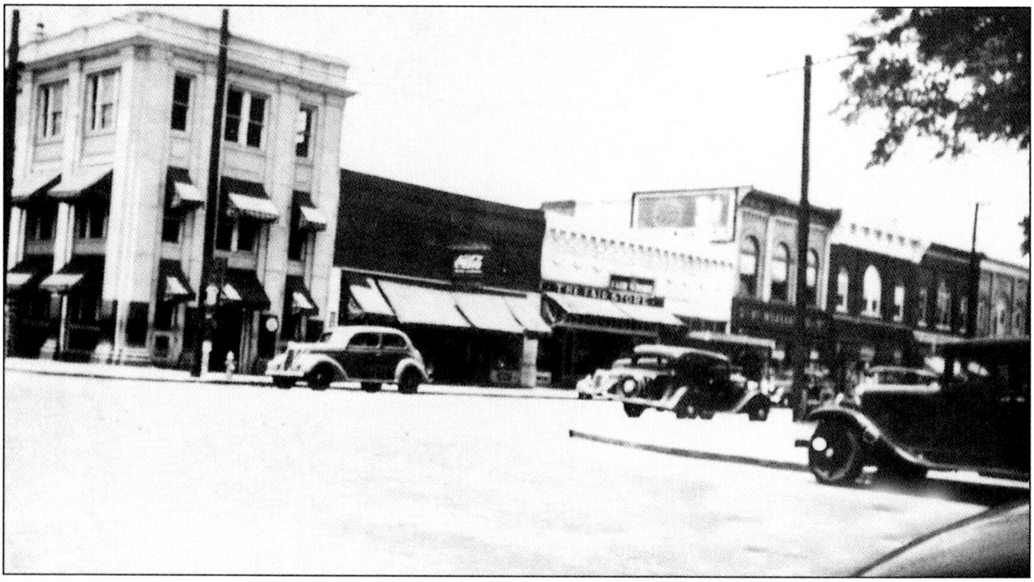

Uptown Statesboro's northwest corner begins with the Bulloch County Bank, which opened in March 1934 in the old First National Bank building. It and the Sea Island Bank were only two banks operating in the town after the Great Depression Next door is Ellis Drugs founded in 1903 by W.H. Ellis and sold in later years to Glenn S. Jennings and "Bunny" Cone. The Fair Store was operated by the Seligman family until they moved their operation to South Main Street. The facades of the remaining buildings in the block have been changed.

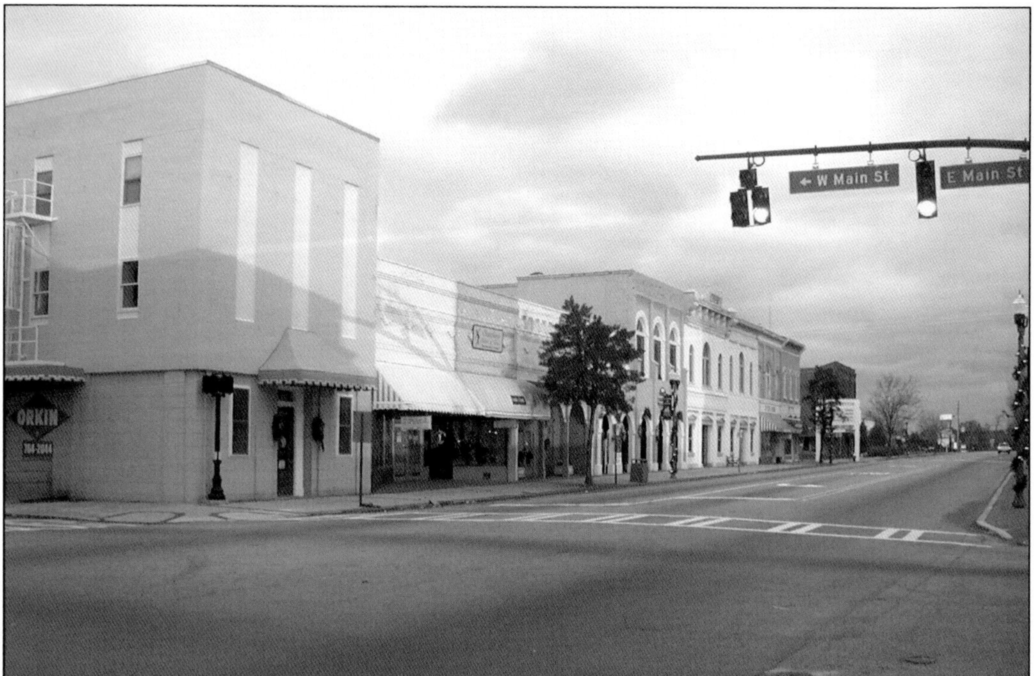

The block shown above in 2003 depicts modern facades on historic structures, as well as new street signs. Note that Orkin Pest Control is located in the basement of the corner building. Spaces once occupied by merchants have been given over to offices and dance studios.

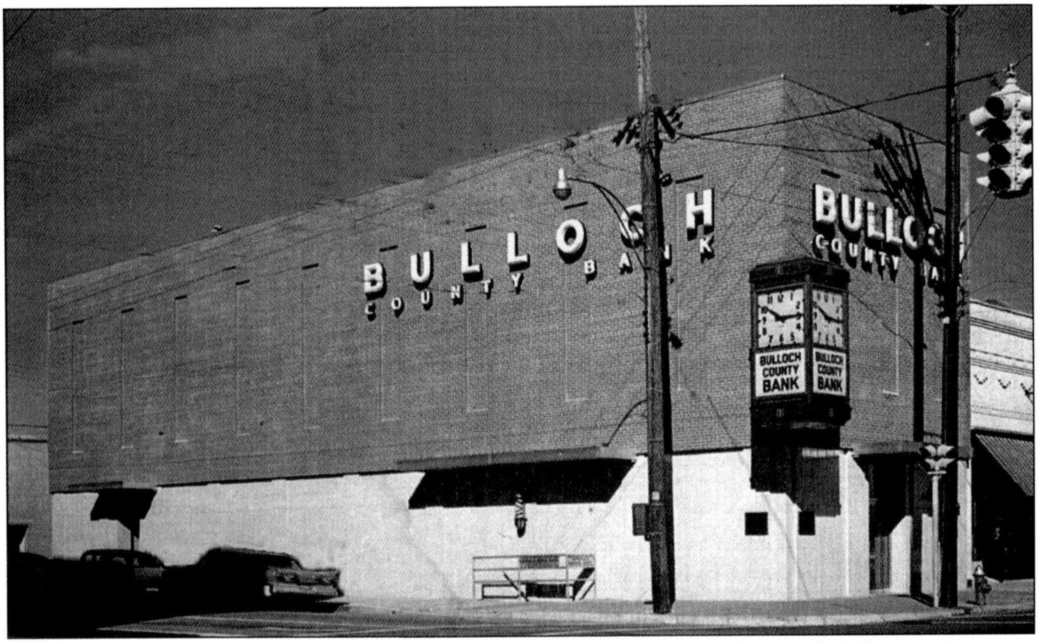

In 1959 the Bulloch County Bank was totally renovated and air conditioned. Offices and storage spaces lined the upper floors. Statesboro's first drive-in banking window with a teller appeared facing the alley behind the bank. Note in the center of the picture a barber pole and railing advertising a barber shop that for decades was located in the basement. The clock on the corner of the building had become a landmark and could be seen from four directions.

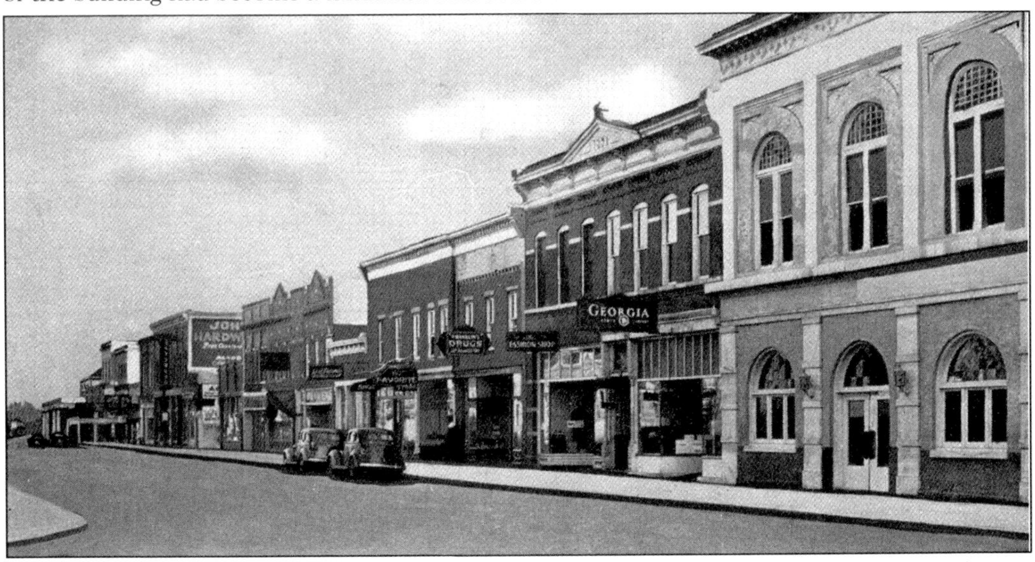

The south side of the first block of East Main Street in the 1950s was the home of some familiar offices and stores. On the corner was the Sea Island Bank, showing a facade added in a renovation of 1950. Down the street were the offices of the Georgia Power Company, Jake Levine's Fashion Shop, Franklin's Drug Store, William Smith's Favorite Shoe Store, Henry Moses's Department Store, Men and Boys Store, City Drugs, and a building which various shops and stores rented. No building in this block stands in 2003. A new Sea Island Bank now occupies the entire block

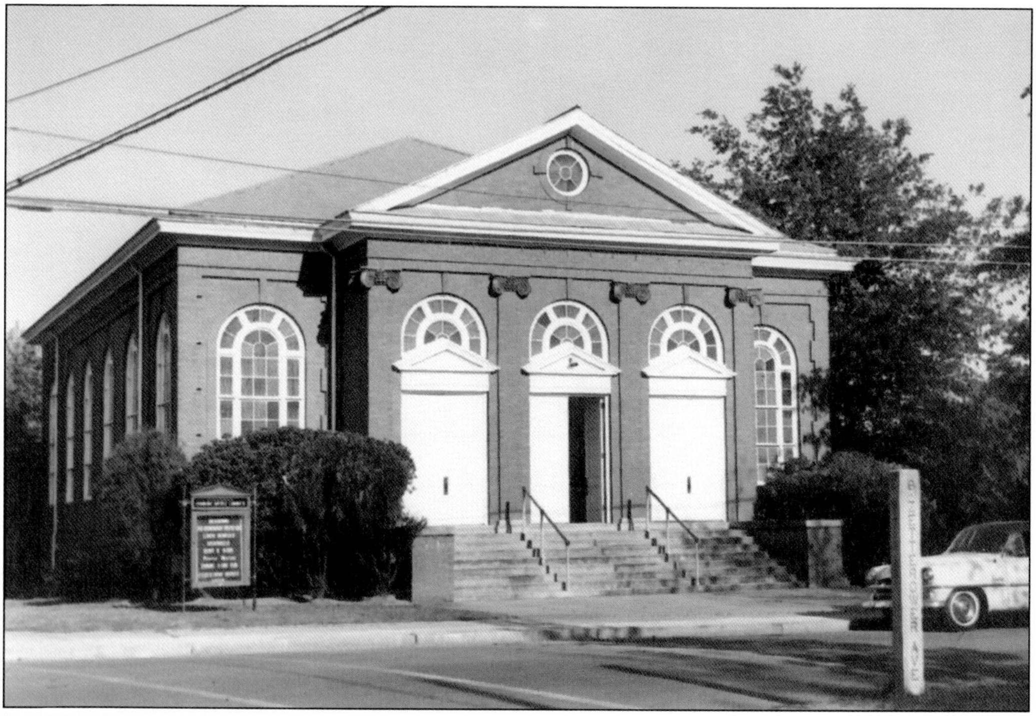

In 1891 the Statesboro Primitive Baptist Church was organized. In 1924 the congregation built a new sanctuary on the corner of North Zetterower Avenue and East Main Street. The building cost approximately $20,000. Elder William H. Crouse was the minister.

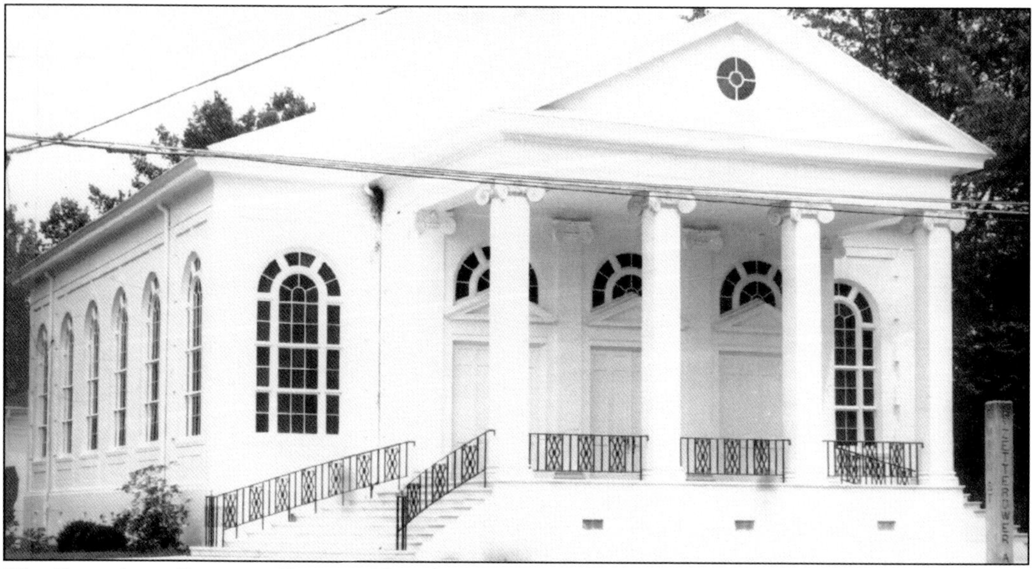

The Statesboro Primitive Baptist Church in 2003 reveals a new white facade which was added in 1961. Square Ionic columns grace the portico, and circular staircases provide an elegant entrance. The church purchased additional property and added a large wing in the 1990s to provide space for Bible classes and a new fellowship hall. A building nearby now functions as an archives for the history of Primitive Baptists. It is said that the church has the largest membership of any Primitive Baptist Church in North America.

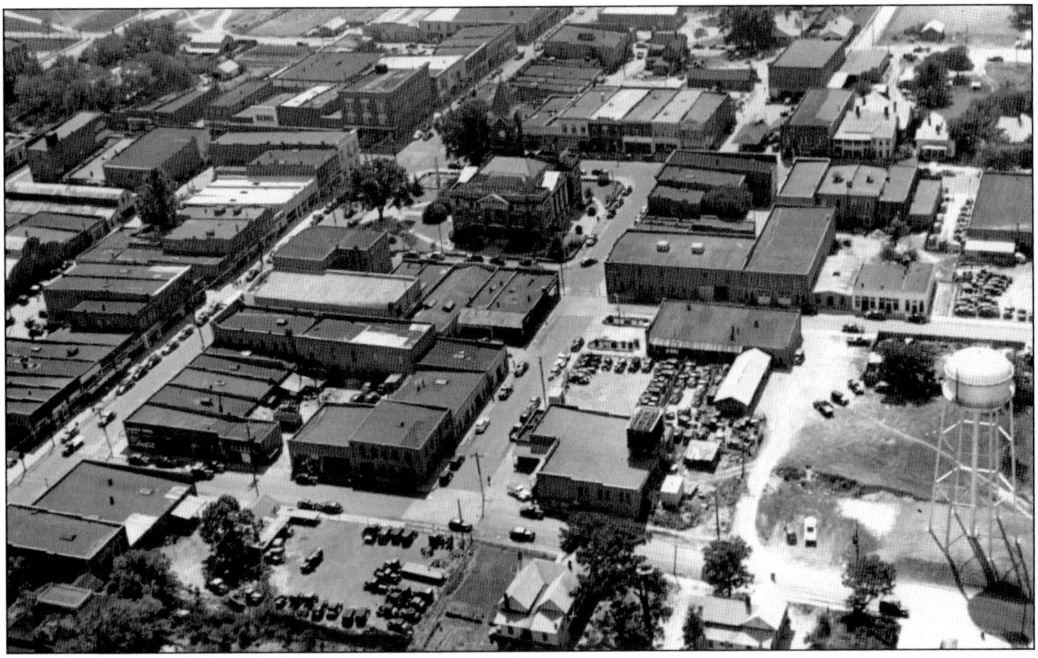

A pre-World War II aerial photograph shows Statesboro in 1941. The perspective, from above Railroad Street near the corner of Hill Street, goes from east at the bottom to west at the top. In the center is the courthouse. Note that Courtland Street ends at Oak Street, and a filling station appears on South Main Street at what became the entrance to Simmons Shopping Center. Uptown served all the shopping needs of Statesboro's 5,000 residents.

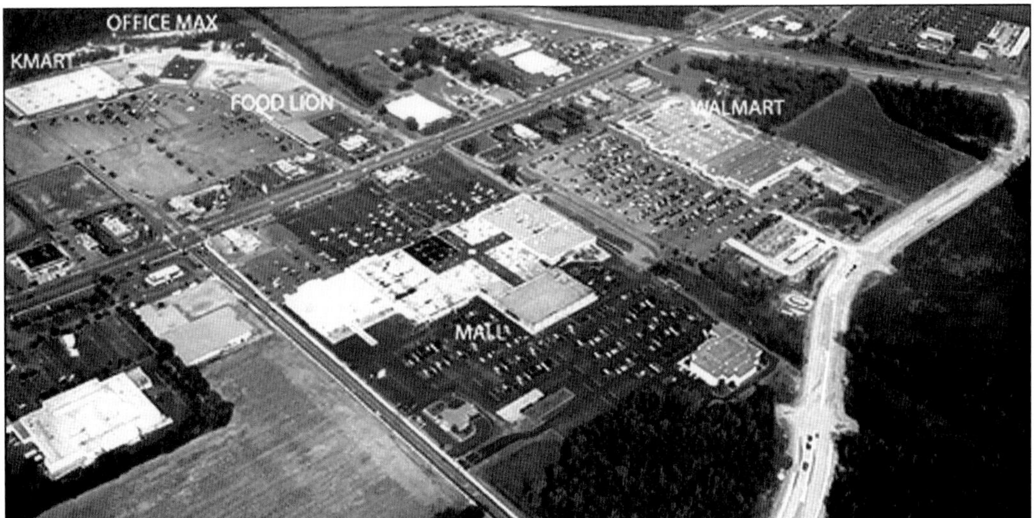

Located on the corner of Northside Drive and Brannen Street, the Statesboro Mall was opened in the 1970s and has expanded to include national retailers and specialty shops. The area east of the mall is occupied by a Wal-Mart Super Store, which in the 1990s became one of the largest stores in the chain. Farther east is Veteran's Memorial Parkway and Lowe's Store for Homes. Across Northside Drive is another shopping center that houses K-Mart, Office Max, and several retail stores. Restaurants and fast food shops appear throughout the area. The divided street on the right is the Brannen Street Extension scheduled for completion in early 2003.

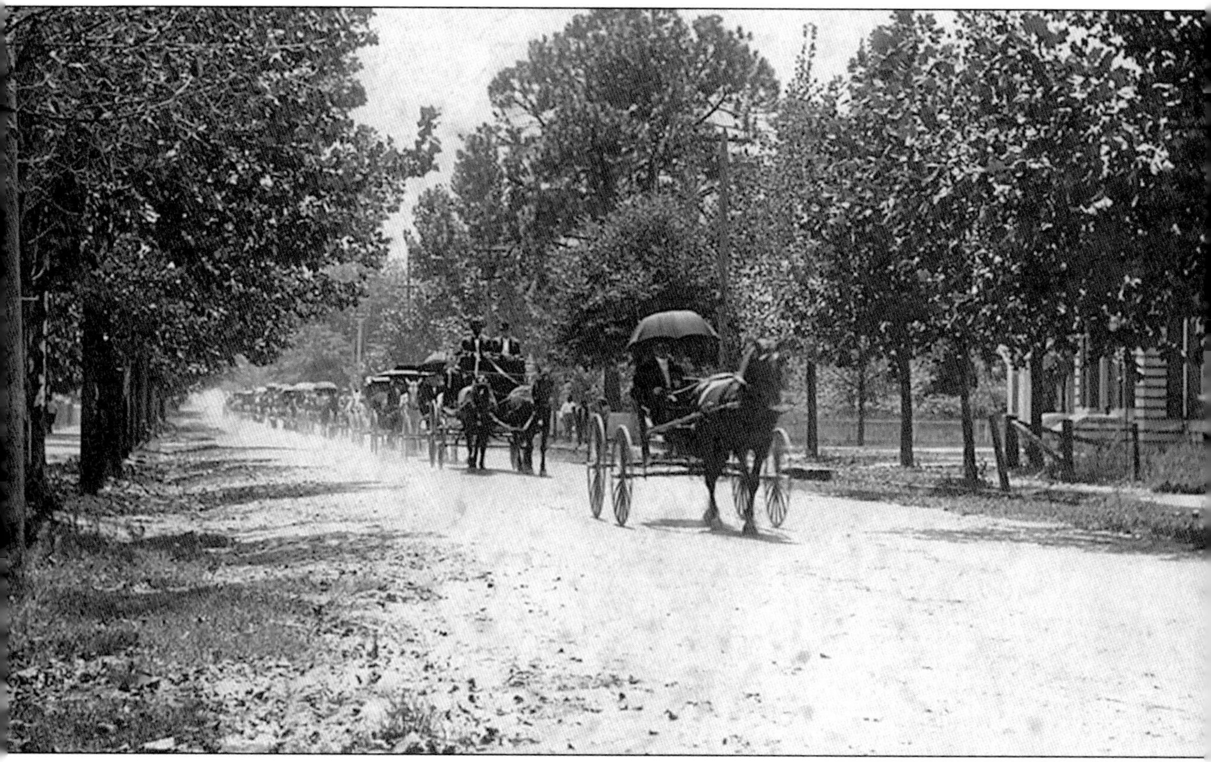

In 1910 a highly successful businessman, Michael Kennedy Jones, died tragically in an automobile accident near Savannah. This rare photograph depicts his funeral procession as it winds its way up South Main Street for his funeral at the Baptist Church on North Main Street. The minister leads the procession, which includes a hearse drawn by a team of horses and a long line of carriages and buggies. The setting is near the Methodist church at the corner of South Main and Cherry Streets. Note the avenue of trees.